Napoleon's Army at Austerlitz

To J. David Markham

Thank you for your friendship and support of my research

Napoleon's Army at Austerlitz

Uniforms and Equipment of the
Grande Armée at the Emperor's Greatest Battle

Paul L. Dawson

FRONTLINE BOOKS

First published in Great Britain in 2025 by
Frontline Books
An imprint of Pen & Sword Books Limited
Yorkshire – Philadelphia

Copyright © Paul L. Dawson 2025

ISBN 978 1 52679 229 7

The right of Paul L. Dawson to be identified as
Author of this Work has been asserted by him in accordance
with the Copyright, Designs and Patents Act 1988.

A CIP catalogue record for this book is
available from the British Library.

All rights reserved. No part of this book may be reproduced, transmitted, downloaded, decompiled or reverse engineered in any form or by any means, electronic or mechanical including photocopying, recording or by any information storage and retrieval system, without permission from the Publisher in writing. No part of this book may be used or reproduced in any manner for the purpose of training artificial intelligence technologies or systems.

Typeset by Mac Style
Printed in India by Replika Press Pvt. Ltd.

The Publisher's authorised representative in the EU for product safety is Authorised Rep Compliance Ltd., Ground Floor, 71 Lower Baggot Street, Dublin D02 P593, Ireland.
www.arccompliance.com

For a complete list of Pen & Sword titles please contact

PEN & SWORD BOOKS LIMITED
47 Church Street, Barnsley, South Yorkshire, S70 2AS, England
E-mail: enquiries@pen-and-sword.co.uk
Website: www.pen-and-sword.co.uk
or
PEN AND SWORD BOOKS
1950 Lawrence Road, Havertown, PA 19083, USA
E-mail: uspen-and-sword@casematepublishers.com
Website: www.penandswordbooks.com

Contents

Acknowledgements		vi
Introduction		vii
Chapter 1	The Need for an Army	1
Chapter 2	Organising the Army	12
Chapter 3	Becoming a Soldier	19
Chapter 4	The Cavalry	34
Chapter 5	Boulogne	42
Chapter 6	The School of Boulogne	58
Chapter 7	Daily Life	69
Chapter 8	I Corps	86
Chapter 9	III Corps	101
Chapter 10	IV Corps	125
Chapter 11	V Corps	147
Chapter 12	The Cavalry Reserve	169
Chapter 13	Everything Else	180
Chapter 14	The School of Boulogne: Success or Failure?	189
Chapter 15	Desertion	205
Chapter 16	Death and Disease	220
Chapter 17	Conclusions	234
Notes		248
Bibliography		260

Acknowledgements

In the preparation of this book, I would like to thank all those who have offered advice and support. I would also like to thank all those who have helped me with my research.

I must single out Yves Martin for his friendship and dedicated support of the project. I must also thank Robert Cooper and Ian Smith for their excellent company during our numerous research trips to Paris. Ian's advice and guidance during our many thousands of hours of conversation over numerous bottles of red wine was, and is, of immense guidance in understanding the wealth of data that we have gathered, to synthesis it into a cohesive narrative. Dan Hazelwood must be also thanked for his editorial and critical comment on my writing. I must also thank Sally Fairweather for accompanying me over the last 15 years to Paris supporting me in the thankless task of photographic archives. Ben Townsend and Martin Lancaster are also due thanks for their comments and insights into the training of the French Army 180+-1805. Frederick Lemaire is to be heartily thanked for allowing me to reproduce images of the artefacts he found during archaeological excavations of the various Camps of Bolougne. Jerome Croyet is to be thanked for permission to reproduce images of the collections at the Emperi museum.

Paris, 5 December 2024

Introduction

I hope this book does two things: fills a gap in published literature about the formation process of the Grande Armée, and provides detailed snapshots of the regiments that became immortalised at Austerlitz. In creating my narrative, I have deliberately – rightly or wrongly – kept clear of nearly all studies of the battle and the camp of Boulogne. I rely instead on eyewitness testimonies and letters and reports written at the time. Why? We already know the outcome of the battle, and most histories of a battle or event are written with hindsight: if you read halfway through an Agatha Christie novel, then flip to the end to find 'who did it', your reading of the remaining part of the book will be tainted by this knowledge. No one knew in summer 1805 Austerlitz would be fought or what the outcome of the campaign could have been. With hindsight, the Grande Armée therefore that fought at Austerlitz is lionised as the 'Best Army' Napoléon commanded. But how do we know this? We have to judge the Grande Armée on what was known at the time before the battle was fought, to make objective judgements.

To do so, we turn to a hitherto untapped set of archive resources: regimental inspection reports, standing orders and correspondence. In order to understand how the army functioned we have to use a combination of regulations and higher-level orders and compare them to how they were enacted at regimental level. For this we have to rely on regimental-level inspection reports, which give us hard facts written by objective observers. In these pages are the records of the logistics, training, and diet of the Grande Armée. I seek to present facts unincumbered by later historians' comments on the army, its training and professionalism. I want to know how the army was viewed at the time, and not after the fact: it is all too easy to fall into the trap of glorifying the Grande Armée rather than viewing it objectively. Rightly or wrongly, I seek to get to the facts as they were known at the time and to assess the army from what was written down there and then. No doubt my conclusions and reporting will be critiqued: yet the facts as they are present an objective view unencumbered by 'rose-tinted glasses'. Each layer of Napoléon's military machine, from the domain of Berthier among the general staff through to regimental level, produced orders of the day and other literature. Almost every day the chief of staff of each camp sent an order of the day for their units: this was transmitted to the divisional generals, who furnished their own orders, and then these orders were passed to the brigade commanders. The *general de brigade* added their own orders, before being issued to the regimental colonel. It is from these documents that I have drawn the bulk of the research material to write this book, supplemented by letters, memoirs and other material produced from summer 1803 through to summer 1805: the years in which the Grande Armée was forged.

Chapter 1

The Need for an Army

In August 1805, after two years of training, Napoléon left the north coast of France with what some regard as the best army he ever commanded to defeat the coalition forces of Austria and Russia. Yet Vienna had not been the original destination of these men; they had been assembled to invade England and Ireland.

The story of Franco–Irish relations stretches back to the seventeenth century: yet since 1792 the invasion of Ireland and the establishment of a French-allied republic in that country to isolate England had been a clear war aim. Remarkably, despite the invasions of 1796 and 1798 being total failures, failure and its inevitability never seems to have crossed the minds of the Irish or French minds. The author explores this more fully in his companion volume *French Invasions of Britain and Ireland:1792 to 1815*, available from Pen & Sword.

In new year 1803, leaders of the United Irishmen – a society formed to liberate Ireland from British rule – travelled to Paris to meet Talleyrand. On the strength of the testimony of these men, an agent working for Talleyrand suggested a series of options for invading Ireland. One of these seems to have been to send a raid in the manner of the 1798 invasion, with the French sending a small professional source of 1,500 NCOs, 300 company officers, and 30 senior officers to take charge of the United Irishmen insurgent force. The plan relied squarely on 15,000 United Irish rallying to the French.[1] How these men were to be trained and armed was never fully explored, or how the obvious language barrier would be addressed. Despite these obvious 'planning failures', the goal was for the French-led United Irishmen to create chaos in Ireland, to keep the British crown focused on domestic policy, and thus unable to interfere with European politics. This had been central to the war aims of the Republic and Directory since 1793: to create a new French ally on Britain's doorstep, and to sow the seeds of discontent in England, Scotland and Ireland in imitation of the British operations in the Vendée. The French plans did not suit the United Irish, however, who reported that the Irish would no longer be 'lap dogs' to the French and no longer be satisfied with half measures and broken promises. The French had to send a strong invasion force or the Irish would 'go it alone'.[2] A secret agent, M. Middleton, was sent to England to report on the political and economic situation: basically, his remit was to assess if England was still ripe for revolution.[3] A second agent by the name of Duverne reported that the public mood, thanks to government propaganda via newspapers and sermons, was now in favour of war, and that that the British government, led by Henry Addington, had begun recruiting for the army and had also mobilised thousands as volunteers.[4]

Emperor Napoléon wearing coronation robes.

After two months' deliberation, Napoléon agreed to send an invasion force to Ireland. On *26 Germinal An 11* (16 April 1803) Napoléon ordered General Berthier to gather information on Ireland and Scotland, to identify landing grounds, and to establish the size of a force needed.[5] Napoléon agreed to invade so long as the United Irishmen could

The Marshal of France in mounted full dress.

mobilise at least 20,000 men to join the French army within the first few days of landing.[6] While the plans were being formulated, France and England were technically at peace for another month. Clearly, this was event planning in case of a rupture of the peace agreement with London. It was increasingly obvious in spring 1803 that as the British Crown had not honoured its part of the treaty, war was inevitable.

When the peace of Amiens ruptured on 18 May 1803, event planning for an invasion did not immediately step up a gear. More pressing actions concerned the invasion of Hanover. Led by General Edouard Mortier, the electorate was overrun. General Jean-Baptiste Bernadotte replaced Mortier during 1804, by which time the number of French troopers in the former electorate was approximately 26,000.

A report was passed over Napoléon's desk on 3 June in which the writer remarked that the United Irishmen and their allies could be relied upon to rise within 24 hours of the landing: tellingly he did not give any numbers. The writer also felt that 40,000 men would be needed to take control of Ireland with a landing in Galway Bay and 'the mouth of Kilmain' – i.e., off the coast of Belfast and Carrickfergus. In order to prevent the English being able to send reinforcements to Ireland, speed was of the essence once troops were landed. The French would, it was estimated, be able to march 30 leagues in 24 hours and would achieve their objective in two days, thus Belfast would fall almost

The Marshal of France in dismounted full dress.

immediately.⁷ After much consideration on the report about Ireland, Napoléon began to formally plan the invasion of Ireland on *5 Messidor An XI* (24 June 1803) when orders were issued to construct sufficient landing barges to accommodate 125,000 men. The expedition was to be ready to sail by *Nivôse* (January 1804).⁸

The French Army Archives hold two reports that may be part of this process. One option for invasion was centred on Wolfe Tone's 1796 plans: a French force of four frigates would sail from Rochefort at the same time as 20 vessels from Brest. The French ships would enter the Bristol Channel and land troops in Wales and lead an insurrection to attack Bristol, while the main force, some 12,000 men, would land in Ireland. A force of 5,000 men would depart from Dieppe and Texel and land in Scotland.⁹ This document is accompanied by a report on Ireland and England. This document outlines a plan to invade Ireland with 24,000 French and Spanish troops, landing in different regions to scatter the Crown forces. A force sailing from Dunkirk landing in England would act as a diversion. The plan was conceived as 'liberating the Catholics of Ireland from English Protestant slavery', and upon news of the Revolution it was hoped rather naïvely that the Irish sailors in the Royal Navy would mutiny and sail their ships to Ireland.¹⁰

For this operation to be successful, the men and equipment had to be transported by a flotilla of small, armed, seagoing vessels that were capable of acting offensively if needed. To this end therefore, the French navy was ordered to embark on a mass construction programme of landing barges and associated craft. Flat-bottomed boats were to be constructed in every port, equipped with sails and oars, and cannon firing at water level. More than 2,000 were concentrated in Boulogne and the neighbouring ports, and these could carry 150,000 men, 11,000 horses and 450 cannon. In order to practise embarkation training, and to weld the disparate republican Army into a cohesive French army, six large training grounds were established: from *Floréal An XI* (May 1803), more than half the French army was assembled in camps occupying Gand, Saint-Omer, Compiègne, Saint-Malo, and Bayonne. Some of these locations, it was quickly realised, were unsuitable, and five camps were created near Boulogne, Montreuil, Bruges, and Bayonne. The troops at Bruges were moved to Ambleteuse, a village a few miles from Boulogne. Following successful negotiations with Spain, the troops at Bayonne were moved to Brest, with the camp in Boulogne serving as a pivot point. Due to the number of men gathered here, it encompassed the Boulogne camp and the close-by towns of Outreau, Ambleteuse and Wimereux. The cavalry and reserve troops were garrisoned at Saint-Omer, Amiens, Compiègne, Arass and Paris. The chances of success of the invasion were all the greater as France had managed to gain the support or neutrality of the other European powers and several engagements with the English flotilla had ended with a French advantage.

Despite Napoléon's intentions, the invasion was not ready by new year 1804. On *22 Nivôse An XII* (13 January 1804) he sent a lengthy dispatch via Berthier and the minister of war to exiled Irish leaders in France and those remaining in Ireland. Napoléon declared boldly that he would not agree peace with England until Ireland was independent:

The General en Chef in mounted full dress. By 1804 this title had been transmuted to General de Division and also Corps Command.

General de Brigade in dismounted full dress.

> The First Consul read with the greatest attention the Memorandum addressed to him by Mr. Emmet on 13 Nivôse. He wants the British Irish to be convinced that his intention was to secure Irish independence. The general who commands the expedition shall be provided with sealed letters, by which the First Consul shall declare that he shall not make peace with England without stipulating for the independence of Ireland, in the event, however, that the army has been joined by a considerable corps of United Irishmen, Ireland will, in everything, be treated as America was in the past war.
>
> Any individual who embarks with the French army will be regarded as French; if he was arrested and not treated as a prisoner of war, the reprisal would be exercised against English prisoners.
>
> The First Consul wants a committee of United Irishmen to be formed. He has no problem with the members of this committee making proclamations and instructing their compatriots on the state of affairs. These proclamations will be inserted in the Argus and in the various newspapers of Europe, in order to enlighten the Irish on the party they must conceive. If this committee wants to make a relation to the acts of tyranny exercised against Ireland by the English government, it will be inserted in the Moniteur.[11]

No promises were made about sending troops to Ireland, however.

With Napoléon now invested in the Irish invasion, General Augereau arrived at Brest on *3 Pluviôse An 12* (24 January 1804) to take command of the Armee d'Irlande. Yet, despite considerable enthusiasm for action, nothing actually occurred.

Thomas Emmet, an Irish leader in exile, prepared on *4 Pluviôse An 12* (25 January 1804) an invasion plan, which was sent to the minister of war. In it, Emmet asked for 25,000 men to invade Ireland and informed the minister that he believed the United Irish in Wexford, Wickford and Dublin were still ready to rise, estimating 6,000 would do so. Furthermore, he recommended the French land at Drogheda Bay and in Waterford, and then advance in two columns on Dublin. Emmet acknowledged the advantage of a quick strike on Dublin being 'incalculable'. Emmet's assumption that United Irish rebels would join along the march towards Dublin was not guaranteed. He offered no suggestion on how to combat the Royal Navy: he assumed that the French fleet would evade the British fleet as they had done at Bantry Bay in 1796: this was naive thinking. Emmet, in a postscript, wrote that notable United Irish leader William Dowdall was in Dublin and he had assured him of support of the United Irishmen, and added that the British garrison was perhaps 70,000, of which 16,000 were militia and 3,500 yeoman 'which posed no threat'.[12]

It took time to build the required landing craft and associated support vessels and months would pass until *19 Fructidor An 12* (6 September 1804), when Napoléon wrote to Berthier:

> Cousin, the Irish expedition is resolved. For this purpose, you will have a conference with Marshal Augereau (general-in-chief of the expedition to Ireland). At Brest

Aide-de-camp in mounted full dress. The light blue brassard on the left arm indicates he is attached to a General de Brigade.

Inspector of Review in full dress. These men ensured – in theory – that the army was well drilled and fed.

there are embarkation facilities for 18,000 men. General Marmont (commander of the Utrecht camp), for his part, is ready with 25,000 men. He will try to land in Ireland, and will be under the orders of Marshal Augereau. The Grande Armée de Boulogne will be embarked during the same time, and will do everything possible to penetrate into the county of Kent. You will let Marshal Augereau know that he will behave according to events. If the information I have from the Irish refugees and from the men I have sent to Ireland are verified, a large number of Irish will line up under his colours when he lands; then he will march straight to Dublin. If, on the contrary, this movement was delayed, he will take up position to wait for General Marmont and until the Grande Armée has landed.[13]

Napoléon wrote to Admiral Honoré Ganteaume the same day to inform him that Lough Swilly was the invasion point.[14] To give Ganteaume a chance of succeeding in avoiding the Royal Navy, Napoléon designed a diversion. Villeneuve would take the Toulon fleet, and Admiral Édouard Missiesy the Rochefort squadrons, and they would sail separately for the West Indies to threaten the various British possessions and reinforce French positions in the region before rendezvousing and returning to combat the British blockade of Ferrol and Corunna. On *21 Nivôse An 13* (11 January 1805) the fleet at Rochefort managed to break out of the blockade, and Villeneuve escaped Toulon while Nelson was in Sardinia. However, having bypassed Nelson's fleet, Villeneuve made it to the Gulf of Lion, where he encountered a heavy storm. At this critical juncture, he turned his fleet around and sailed back to Toulon. The golden moment had passed.

In order to prevent invasion, England, the banker of the Napoléonic wars, however, formed a third coalition against France. With English gold, and a deteriorating political situation since the execution of the Duc d'Enghien, by August a European war was inevitable, and France faced the combined armies of Austria and Russia. The camp in Boulogne was struck on *29 Thermidor* (17 August 1805). On *6 Fructidor* (24 August) the army, which had been heretofore known as the *Côtes de l'Océan* (the Ocean Coasts) became the Grande Armée (Great Army). The same day it headed for the Rhine by forced march.

Chapter 2

Organising the Army

The army that Napoléon assembled at Boulogne comprised three arms: infantry, cavalry and artillery with associated support services. During the peace of Amiens, Napoléon had time to rebuild the French army in the form he envisioned for it. Swept away were the revolutionary *demi-brigades* in favour of regiments once more.

Demi-brigades had been created by the decree of 21 February 1793. In order to combine the discipline of the old regulars with the revolutionary zeal of volunteers, one regular infantry battalion and two volunteer battalions were formed into *demi-brigades de bataille*. Each battalion comprised eight companies, one of which was the elite grenadier company. A grenadier company comprised one captain, one lieutenant, one *sous-lieutenant*, one sergeant major, two sergeants, one *fourrier* (quartermaster corporal, in essence the company clerk) four corporals, four chosen men, 48 grenadiers, and two drummers. Fusilier companies had an additional sergeant, two corporals, two chosen men and 19 fusiliers. On 22 November 1793 grenadier companies were made the same strength as fusilier companies, each company now mustering 104 men. Attached to each *demi-brigade* was a company of artillery manning six 4-pdr field guns. The rank of chosen man was removed. The decree was not put into practice until *21 Nivoise An 2* (8 January 1794).[1]

The decree of 18 *Nivoise An 4* (8 January 1796) consolidated the 238 existing *demi-brigades* into 140 new *demi-brigades*; 110 line infantry *demi-brigades* and 30 light infantry *demi-brigades*. Henceforward, a *demi-brigade* in theory mustered 96 officers and 3,300 men, the men now wearing a national blue coat (*habit*) with white-sleeved waistcoat (*veste*), knee breeches (*culottes*) as well as white and black and linen gaiters. He also had an ammunition box (*giberne*) with its belt *(banderole)*, as well as his backpack (*havresac*), and for corporals, grenadiers and *sous-officiers* (sergeants, *fourriers*, sergeant majors) a sabre and its belt (*baudrier*). He would also have his *chapeau* and off-duty cap (*bonnet de police*).

The decree of *21 Nivôse An 6* (January 1798) disbanded the regimental artillery. The decree of *23 Fructidor An 7* (9 September 1799) consolidated the existing *légère* formations into 26 *demi-brigades* of 4 battalions, all this changed again with the decree of *9 Fructidor An 8* (27 August 1800), when four new *demi-brigades* were created by dissolving the 3rd battalions in the 3ᵉ, 5ᵉ, 8, 16ᵉ, 18ᵉ, 20ᵉ, 25ᵉ, 26ᵉ, 28ᵉ, and 29ᵉ and the manpower spread between the various *demi-brigades* to bring them up to strength. Simultaneously, the *Ligne demi-brigades* were reduced to two battalions. On *4 Brumaire An 10* (26 October 1801) a new equipment regulation was issued. It sought to bring some semblance of order to the army now it was for the first time in nearly a decade on

War Commissioner in full dress. These men acted as a quality control system – in theory – for the rations, clothing and equipment supplied to the army.

Colonel of line infantry, c.1805.

a peacetime footing and in thorough need of a shakedown in organisation.² The major change to the uniform of the infantry had been the introduction of *voltigeur* companies with the decrees of 13 March 1804 and 24 September 1804 in regiments of light infantry only. They were armed with light cavalry *mousquetons*, and allowed chamois collars to their clothing.³ Voltigeurs were added to *Ligne* regiments and allowed to wear epaulettes from 19 September 1805, which were to be yellow.⁴

The Cavalry

Upon becoming Consul, Napoléon inherited 25 regiments of heavy cavalry. The heavy cavalry was broken down into two types: the *Cavalerie*, who were issued long, straight sabres, and the two regiments of *Carabiniers* armed with muskets. The latter were the *Grenadiers à Cheval* of the Imperial Guard and their equivalents in the Line, the *Carabiniers à Cheval*. These were, in theory, the big men on big horses who were held in reserve exclusively for service in battle. Due to their large size and heavy armour, which increased their protection from enemy cavalry and infantry alike, the heavy cavalry was Napoléon's decisive combat arm that could deliver a devastating blow upon enemy units when employed properly.

The great innovation of 1801 to 1803 was the formation of 12 regiments of *cuirassiers* – the iconic French heavy cavalryman, whose uniform changed little from Austerlitz to the Marne in a period of over 100 years.

The 1e *regiment de cavalerie* became the 1e *regiment de cavalerie-cuirassiers* by a decree *of 18 Vendémiaire An10* (10 October 1801), complementing the 8e *regiment de cavalerie-cuirassiers*, which had been created over a hundred years earlier. The 2e, 3e and 4e followed suit by a decree of *20 Vendémiaire An 11* (12 October 1802). On *2 Nivôse An 11* (23 December 1802), the 5e, 6e and 7e were also added to the new arm, which, with the 8e, comprised eight regiments. Less than a year later, *1 Vendémiaire An 12I* (24 September 1803), the arm was increased to twelve regiments with the addition of 9e, 10e, 11e and 12e regiments of cavalry. Each company comprised a captain, one lieutenant, two *sous-lieutenants*, a sergeant major, two sergeants, one *fourrier*, four corporals and 54 troopers and a trumpeter.⁵

In addition, under the terms of the decree the remaining regiments were disbanded:

13^e *Cavalerie* became the 22e *Dragons*
14e Cavalerie became the 23e *Dragons*
15e *Cavalerie* became the 24e *Dragons*
16e *Cavalerie* became the 25e *Dragons*
17e *Cavalerie* became the 26e *Dragons*
18e *Cavalerie* became the 27e *Dragons*
19e *Cavalerie* was disbanded into the 9e, 10e and 11e *de régiments de cuirassiers*
20e *Cavalerie* was disbanded into 12e *régiment de cuirassiers* and 23e *régiment de dragons*
21e *Cavalerie* was disbanded into 24e and 25e *régiments de dragons*

22ᵉ *Cavalerie* was disbanded into 9ᵉ and 12ᵉ *de régiments de cuirassiers*
23ᵉ *Cavalerie* was disbanded into 5ᵉ, 6ᵉ and 7ᵉ *de régiments de cuirassiers*
24ᵉ *Cavalerie* was disbanded into 1ᵉ and 8ᵉ *de régiments de cuirassiers*
25ᵉ *Cavalerie* was disbanded into 2ᵉ, 3ᵉ and 4ᵉ *de régiments de cuirassiers*

The dress of the French line infantry at the camp of Boulogne had changed little since 1796. We see left to right a *voltigeur* of light infantry – note yellow collar and cuffs to the *habit*, the former being non-regulation – an officer of line fusiliers, a line grenadier and lastly a fusilier of the line wearing the felt *chapeau*. Note that he carries a greatcoat, a regulation item since 1803.

Organising the Army 17

Officer of light infantry, c.1805.

As well as heavy cavalry, Consul Bonaparte inherited regiments of light cavalry and dragoons.

Dragoons historically were soldiers who rode into battle on horseback and fought on foot, armed with a musket. The first regiment raised in France was in 1635 – the ancestors of what became the 2ᵉ *Dragons*, the 1ᵉ regiment was not formed until 1656, the 3ᵉ was formed in 1649 by the Duke d'Enghien, the 4ᵉ was formed in 1667 and the 5ᵉ in 1668. The last of the *Anciene Régime* regiments was formed in at Metz in 1744, the 18ᵉ *Dragons*. The 19ᵉ *Dragons* was formed 27 February 1793, as was the 20ᵉ *Dragons*. The 21ᵉ *Dragons* was formed in April 1796. Under the reorganisation of *1 Vendemiaire An 12*, the 7ᵉ *Bis Hussard* became the 28ᵉ *Dragons*, so too the 11ᵉ *Hussard* became the 29ᵉ *Dragons*, and the 12ᵉ *Hussard* the 30ᵉ *Dragons*.

In theory, dragoons could operate equally as well as light cavalry or as battle cavalry for charges. Since 1789, the number of light cavalry regiments in the French Army had more than doubled in number, with 26 regiments; light cavalry was of increasing importance in picket and patrol work as well as screening the army, leaving the heavy cavalry for the shock of the charge. The *chasseurs à cheval* cost less to clothe and equip and train.

Chasseur of light infantry, c.1805. Hoffman shows us the theoretical dress of the various regiments of light infantry as they could have appeared at Austerlitz.

The most flamboyant regiments of the French Army after the imposing *cuirassiers* must surely have been the gaudily dressed hussars. The hussars at the time of Napoléon coming to power comprised 14 regiments, and six existed well before 1791. The famous 7ᵉ *Hussard* were formed in 1792 along with the 8ᵉ; the 9ᵉ, 10ᵉ and 11ᵉ came along in 1793; the 12ᵉ in 1794; the 13ᵉ in 1795 in its first incarnation, and the 14ᵉ in 1814. The 13ᵉ had been disbanded in 1796.

Chapter 3
Becoming a Soldier

So how did one become a soldier? This chapter seeks to answer that question. Firstly, how did men join the army and 'discover soldiering'?

Two routes were open to joining the army: either of your own free will, or being told to do so by the state via conscription. Conscription dated back to the dark days of 1793: following the military setbacks of 1792 that threatened the existence of the republic and an army crippled by desertion, the government resorted to conscription to regenerate the armed forces. The first *Levée* came in February 1793, to call into the army 300,000 troops. Each *département* would supply a particular percentage of the 300,000 through recruiting volunteers. This was repeated on 23 August 1793. Historian Alan Forrest holds that 'the *levée en masse* meant much more than a simple call to patriotism. It included a direct appeal to civic virtue and public responsibility.'[1] The *Levée* of August aimed to create an army a million strong. The *Levée* was carried out by municipal authorities under the close supervision of local Jacobin clubs and representatives-on-mission. The measure was deeply resented, and it is little wonder that the levy ultimately failed to raise a million-man army; despite this, however, the *Levée* did succeed in its principal goal, that of 'getting a large number of men into uniform in a very short time'.[2]

Conscription was formally established with the Jourdan-Delbrel Law of 1798. Hence forward, on an annual basis men aged between the ages of 20 and 25 were registered in five classes by the prefects of each department, aided by their assistants and the mayors. General Jean Lacuee was placed in overall charge of conscription. An innovation of the system was that substitutes were allowed, albeit at a set fee. This was an overtly political act: it meant that the sons of the middle and upper class and wealthy industrialists could 'buy their freedom' from any obligation to serve the state. It placed the burden squarely on the poor and working classes. The days of 'liberty, equality and brotherhood' were over. Money bought privilege.

Change came again with the decree of *1 Vendémiaire An 12* (23 September 1803): rather than local selection of men to be sent to the army, it was changed to the one of drawing lots. All those who were called up and unfit for service had to pay a fine of 50 to 100fr. All family bread winners, married men with children, men with a brother already in the army, the only son of a widow, the eldest of three orphans or a man with a father aged 70 or over were exempt from military service; substitution was forbidden until the law of 26 August 1805, which recognised the reality of paid substitutions, and placed the burden of conscription increasingly on the poorer classes.

The annual lot drawing took place in each commune, under the direction of the local mayor, with an officer of the Gendarmerie in attendance, as well as an army officer to

20 Napoleon's Army at Austerlitz

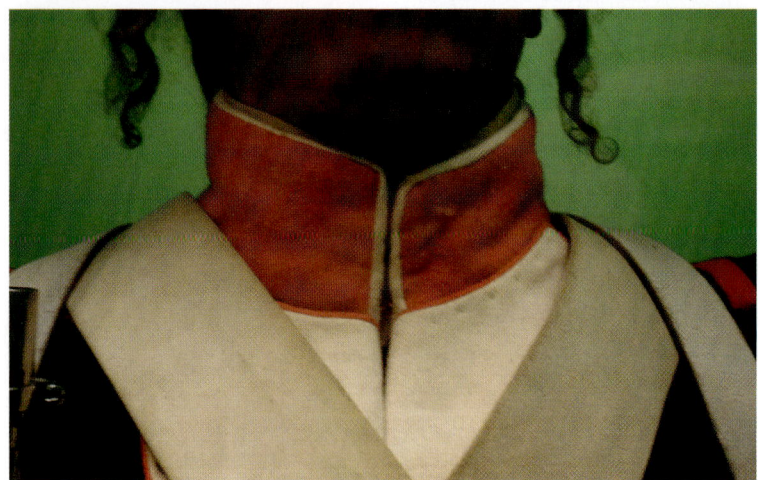

This mannequin comprising a melange of original items from the epoch gives a good impression of how French line infantry looked at Austerlitz. (*Musée de l'Empéri, Collections du Musée de l'armée, Anciennes collections Jean et Raoul Brunon*)

act as witness. A numbered ballot for each man of each commune who had reached the minimum age to be conscripted was placed in an urn. Each prospective conscript drew a ballot out of the urn; low-numbered men were taken first, higher-numbered men were called up later in the year or left at home until called up. In 1813 Napoléon drew heavily on the men not called up in 1809–12 to fill the ranks of his army along with the men of the class of 1813.

The end result of this process meant that the army that was camped at Boulogne was an eclectic mix of veterans of the Revolutionary Wars and some 'old-timers' from the Army of the King forming the cadres to an ostensibly conscript army that had never seen action. When we look at the 3e *de Ligne* at the time of the review on *24 Vendémiaire An 12* (17 October 1803), 558 men had enlisted before the *levée en mass* of 23 August 1793, out of 2,509 men under arms, 1,626 of which had experienced combat during the Revolutionary wars. Of the pre-1793 men, 43 had served before the Revolution, and the oldest man had enlisted in 1775.[3] Between forming up at Boulogne and marching to Vienna, over 400 conscripts would arrive.[4] Thus, of the 2,509 men under arms in August 1805, roughly 36% of the regiment had never been in action, with Austerlitz being their baptism of fire.[5]

The 3^e *de Ligne* was not unique, far from it. Of the men in the 4^e *de Ligne* on *17 Thermidor An 13* (5 August 1805), we find 35 men had served in the regiment before the Revolution, while 381 had volunteered between 1789 and 23 August 1793.[6] Of the regiment's 2,396 men under arms, 857 men, 35%, had any combat experience prior to Austerlitz.[7] Regardless of the hours of training, it would not have prepared the men to see

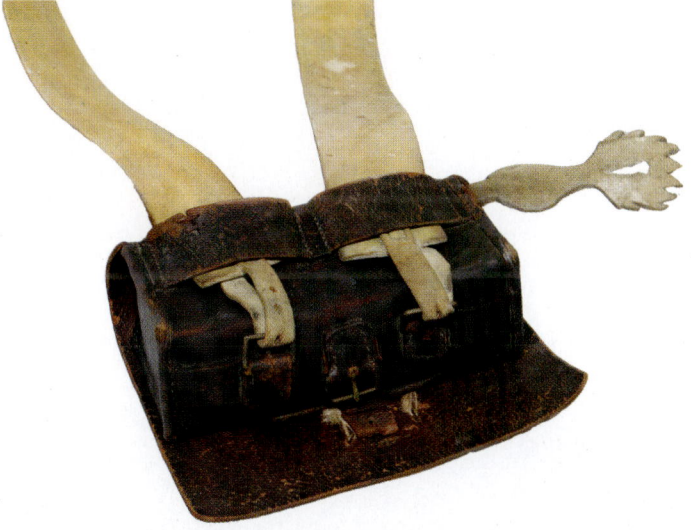

A grenadier's *giberne* carried on a fusilier's cross belt. We can see how the belt is fitted to the *giberne*. It is missing the leather straps to carry the *bonnet de police*, but the loops remain to fit the straps to. (*Private collection*)

their friends killed and maimed, or trained them to the sounds, sights and horrors that they would have endured. The 8ᵉ *de Ligne* on *27 Prairial An 13* (16 June 1805) had 2,546 men in three battalions. Just 23 men were veterans from the Royal Army, 121 had volunteered to join the regiment between 1789 and August 1793, with a total of 1,300 (51%) having combat experience.⁸ One hopes these veterans were concentrated in the war battalions. Brigaded with the 8ᵉ was the 45ᵉ *de Ligne*. On *1 Prairial An 11* (21 May 1803) the regiment had 61 men who had served before the fall of the Bastille and 219 had volunteered before the *levée en masse*, and in total 919 men had seen combat out of 1,786 men, 51%.⁹ By *1 Vendémiaire An 14* (23 September 1805), the regiment mustered 2,626 men, reducing the quota of combat veterans to 34%.¹⁰ Indeed, 840 conscripts had arrived over the previous year and were 'little more than children … many standing under 5 feet in height … have a weak and poor constitution'.¹¹ We suppose the 45ᵉ was far from 'a crack regiment'. Also serving with the 8ᵉ was the 54ᵉ *de Ligne*. Just 13 men had served the Army of the King on *1 Vendemiaire An 12* (24 September 1803), with 269 joining the regiment before August 1793, with a total of 1,158 men having been in action out of 1,446, 80%. After that date 600 conscripts had joined the unit: in total 1,414 men joined and 1,189 left. This brought the regimental strength to 2,198 men, of whom 52% had seen action by October 1805.¹²

French light infantry *schako* of the first issue, in use from 1800. Offering greater protection to the head than the *chapeau*, it was the model on which the 1806 *schako* was based. Some models of the light infantry *schako* as late as 1803 had detachable peaks. (*Musée de l'Armée*)

In the same division were the 94ᵉ and 95ᵉ *de Ligne*. The 94ᵉ had just 17 men who had served in the Royal Army and all had set off to Ireland with General Hoche. Another 198 had volunteered between the fall of the bastille and August 1793, with 1,207 men having seen action by *22 Nivôse An 12* (13 January 1804), when the regiment mustered 2,162 men.¹³ On *16 Thermidor An 13* (4 August 1805), the regiment mustered 2,130 men, of which 1,115 were conscripts who had joined the regiment, thus 51% on this date had been in action.¹⁴

We see that the men assembled were a mix of 'old hands' and fresh-faced recruits: the coming campaign was their baptism of fire and inauguration into the world of soldiering. Stiffened by veterans, these men became the nucleus – if they were lucky to survive – of the armies fielded at Friedland, Wagram and elsewhere.

The Regimental Depot

Once given a clean bill of health, the men were marched by the Gendarmerie to the depot of whichever regiment needed replacements.

 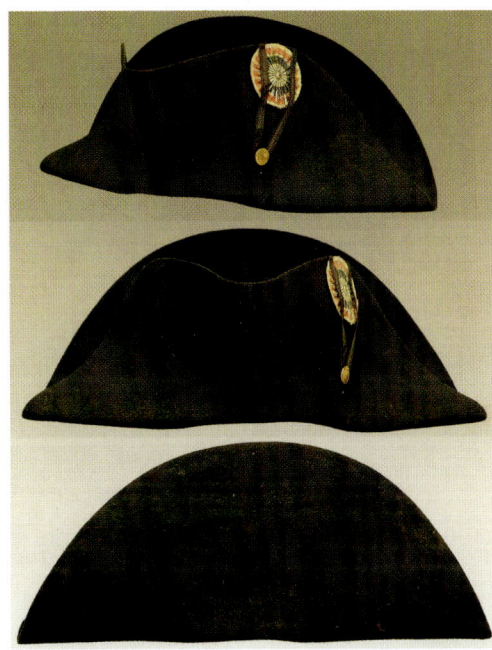

A French fusilier's *chapeau*. Totally useless in offering head protection, and often simply collapsing in wet, this was the traditional headdress of the French solider until well into 1808. (*Private collection*)

The formal framework for instruction was part of the reorganisation of the army under the terms of the decree of *1 Vendémiaire An 12* (24 September 1803). The decree outlined that every regiment was to have three battalions: two were classed as 'war battalions' and the third was a training or depot battalion. It was in the depot under the orders of the regiment's major that the men were given their basic training, clothed and equipped. It was the major who oversaw that the regimental workmen produced the necessary number of uniforms required. Upon arriving at the regiment's depot, the conscript's name would be entered in the *contrôle nominatif troupe* and he was assigned to an ordinary, i.e. mess, as well as his squad, and allocated bunk in the barracks. He was then sent to the quartermaster to be issued his uniform. The following the day the new soldier began his basic training, upon completion of which he would be posted to one of the two war battalions.

The 'Rules and Regulations for the Field Exercise and Manoeuvres of the Infantry of 1 August 1791' was the set text of 'necessary knowledge' for officers and men alike in the infantry. Upon joining their unit 'john raw recruit', or in this case the conscript, was handed over to the corporals for initiating in military and basic training:

When a recruit arrives in a squad, after he has been registered, the corporal will make sure he can do the required drill, he will then assign him to the class to which he believes he can go. If this recruit does not know anything at all, the corporal will instruct him for eight days of the means to turn his head squarely at the pivot, to position himself well and to march the various steps prescribed by the regulations on the exercise of infantry. At the end of the eight days of this school, he will make him take up arms and exercise him in the handling of arms, in charge and in fire; the duration of the exercise should never be more than an hour during which there will be only two or three short rests.

Each corporal will exercise the recruits of his squad twice a day, morning and evening, at the hours prescribed.

Every *decade*,[15] the corporal will read to his squad the rights of men as soldiers, the crimes and punishment of military law and some articles of the theory on the service of garrisons or campaign, according to the circumstances. Until a recruit is fully trained, the corporal must never tire of speaking to him about his training and as long as the recruit has aptitude for the military state, the training of the corporal will be neither painful nor of long duration, and by instructing his recruit he will strengthen himself in the knowledge and the principles of his profession.[16]

Soldier's uniform coat or *habit* of the type worn at Austerlitz. (Musée de l'Armée)

For those readers who went through armed forces basic training, the routine and details will feel familiar. More details about the duties of the corporal-instructor can be found in a document from 1805:

> He shall pay the greatest attention so as not to put the young soldier off from learning his trade, by his brusqueness, nor by his impatience. All men do not learn, or contribute equally or at the same pace, to being taught; patience and calmness shall be the greatest virtue of the instructor. He shall study the character and intellectual capacity of each man who he is to instruct, and shall use these insights to determine the tone and vigour of the lessons.
>
> These lessons shall not be of too long a duration; it is infinitely preferable to repeat (the lessons) more often.
>
> The corporal-instructor shall follow exactly the lessons prescribed by the exercise regulations, and shall never depart from them.
>
> He shall not proceed to the second lesson until the recruit is perfectly at ease with the first; without which his instruction will invariably be wanting: undue haste in this matter is a most dangerous vice.[17]

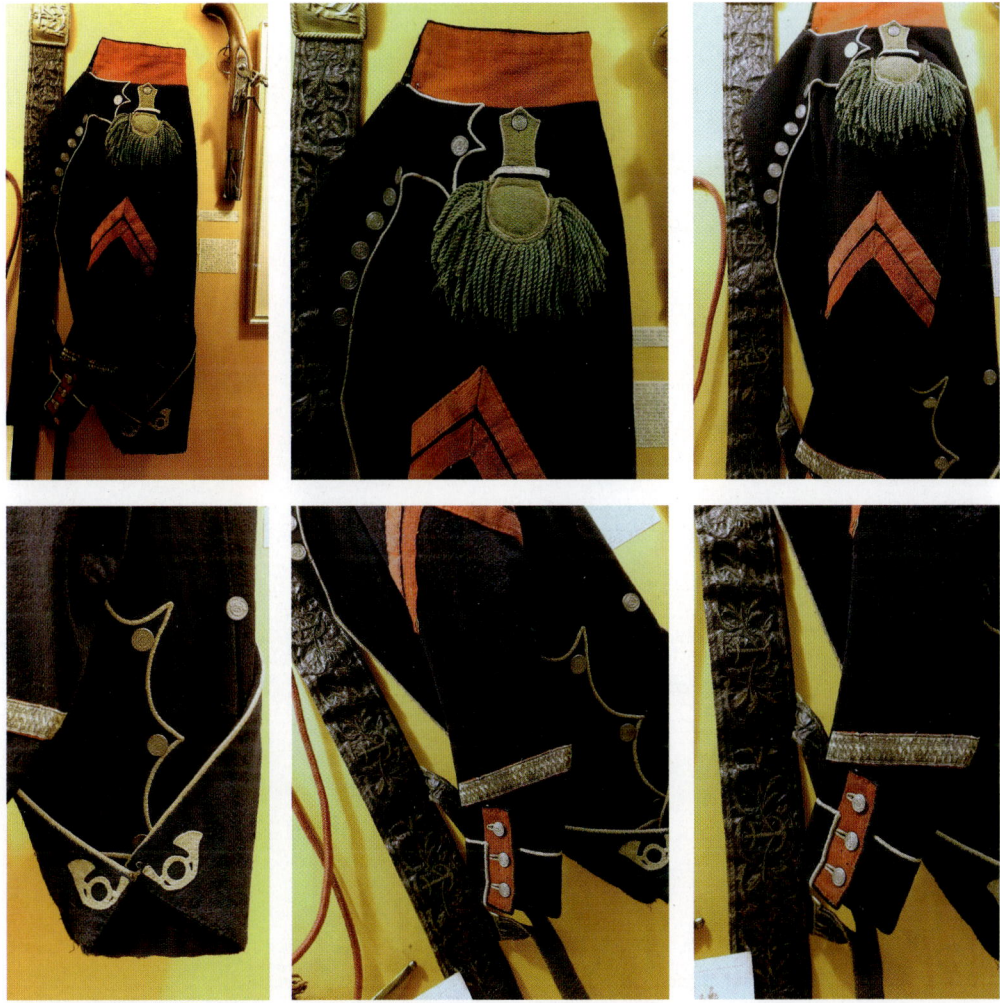

Sergeant's *habit* of light infantry of the type worn at Austerlitz. (*Musée de l'Empéri, Collections du Musée de l'armée, Anciennes collections Jean et Raoul Brunon*)

Then as now, training was broken down into 'bite-sized chunks'. Conscripts were initially trained individually in the School of the Soldier (*école du soldat*). For infantry, cavalry and artillery, this meant learning how to stand as a soldier, how to march and carry out basic manoeuvres as a formed body of men. One of the first lessons a conscript learned was how to stand without moving for 15 minutes. In addition, the men were taught how to handle their musket, and to load and fire it in twelve movements. Montesquiou-Fezensac, who joined the 59ᵉ *régiment de la Ligne* in 1804, recounts that when he started to 'learn the drill', which he found 'rather hard … the musket seeming heavy for lack of practice'.[18]

Once these skills were mastered, the infantry moved to the platoon school – *école du peleton* – and the cavalry men began to take their first lessons in equitation. Gunners were passed to the gun teams to learn their duties.

For the infantry, the *école du peleton* used the same material as already taught but applied it to small formations of men up to company strength. The next level of training, the School of the Battalion – *école du bataillon* – focused on formations and their manoeuvres. The final stage consisted of full regimental manoeuvres, which concerned marching in line and column, including transition to line of battle, as well as brigade movements.

During initial instruction, conscripts were drilled three or four times a day. The instructor would record the progress of their conscripts, noting the dates that they had achieved basic competency, before being sent to a war battalion. Jean-Baptiste Boisson, writing in 1809, recounts how 'horrific training' began the day after his arrival with the 2e *Légère*, writing 'the *sous-officiers* allowed us hardly any respite. We had to repeat the "Attention" and "At ease" positions a hundred times.' He adds 'we had to learn the march step, two feet in length from one heel to the other, seventy-six paces per minute; that's what the sergeant kept yelling at us. We were also initiated into the mysteries of the oblique step.' Constant drilling was exhausting, and when evening came, as Jean-Baptiste Boisson admitted, 'we were done in.'[19]

The key to being a good soldier was being able to 'shoot straight'. Under the 1791 regulation, target practice was to be a regular occurrence. For this purpose, a battalion was allocated 250kg of power and 125kg of shot. The targets used were roughly the same height as the average soldier, 5ft 6in tall and 21in wide, and were to be fired at from 300ft, 600ft and 900ft. At the first two ranges, the men were instructed to fire at the middle of the target, at 900ft at the top third.[20]

Officers, like their men, wore greatcoats on campaign. This officer is typical of those seen at Austerlitz. (*Musée de l'Empéri, Collections du Musée de l'armée, Anciennes collections Jean et Raoul Brunon*)

A soldier's training also included 'physical jerks'. The regulation of 5 April 1792 recommended conditioning soldiers about to embark on campaign by exercising the men on route marches in FSMO – field service marching order – i.e., with arms and full equipment. Over time the marches were to grow from a few miles to ten or more, and as

Off duty, officers and men alike wore a fatigue cap or *bonnet de police*. This is an officer's example – those of soldiers were broadly similar – presumably for an unknown regiment of *Chasseurs*. This example is notable as its cut is markedly different to preserved examples for other ranks. (*Collection de l'Office du Tourisme de Pontarlier. Dépôt au Musée municipal de Pontarlier, France*)

the men became fitter they would take place in full midday sun. Bardin's infantry manual of 1807 suggested that light infantry and *voltigeur*s ought to be able to swim, run, leap ditches and climb.

Education was not forgotten; the 1792 Police Regulation for the internal discipline of a regiment stated that from 1 October to 1 May each year, each regiment was to form a school to teach reading, writing and basic arithmetic. The school room was to be set up in a barrack and furnished with tables and benches. Books, text books, pens and paper were provided by a bounty from the war ministry: as we shall see, the regimental schools were vital at keeping up morale.

Clothing the Soldier

As with the modern-day armed forces, the clothing that was issued to a 'squaddie' was done so on a regulated basis, each item being described by a series of dress regulations. Each item of clothing had a specified duration period. A *habit* (the uniform coat) had to last two years, a bearskin 20 years, a pair of *culottes* a matter of months. Every year a regiment would be inspected, and the condition of the clothing assessed. A return of all the clothing to be struck off/disposed of was made, and the appropriate number of new items ordered. Clothing and equipment needing repairs was also logged, as was how many items had been repaired since the last inspection. The soldier was responsible for the repair of their own clothing and any costs associated. Likewise, if they lost items, they had to purchase replacement items – in many ways a soldier ended up paying to be in the army when these deductions were taken into consideration. It was very much make do and mend by the time the cloth items of equipment were coming to the end of their service life. These inspection returns are a fantastic resource for outlining what a regiment actually wore rather than the theory based on the regulations. The two often did not agree in practice. The regiment's clothing and equipment was overseen by the regiment's

Austerlitz was the first battle in which the newly created *cuirassiers* took part. This mannequin, comprising original uniform items, gives an excellent impression of how a *cuirassier* looked in parade dress. (*Musée de l'Empéri, Collections du Musée de l'armée, Anciennes collections Jean et Raoul Brunon*)

clothing officer. His work was overseen by an Inspector General. The lieutenant clothing officer had to oversee the purchase of all items of equipment and clothing for the *sous-officiers* and men. Officers provided their own uniforms and equipment. The regimental council oversaw that the items purchased on the regiment's behalf were of good quality, that they matched the model items sent by the War Ministry, and that the cost of purchase was as agreed in the contract. All receipts had to be lodged in separate account books that were overseen by a Commissioner for War. This was to ensure that officers did not pocket money off the regiment obtaining contracts. The specification for each item of uniform was recorded in a Register of Uniforms (*registre de tenues*). The Commissioner for War was to ensure that items purchased matched this register. All deliberations of the council in obtaining contracts for clothing and equipment from contractors were to be recorded so that the Commissioner for War could see how and why a regiment chose a certain contractor.

At company level the company sergeant major had charge of the *Livre de Detail*: in this book each man in the company was recorded, along with what items of clothing and equipment he was issued and when, as well as the fines levied against him for damaging regimental clothing. The men of the Grande Armée were paid professionals. They were paid, in theory, weekly, according to rank and status. In all cases, the pay was subject to a number of deductions for communal funds (masses), which left very little actual money. The purpose of the pay was actually not to give the soldier pocket money to spend on wine, women and gambling but so he could pay for fines, pay repair bills for his clothing and equipment, purchase soap and cleaning equipment and if needed buy new items of clothing. All repairs were carried out under the auspices of the *caporal-fourrier*. Minor repairs were to be carried out to clothing and equipment by the soldier; for more major repairs, the *caporal-fourrier* took the soldier and his damaged items to the captain clothing officer, who authorised the regimental workmen to undertake the repair. If the repair was judged to be the fault of negligence of the soldier he had to pay for the work or a replacement item from his pay.[21] It is these fines that the sergeant major wrote diligently in his book.

A soldier's clothing was financed by three distinct 'funds'. The most important fund was the *1ᵉ Masse*: this provided the man on joining the army with his complete uniform.

Second in importance was the *Masse General*, or general fund, from which the

On campaign, officers, like their men, wrapped themselves in voluminous cloaks. (*Musée de l'Empéri, Collections du Musée de l'armée, Anciennes collections Jean et Raoul Brunon*)

soldier's next issue of clothing was paid. The fund was set at 48fr 29 centimes per man per year in the line infantry, and some 49fr 53 centimes for a soldier in a light infantry regiment. From this fund, the regimental Council of Administration drew its necessary funds to buy raw materials, equipment and headdress as well as to pay the regimental workmen. It also covered sundry items such as the epaulettes of the *adjutant-sous-officiers*, lace for rank stripes, service chevrons, musicians and drummers, plumes and pompoms. The fund was to provide a soldier with his full issue of uniform and equipment upon arrival with his regiment, which included two shirts, a black stock with buckle, a pair each of linen and woollen socks, two pairs of shoes, a pair of black twill gaiters, a pair of grey linen gaiters, his ration bag (*sac a distribution*) which was so large that it could be used as a sleeping bag, his *havresac*, two cockades, vent prick and musket worm as well as other sundry items. In addition, the fund covered the repairs to uniform and equipment that were not due to negligence of the soldier.[22]

The third fund was the 'linen and shoe fund'. The fund paid for supplementary items to the bare minimum uniform provided by the clothing fund. The fund paid for the soldier to have a third shirt, three white stocks, an additional pair of linen socks, two handkerchiefs, a third pair of shoes and cleaning kit. Prior to 25 April 1806 it had also allowed for a pair of white parade gaiters but it was then switched to pay for a pair of linen overalls. The fund was paid for at the rate of 12 centimes a day for *sous-officiers* and 7 centimes for other ranks.[23]

Everything bar weapons was made 'in house' where possible, or if not then purchased by the regiment from civilian contractors. Every year a third of the regiment's cloth work was replaced, so every 36 months a soldier received a new *habit*.[24] Each year the council of administration, acting with the clothing officers, drew up a store's inventory of the regiment, as well as gathering the parade states of the items of equipment and clothing issued. It is as if clothing had a specific lifespan. Each time an item was inspected it was classed as either new, in need of repair, due to expire, or expired and in need of replacement. From this data the clothing officer was able to report the total number of items needing to be replaced or repaired. The contracts for repair of clothing have not survived, but the minutes drawn up by the council of administration do.[25] Under the terms of the 1791 regulation, the War Administration supplied regiments directly with the broadcloth, tricot, serge and linen to make *habits*, *vestes*, *surtouts*, *culottes* and *bonnets de police*. The war administration also provided grenadiers' bearskins, *gibernes* with belts, sabre belts, musket slings.[26]

A stunning example of a *cuirassier* officer's helmet. (*Musée de l'Empéri, Collections du Musée de l'armée, Anciennes collections Jean et Raoul Brunon*)

The regimental council of administration was responsible for shouldering the cost of producing the clothing and equipment in house as it was made by the regimental craftsmen, as well as the provision of lace for trumpeters, gold, silver and worsted lace for rank and service stripes, the epaulettes for adjutants, and the lace for the *bonnets de police*, *chapeaux*, plumes, shoes, socks, underwear etc.[27] Therefore, each regiment was responsible for the clothing of each man in the regiment with little or no reliance on external contractors.

Shoes, *havresacs* and other one size fits all items were mass produced. Shoes came in three sizes. *Schakos* came in three sizes. Cloth uniforms came in three sizes. This allowed for standardisation and thus ease of production. Ideally each conscript was to receive his issue uniform and then have it fitted to him by the regimental tailor – this perhaps seldom happened unless a regiment was on garrison duty. Leather items were ordered from manufacturers, as were metal fittings like buttons. Headdress was also outsourced. If made in house or bought in, *marches* would be prepared for agreement by the regiment's administrative council, who would oversee the work and inspect the quality of the workmanship or materials. Each regiment it seems kept a sealed pattern for each item of equipment that was the established model to be copied by suppliers.[28] Due to shortages of buff leather, blackened cow hide was used to make cross belts and other items. An order given to the Army of the Rhine, dated 18 April 1793, stated that blackened cow hide was to be used due to the scarcity of buff leather. General Schauenbourg notes in an inspection of the 31e *Demi-Brigade* in Strasbourg on *15 Pluviôse An 5* (3 February 1797) that all the musket slings, *giberne* belts and *baudriers* were made from blackened cow hide. The practice was – in theory – abolished on *11 Thermidor An 8* (29 July 1799), yet General Schauenbourg, in a report of *30 Pluviôse An 10* (19 February 1802) for the 110e *Demi-Brigade* stated that the majority of *giberne* belts and *baudriers* were made from blackened leather, of which a part had been bleached. On *3 Nivôse An 14* (24 December 1805), Marshal Kellerman wrote to the Minister for War, General Clarke, that he found in the stores at Strasbourg a great quantity of *giberne* belts and *baudriers* as well as musket slings made from blackened cow hide, which he had to issue to conscripts as they passed through the depot as no buff

An other ranks *cuirassier* helmet: Not of the earliest model issued, however it gives a good idea of a trooper's helmet. (*Private collection, France*)

First model *cuirass* and officer's *bonnet de police*. (*Private collection, France*)

items existed.[29] It would not be until after the Battle of Jena that all the blackened cow hide equipment was removed from service.

As well as relying on regimental-level production, Berthier, as Minister for War, ordered that a huge stock pile of clothing and equipment was to be created at Amiens:

10,000 *habits (d'infanterie)*
10,000 *vestes (d'infanterie)*
20,000 *culottes en drap (d'infanterie)*
400 *habits d'artillerie, sapeurs*, etc (or the cloth to make them)
250 *uniformes de hussards* (or the cloth to make them)
250 *uniformes de chasseurs* (or the cloth to make them)
150 *uniformes d'artillerie à cheval* (or the cloth to make them)
1,000 *habits de dragons* (or the cloth to make them)
1,000 *vestes de dragons*
500 *culottes de peau*
60,000 infantry *capotes*
500 *manteaux de hussards, chasseurs ou canonniers à cheval*
1,000 *manteaux de dragons*
400 grenadier bearskins
10,000 *chapeaux*
500 light infantry *schakos*
250 dragoon helmets
50,000 shirts
25,000 pairs of stockings
10,000 pairs of black gaiters
1,000 pairs of *hussard* boots
2,000 pairs of dragoon boots
80,000 pairs of shoes

Equipment
10,000 *havresacs*
5,000 *porte gibernes*
5,000 *baudriers*
250 *porte-mousquetons*
500 *ceinturons*
500 *bretelles de fusil*
500 bayonet scabbards
50 drums
100 drum carriages
100 pairs of drum sticks
5,000 *gibernes*
1,000 pairs of spurs

Harness

250 *hussard* saddles
500 *dragon* saddles
250 *hussard* bridles
500 *dragon* bridles
250 *porte manteaux de hussards*
500 *porte manteaux de dragons*
2,000 nose bags
1,000 curry combs
1,000 sponges
250 saddle blankets
50,000 horse shoes
200,000 shoe nails[30]

Berthier also ordered a complete array of campaign equipment that included cook pots, canteens, shovels, spades, axes and 80,000 personal canteens. This stockpile was to be used to issue on campaign and to make up for the regimental shortages: of course, the state ordering vast quantities of items, simultaneously to regiments placing vast orders, meant that as supplies of material dwindled, costs rose and both regiments and the state were competing against each other to obtain items. Despite this seemingly chaotic situation, it remained in place until 1822. The process whereby the state obtained items was overseen by the Clothing Directory at the Ministry for War, set up in summer 1800.[31]

Austerlitz marked the use of dragoons as second-line cavalry, performing duties of picket and patrol work, as well as charging in the line of battle. This officer's helmet is typical of those worn during the battle. (*Musée de l'Empéri, Collections du Musée de l'armée, Anciennes collections Jean et Raoul Brunon*)

Chapter 4

The Cavalry

The cavalry needed two things to be effective: men who could ride, and horses. Training of both took time.

As Minister for War, General Bernadotte had, by and large, swept away the corruption of the revolutionary epoch where colonels bought their regiment's mounts, and replaced it with a centralised system, less open to fraud, in September 1799. This logical and eminently sensible system was abolished by Consul Bonaparte on *1 Prairial An 10* (21 May 1802), reverting back to the previous system.[1] For this, both Bernadotte – quickly making an enemy of Bonaparte – and Inspector General of Cavalry Antoine Bourcier heavily censored Bonaparte, the latter lamenting that colonels who knew little about horses got themselves swindled by unscrupulous dealers. Others, he noted, were in league with the horse dealers and swindled the government by purchasing horses totally unsuitable for purpose at a much lower price than the government allowed, asking for reimbursement of the horses at the set price and pocketing the difference.[2]

Trooper's helmet of the type likely worn at Austerlitz. (*Private collection, France*)

The most flamboyant of all the cavalry at Austerlitz were the French hussars. This sergeant's *dolman* of the 9e regiment is typical of those worn at the battle. (*Collection Office du Tourisme, Fontainebleau*).

To rectify some of the misgivings, on *18 Brumaire An 12* (10 November 1803), the Minister-Director Dejean issued 'Instructions for service in remounts'. Inspectors General were placed in charge of selecting horses for purchase, while the regimental colonels handled the paperwork. The instructions laid out the amount of money allocated per year for remounts as follows:

*Carabinier*s and *cuirassiers*	71.43fr
Dragoons	65.72fr
Chasseurs and hussars	51.43fr
Horse artillery	65.72fr
Train artillery bans	51.43fr

These funds were partially raised by selling worn-out horses – casting – as well as government funds. The sale of horses was monitored closely, the sale having to be verified by a vet, an inspector and *Commissaire de Guerre*. The decree also fixed the price of mounts, ranging from 500.00fr per horse in the heavy cavalry to 460.00fr for dragoons,

Incredibly rare *dolman* for a trumpeter of the 9e *Hussard*. Yellow with sky blue facings and black braid, it is a highly distinctive uniform. (*Musée de l'Empéri, Collections du Musée de l'armée, Anciennes collections Jean et Raoul Brunon*)

On campaign, many hussar officers wore a much more sombre uniform comprising a *habit*. This example belongs to the 5e *Hussard*. (*Musée de l'Empéri, Collections du Musée de l'armée, Anciennes collections Jean et Raoul Brunon*)

and 360.00fr for *chasseurs*, hussars, and the artillery and train. The purchase of horses was to be authorised by the regimental administrative council, which delegated an experienced officer to make a transaction. To give an idea of the sums involved, a dragoon regiment, for example, had 906 men and 596 horses; its authorised *masse de Remonte* was 596 × 65.72fr = 39,170fr, which allowed the purchase of about 106–110 new mounts per year.[3]

Article IV of the aforementioned 'Instructions' specified the regions (with their corresponding breed of horse) that were supposed to furnish mounts for the various branches of cavalry. For example, Mecklenburg in Germany was designated for *cuirassiers*, l'Eure or la Manche for dragoons, Ardennes, du Cantal, des Pyrenees for light cavalry, and the like. Next, Art. VI provided a chart for the preferred height of the

A trademark item of apparel of the hussars was their sabretache, here we see an example of the 8e regiment. (*Musée de l'Empéri, Collections du Musée de l'armée, Anciennes collections Jean et Raoul Brunon*)

mounts (in the new metric system, along with the old one, based on *pieds* and *lignes*). *Cuirassier* horses had to stand 15.1hh to 15.3hh, dragoons 14.3 to 15.1hh and for the light cavalry 14hh to 14hh. The minimum age of acceptance for purchase was four, the maximum was ten.

The horses were selected for purchase by the Inspectors General aided by the officers of the regiment, who dealt directly with the dealer. The horses had to fit to a tight requirement for shape, size and confirmation. Upon arrival with the regiment the purchased horses were examined by a vet, assisted by a *commissaire de guerre* or *sous-inspecteur aux revues* (assigned to a particular military district) and, in the absence of one or the other, by a member of the civil authorities, after which the horses might be transferred to the unit and the dealer paid in full there and then.[4]

Obtaining the horse was just one part of the process: they had to be 'backed' and trained to be ridden. This took almost a year of hard work by the allocated regimental staff. The process of backing a horse and training it was overseen by the riding master and 'rough riders'. It relied on skilled horsemen. The position of riding master was created on *15 Germinal An 5* (4 April 1797) and ranked as a corporal, becoming a post of prestige by the middle years of the Empire with the rank of captain.[5] The riding master of a cavalry regiment schooled the men and conscripts to make them competent riders, who had to be able to carry out eight basic movements and show their competency at them

The Cavalry

This elegant dragoon officer of the 23e regiment gives a good impression of how many officers would have looked at Austerlitz. (*Musée de l'Empéri, Collections du Musée de l'armée, Anciennes collections Jean et Raoul Brunon*)

to the satisfaction of the riding master. The riding master was to have passed the 18-month course at the Military Riding School: at least that was the theory. Officers and select *sous-officiers* were taught here to ride to a high level to be the instructors of the future at the cavalry schools. It would be these men who would train new recruits to the cavalry. On *11 Nivôse An 13* (1 January 1805) General Bourcier reported to the Minister for War that the *dépôts* of the *cuirassiers* and *carabinier*s comprised of officers unfit for service with the army and were incapable of training mounts and men, and in consequence should be replaced by officers better suited for the purpose as riding masters.[6] Furthermore, Bourcier ordered the regimental colonels to ensure their *dépôts* had one captain and five lieutenants appointed, a minimum of two from the Equitation School at Versailles, and the existing officers retired. Furthermore, Bourcier passed orders that Inspectors General of the Cavalry were to appoint six captains, five lieutenants and five *sous-lieutenants* to act as assistant inspectors to directly oversee the activities of the *dépôts*, and to

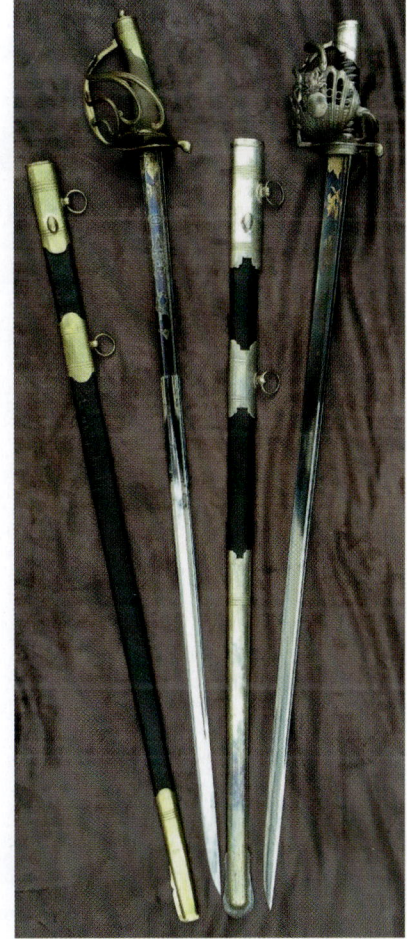

Trooper's (left) and officer's sabres of line dragoon regiments. (*Private collection, France*)

ensure horses were broken correctly to the regulations of 1788, which is discussed later in this book.[7] This all took time to implement, and we do wonder what the quality of training received before the cavalry left for Vienna was actually like.

Training the Men

The third part of organising a cavalry regiment, and time-consuming, was training the conscripts to ride. The vast majority of the conscripts taken into the mounted arm had never ridden a horse, thus it would take time for cavalry commanders to train their men and mould their new commands into combat forces.[8] The new cavalry troopers and artillery drivers were drilled in the art of equitation for several hours a day, for at least six months, which allowed troopers to at least remain in the saddle during reviews and carry out basic field manoeuvres.[9] Jacques Chevillet, who joined the 8e *Chasseurs à Cheval*, had never sat on a horse in his life:

> I had to go to exercises to learn how to become a good horseman, which cost me the pain of falling off my horse every day in the riding school, since these first exercises were done with only a folded blanket strapped to the horse's back. I could not get the knack of staying on the horse with my short legs and kept rolling off like a package, especially when beginning the trot or gallop. I tried to make myself more secure by closing my legs and clutching the mane, but my Chiml [his horse] was crafty, like all old trumpeters' mounts, and was not above putting her head between her legs and bucking until she had thrown me off. Luckily, I never got badly hurt: someone soon put me back up saying, 'Stay up there you little bugger!' There was no point in being disheartened, and gradually I began to get the hang of it; you only need determination to get what you want.[10]

Austerlitz marked the transition for the *Chasseur à Cheval* regiments away from hussar dress to their own unique style, as exemplified by this example of the 22e regiment. (*Musée de l'Empéri, Collections du Musée de l'armée, Anciennes collections Jean et Raoul Brunon*)

It was essential that every man in the regiment knew their drills and could ride to the same standard. It was just as essential every man knew how to care for their horse. Horses were expensive, so the new recruit's first lesson was on a dummy horse, and then an 'old nag' school master. He learned to use his sword on a wooden horse – it was easy to repair if an ear was lopped off, unlike the real thing. The conscript had to be able to ride the following manoeuvres to the satisfaction of the riding master before being allowed to join a company and leave the training dépôt:[11]

1) to mount and dismount, 2) the position of the horse at the halt and the riders' position. 3) to understand the use and effect of the reins, the bit and bridle, the legs and the spurs (as well as their correct position on the boot). 4) to learn the paces of the horse on the lunge without and then with saddle and to clear hurdles without falling off. 5) to ride the paces of the horse with saddle but without stirrups or bridle, to ensure the rider could move his horse using his body weight (seat) and legs,

Although not glamorous, the artillery were an important factor in Napoleonic battles. This is an example of a line foot artillery *giberne*. (*Private collection*)

Dressed as hussars, we see a gunner's *dolman*, the horse artillery considered themselves a cut above the foot artillery. (*Musée de l'Armée*)

An iconic object: a bearskin of the grenadiers of the old guard, worn from Marengo to Waterloo. (*Musée de l'Empéri, Collections du Musée de l'armée, Anciennes collections Jean et Raoul Brunon*)

A gorget belonging to an officer of the Old Guard. (*Private collection, France*)

Officer of *Chasseurs à Pied* of the Old Guard. (*Musée de l'Empéri, Collections du Musée de l'armée, Anciennes collections Jean et Raoul Brunon*)

leaving his hands relatively free to handle his sabre, pistols or musketoon. This deepened the rider's seat, and sweated off excess fat. He did all his movement with his arms folded across his chest to give him a truly independent seat. 6) To be able to ride the three paces with bridle and stirrups, and to learn in the three paces, the oblique march, a turn to the left and right, to about face and to wheel left or right. 7) to maintain his arms and equipment. 8) to ride a course of heads.

In addition, he had to be able to correctly tack his horse up, know how to care for his saddle, bridle, and bit. Three times a day each trooper, under the command of a sergeant, had to don their stable clothing and groom their horses, muck their stables out, and learn that to sponge a horse's dock before its eyes was as serious as tightening a girth around a horse's stomach swollen from a recent feed.

The soldiers in the artillery train had an even harder task: they had to learn how to ride, how to harness a pair of horses and how to drive both the pair of horses they were responsible for, but also in a team of four or six. They had to care for not one horse, but two. Unglamorous and labour intensive, without the artillery train, the army had no artillery, stores waggons or siege train.

Trooper's sabretache of the *Chasseurs à Cheval* of the Imperial Guard. On campaign, this item was protected with a leather cover. (*Private collection*)

This *pelisse* belonged to a sergeant of the *Chasseurs à Cheval* of the Imperial Guard, who daily escorted the Emperor. (*Musée de l'Empéri, Collections du Musée de l'armée, Anciennes collections Jean et Raoul Brunon*)

An exceptionally well preserved bearskin of the iconic *Grenadiers à Cheval* of the Imperial Guard. (*Collection de l'Office du Tourisme de Pontarlier. Dépôt au Musée municipal de Pontarlier, France*)

Chapter 5

Boulogne

Having completed their basic training, men were marched off in groups of 50 to 100 to join their regiment. Unlike during the Revolutionary Wars where conscripts were hastily sent into action, now, at a time of relative 'peace and plenty' time could be devoted to training both the 'old sweats' and new hands. This would become the *raison d'être* of the camp of Boulogne.

Building the Camps

From the outset, the camps were seen as fairly permanent installations. About the laying out of the camps, Marshal Soult commanding IV Corps ordered on *30 Fructidor An XI* (17 September 1803):

> The troops will be barracked in three lines, there will be 9 barracks per company.
> The barracks will measure 12 pied long, by 12 pied wide. Will measure 2 pied at the lamp pit – *cul de lamp* – and will be open at the gable end. The barracks will be sunken into the ground by 3 pouce.
> There will be 4 pied between each barrack of the company and an 8 pied interval between companies.[1]

The barracks Soult describes were bell shaped and in essence a permanent construction of a tent. The excavated barracks from Ney's VI Corps are rectangular with no *cul de lamp*.[2] Soult added that behind the nine rows of barracks came those of the *sous-officiers*, and beyond the third line were the 'company kitchens, each to measure 6 pied by 12 pied'.[3] Beyond the kitchens came, according to Ney, 'the Surgeon-majors, adjutants, *sous-officiers*, drum majors and musicians, launderers and *vivandières*, will barrack on the same line as the *sous-officiers*' accommodation. The grenadiers occupied the barracks at the right-hand side of each company, along with the sergeant major and *fourrier* of the company.'[4] Construction of the huts did not begin immediately, as Jacques Bellavoine of the *55e de Ligne* tells us:

> it was in the 1st Vendémiaire year 12 of the Republic (24 September 1803) where we were given a field to make our home. The General Commanding the Division told us: this my children is your destination; in two or 3 days, we will bring you wood to make your huts [...] we slept for 4 or 5 nights under the stars.[5]

Excavated soldier's hut from the camp of Boulogne. The ground plan is worth comparing with this contemporary representation of the huts at the camp. Some are made from timber planks, others from stones, rendered white. In both cases the roofs are, we assume, thatch or turf. With no drains and little ventilation, these huts became extremely squalid. With 30,000 men in the same camping area for 18 months, the lack of space for latrines, middens – and rubbish disposal in general – fuel and food resources, meant that the camp became hell on earth. (*Frederick Lemaire*)

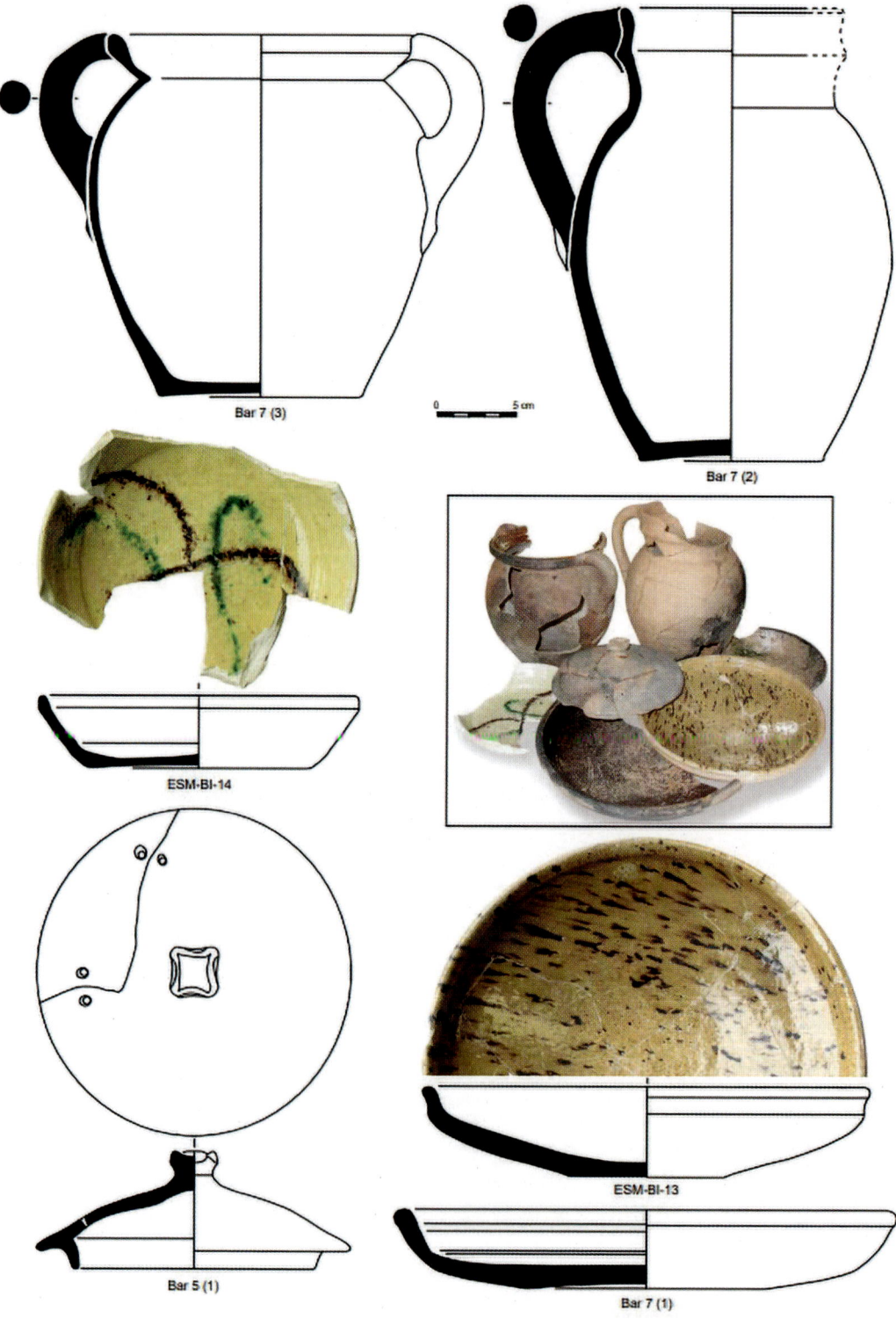

Recovered storage vessels and other ceramic items from an excavated soldiers' hut in the Camp of Boulogne. (*Frederick Lemaire*)

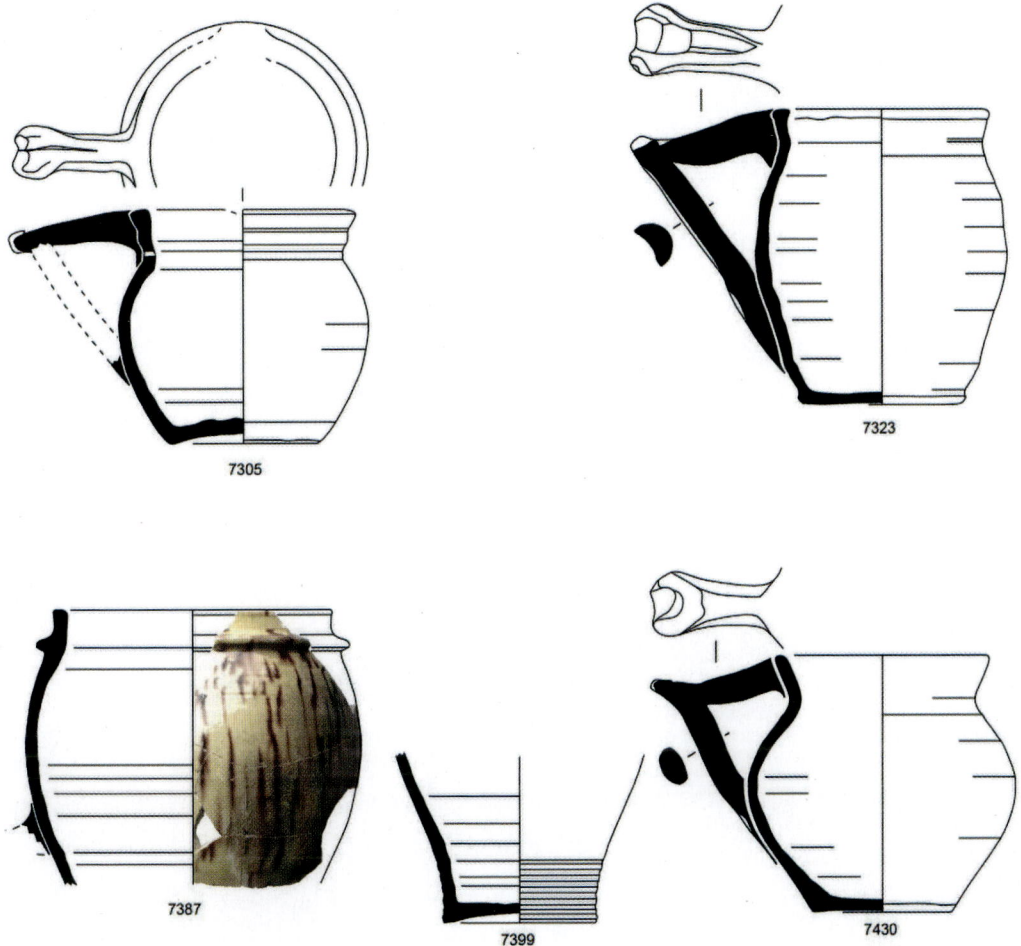

Recovered pitchers and other storage vessels ceramic items from excavated soldiers' huts in Boulogne. (*Frederick Lemaire*)

Beyond the soldiers' accommodation were the officers' lodgings. Officers of the same company were to have a single barrack, their servants having their own separate accommodation. Each officer on the staff had their own barrack, at least in theory.[6] The future General Marchand reports that officers – being gentlemen – did not build their accommodation themselves and instead had to pay for it:

> those who are most to be pitied in all this are the soldiers and the officers … They are supplied with wood, straw, and turf, and with that they make themselves barracks […] The officers are obliged to employ their soldiers to build their barracks, and they pay them like day labourers, which is quite expensive for them. The colonels' hut costs them up to 400 F.[7]

Unlike the infantry, the cavalry was quartered in churches, monasteries, barns and other large spaces. As well as using buildings, thousands of men spent years under canvas: a

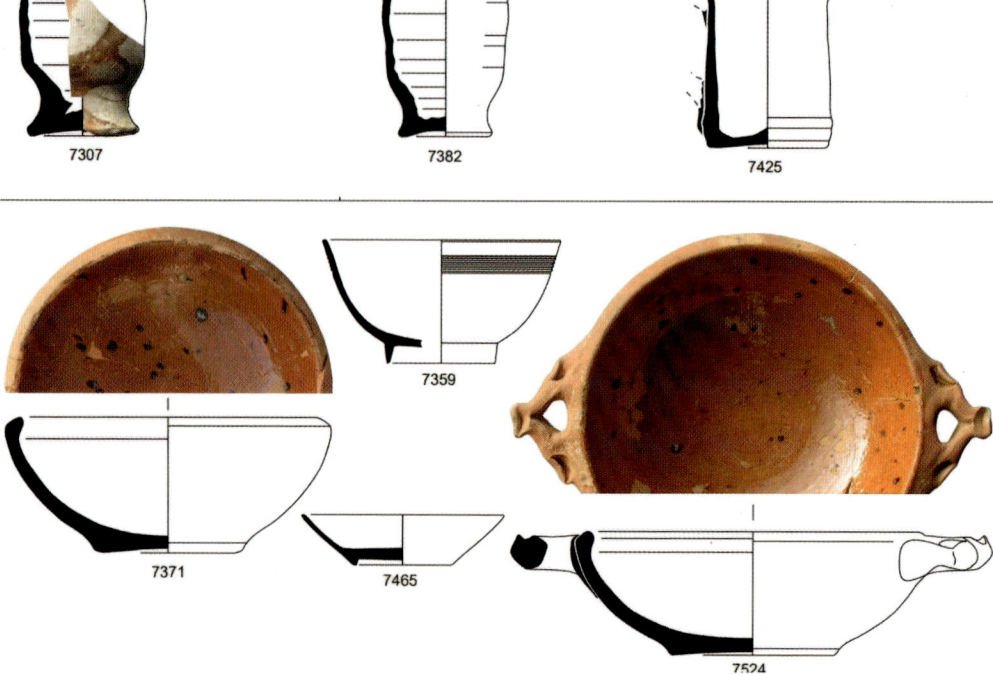

Recovered storage vessels and other ceramic items from excavated soldiers' huts in Boulogne. (*Frederick Lemaire*)

report from early October 1803 reports that 3,076 16-man tents were in use, sufficient accommodation for almost 50,000 men.[8] Not all soldiers had to endure these conditions. Soult ordered on *7 Vendemiaire An 12* (30 September 1803) that the 75ᵉ *de Ligne* were to be lodged in permanent barracks in Saint-Omer, the 72ᵉ *de Ligne* were to lodge with the townsfolk of Saint-Omer and the 88ᵉ *de Ligne* were to be lodged in the villages surrounding the town.[9] The following day the 24ᵉ *Légère* were to bivouac around Boulogne.[10]

However, it was the 'home-made' barrack that was the most common form of accommodation.

We are fortunate that we have the personal letters and orders of Jean Nicholas Soult and his 'trials and tribulations' in getting his corps established in its encampment. One of his first actions was to issue an order on *2 Vendémiaire An 13* (25 September 1803) that straw was to be issued over the next 15 days for the men to roof their huts.[11] Presumably the men had already built the frames from whatever material – likely timber – was to hand. However, getting materials to the camps proved a major stumbling block, so much so that a week later, on *9 Vendémiaire*, Soult ordered that regimental commanders were authorised to hire civilian waggons to transport wood and straw to allow the men to build their huts. Once the huts were completed Soult ordered the kitchens to be the next buildings to be completed.[12] Vandamme 'was given a kick up the backside' on *15 Vendémiaire* (8 October 1803) to ensure his men had completed their huts within the next two days: his was the only division needing this prompting.[13] The following day,

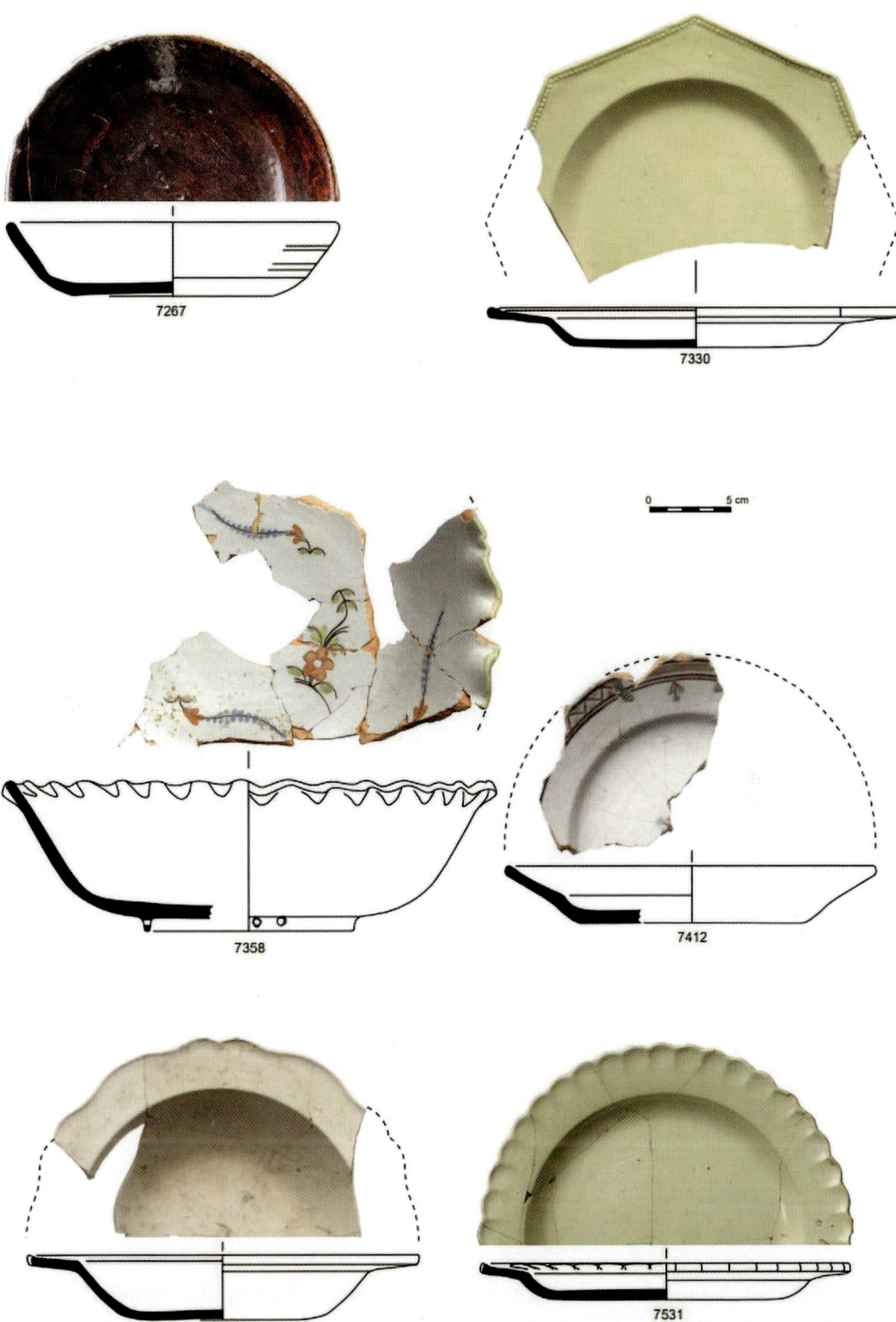

Recovered soldiers' bowls and plates from excavated soldiers' huts in Boulogne. (*Frederick Lemaire*)

Soult made a tour of the encampment and 'chewed out' the colonel of the 43ᵉ *de Ligne* for not ensuring that his men had completed their huts. In reply the colonel pleaded that he had done everything possible to ensure completion with the limited number of waggons at his disposal. Soult passed orders for the colonel to requisition transport – 15 wagons – to move the wood necessary to complete them. From Soult's pen came a second order that stated all huts were to be completed by the *17 Vendémiaire* (10 October 1803).[14]

The huts seem to have been fairly ramshackle affairs. The straw roofing seems to have been simply 'heaped over' the rafters of the huts rather than being thatched by a specialist. Being bult on the exposed coast, the camps were at the full fury of winter storms. It comes as no suprise given the ramshackle nature of the hits, that Soult ordered on *26 Brumaire* (18 November 1803) that straw was to be issued with all haste to allow the men to repair the roofs. Many colonels had reported that a lot of huts were in need of replacement as autumn gales had torn the roofs off or had blown the structures into the sea.[15] Brun-Lavainne, a musician of the 46ᵉ *de Ligne*, writes:

> As for housing … our camp comprised three rows of thatched roofs going down to the ground covering a pit dug in the ground […] a fourth row for kitchens and police rooms; a fifth for non-commissioned officers, musicians and canteens; further on, the officers behind their companies; further still, the battalion commanders, and finally behind all the rest, the colonels […] To return to our barracks, their structure was not beautiful, but we were there comfortably during the summer. It was quite another thing when the rainy season had soaked the earth and the waters, finding a clear passage through the thousand little channels dug by moles, mice and other inhabitants of these subterranean dwellings, came to invade our apartments […] One day, returning from the parade in torrential rain, we found one of the two barracks assigned to the accommodation of the musicians of 46ᵉ, precisely the one where I slept, converted into a pond where we could see floating, ducks and swans, linen, music paper, straw, love letters and *bonnets de police*. We immediately set to work with our cans and bowls to dry out this unwelcome piece of water; but while we were occupied with this work, the roof, being no longer supported on the sides, collapsed on us and filled our damp dwelling with its debris. We got out of it, well, I don't quite know how; and we were forced to take refuge in the second hut where our comrades huddled together to make room for us.[16]

One gets the feeling these temporary huts were rather damp, cold and a distinctly unpleasant space to spend a winter. Following the storms, he reports the replacement of ad hoc huts with stone: 'to begin our new construction and give it solidity, we resolved to build along the walls of our pit, which retained its shape and dimensions, a stone wall taking from the bottom and rising about half a metre above the level of the outside ground'.[17]

Even when built with stone, the living conditions in the huts were not conducive to good soldiering, as Raymond Aimery de Montesquiou-Fezensac describes:

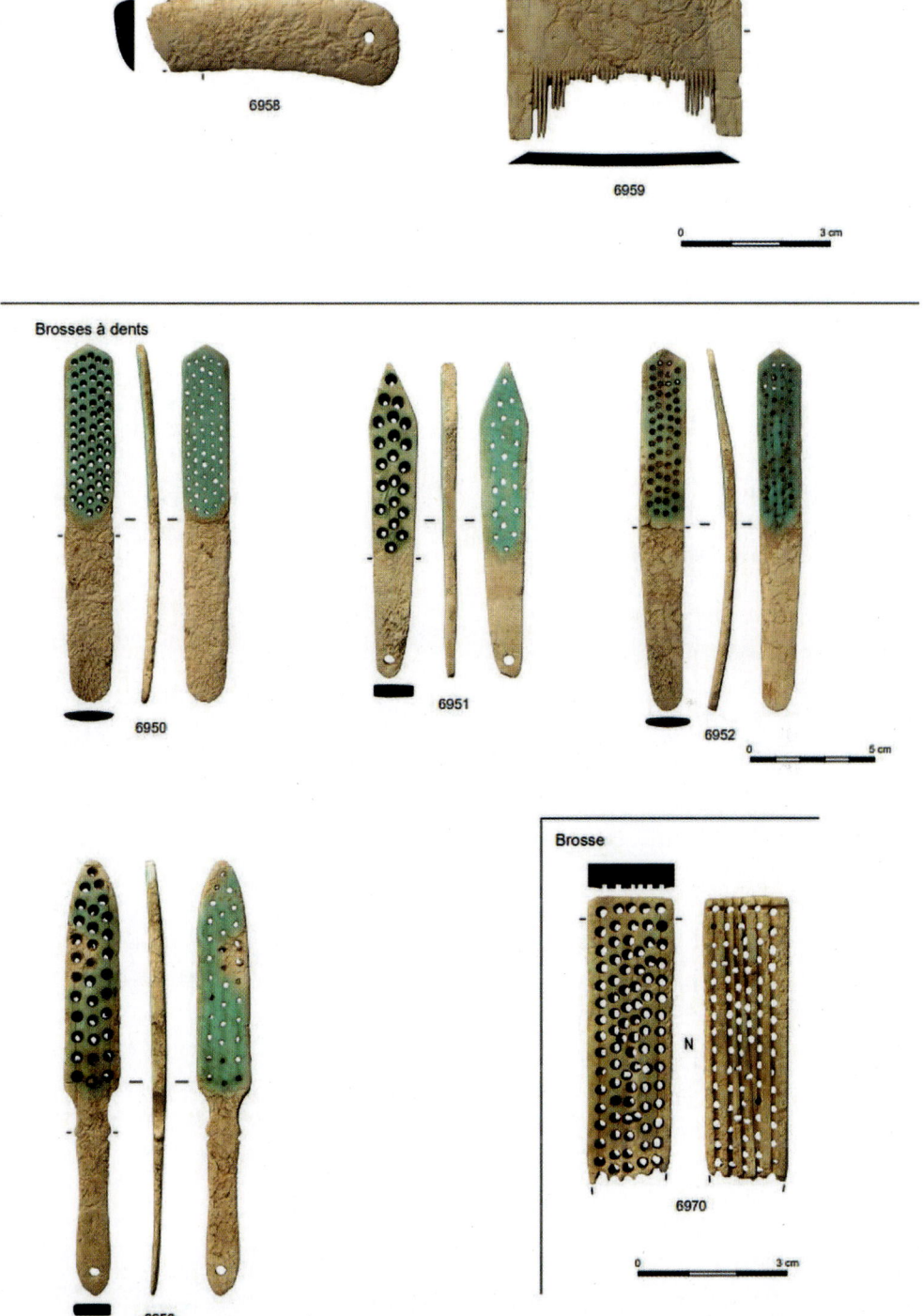

A soldier's lice comb, uniform brush and habit brush excavated from a soldiers' hut in Boulogne. (*Frederick Lemaire*)

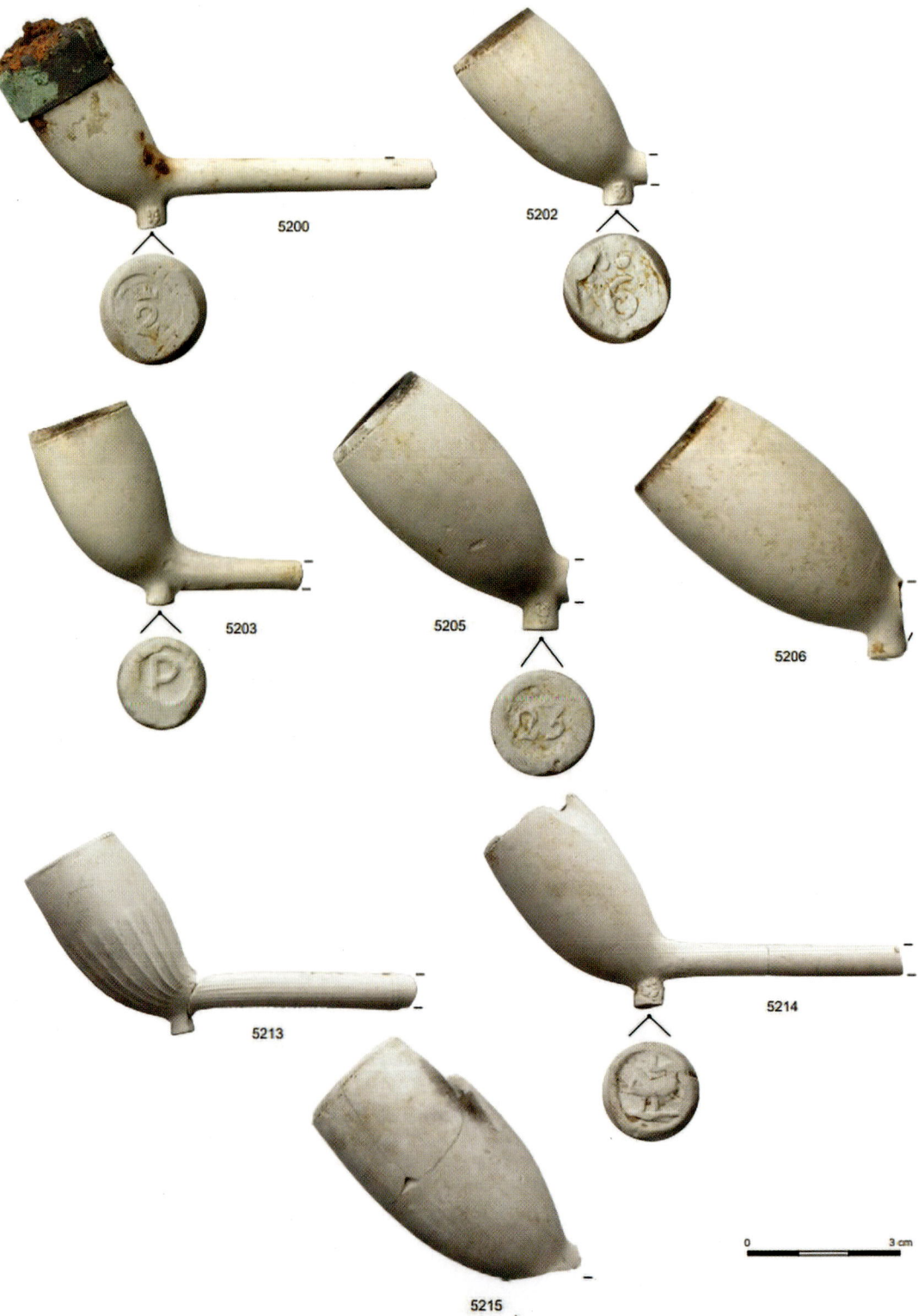

Fragments of soldiers' pipes from excavated soldiers' huts in Boulogne. (*Frederick Lemaire*)

The huts were dug one metre underground, which made them very wet. The bed consisted of a large cot in which straw was spread; on top, a wool blanket. Each man lay down on this blanket, wrapped in a canvas bag, the haversack serving as a pillow; They then spread a woollen blanket over the top of them. We slept together, and yet separately.[18]

Assembling hundreds of thousands of men in a single area, while an excellent idea for conducting large-scale training, placed impossible strain on the resources of an area. Each of the camps had the population of a small town: men and horses needed feeding, wood for fires, repairing the huts, etc. As could be reasonably expected, the huge demand placed on local supplies of straw and wood meant that by *29 Brumaire* (21 November 1803) some Generals of Brigade were complaining to Soult that the cavalry had no straw for their stables, and wood was running out, or had run out, for repairing the huts, heating and cooking.[19] A few days later, on *3 Frimaire* (25 November), Soult authorised his corps to hire 60 to 70 men, to be paid 50 sous per day and provided with a loaf of bread, to extract wood from the Forêt du Boulogne to provide fire wood.[20]

The timber contained in the National Forests was, however, strictly 'off limits' to the men at Boulogne: it was allocated primarily to the needs of the French Navy to construct the invasion barges. When Army Headquarters caught wind of Soult's actions, he was severely reprimanded and on *18 Pluviôse An 12* (8 February 1803) passed orders to his divisional commanders that they were to prevent the men gathering timber from national forests to repair their huts or for fire wood. He ordered that if timber was needed, regiments had to make special requests for timber directly to the *Chef d'état Major General* (Bonaparte's chief of staff) as timber was in short supply and directed to the needs of the navy and artillery.[21]

Soldiers ate from a communal bowl in the line, their spoon was personal property. Two soldiers' spoons were recovered from soldiers' huts in Boulogne. (*Frederick Lemaire*)

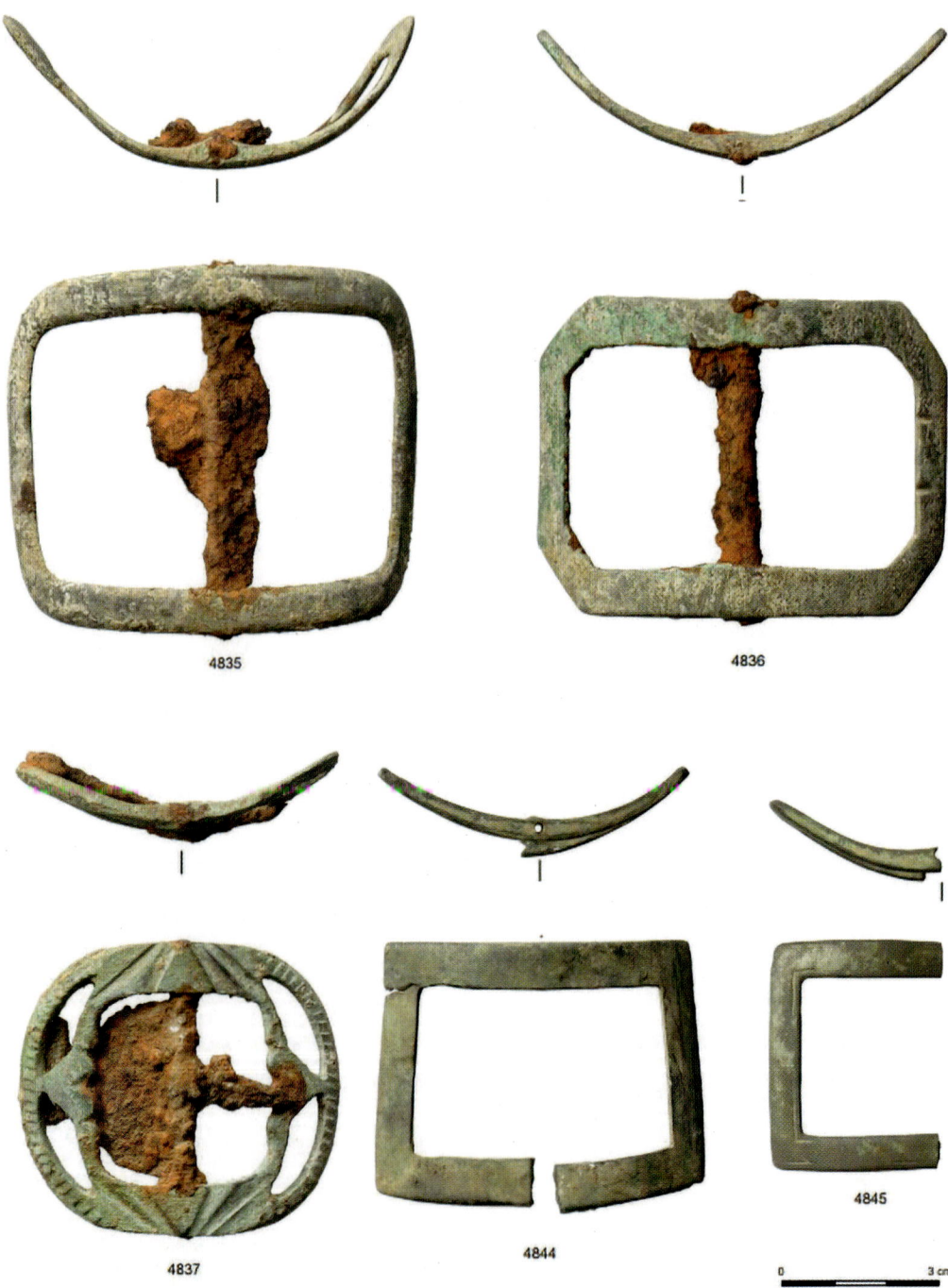

Shoe buckles from Boulogne. (*Frederick Lemaire*)

Future Marshal Suchet complained that: 'It is easier to form camps and organise them promptly when you are close to a good fire and the caress of a pretty girl, than when on the edges of the English Channel; we have to constantly fight against the wrath of the seasons, against the appalling whistle of the wind.'[22] He added in a second letter to his brother 'you were far from correct in thinking that in France there wasn't any difficulty in establishing oneself well, you need to know that in the Department of Pas-de-Calais the forests are a very long distance from the sea and that the establishment of our camps devours a lot of wood; you can easily imagine it when you learn that there are nine barracks per company, that it takes two whole rows for those of the officers, majors, as well as the kitchens and pavilions for chefs.'[23] All ranks suffered from the cold and damp.

An idea of the amount of materials needed to make each regiment's huts can be garnered from Soult's order of *28 Messidor An 12* (17 July 1804), which allowed 1,755 bales of straw to the 72^e *de Ligne* to construct the roofs of their huts.[24] The army was asset stripping the north French coast: robbing the local population of timber, firewood and straw – which of course they would be reimbursed for, as soon as they had completed and submitted the correct paperwork, and the War Ministry had processed the request, often months, if not years later.

Ney, in a letter of *4 jour complémentaire An 12* (21 September 1804), reports that after a year in almost constant use, he had to almost totally rebuild his camp before the winter storms lashed the coast, adding:

> the barracks in general had been badly made in principle, the soldiers were beginning to suffer from it, and the engineers did not even have a wheelbarrow to give them to remove the sand which encumbered their dwellings.
>
> Despite all these contradictions, I ordered the re-establishment of the barracks of all the regiments. We have been working on it tirelessly for 20 days and I have the hope that before *Brumaire* it will also be beautiful and healthy, and that it will be able to last all winter and even next summer. These works, however immense they may be, will cause no expense to the government since the same materials are used again; the soldiers extract the stone from the quarries they have dug themselves and build houses instead of barracks. To facilitate the transport of these materials, I have ordered the Commander of Engineers to provide two wheelbarrows per company, but according to your Excellency's letter, this officer has the right to refuse them to me. It is very painful for me to see my authority compromised for objects of such small importance, but despite this inconvenience, and although I have not a penny of encouragement to give, other than from my own funds, the barracks will be finished and when the Emperor sees the camps again, I dare to hope that his majesty will deign to be satisfied with my operations.[25]

In a letter of *8 Vendémiaire An 13* (29 September 1804) Ney redoubled his demands for timber, noting that:

> this resource is far from being sufficient for the restoration of the barracks, which having been built on the principle of promptness and speed, have been absolutely degraded by the bad weather that reigned this year. I am therefore forced to pray your excellence to give orders to make me at my disposal 25,000 poles, 56,000 rafters,

200,000 beams and 1,200 fagots. I also ask you to recommend forestry agents to put the greatest activity in the delivery of this material, the bad season approaches and if the restoration of the barracks does not take place promptly, the soldiers' health would be affected.

Ney added 'the strictest economy must preside over this work' and 'that we even use stones and other materials for the construction of kitchens and part of the barracks, which reduces considerably the consumption of wood.'[26] Ney added some days later:

I must instruct your excellence that I was forced to have the barracks renewed almost entirely and that for more than a month the soldiers have been working day and night to extract stones and build barracks of a construction solid enough to last ten years. But since that time, it was impossible, despite my repeated requests

Bottle necks from Boulogne. (*Frederick Lemaire*)

to obtain the required amount of straw and blankets. Deliveries already made are insufficient, so much so the soldier is almost reduced to bivouac. It has rained without interruption for ten days, which deteriorates the buildings and rots the little straw that we had.[27]

Later the same month Ney ordered that there:

will be built behind the front of each regiment three barracks for the following use: the two smallest, placed in the centre and behind the 1st and 2nd battalions will serve as armouries and dance rooms, the third placed at the same height as the previous ones in the interval of the battalions will serve to bring together the officers of the corps to maintain the theoretical instruction on manoeuvres, and learn to give orders.[28]

Clearly the lack of a classroom to learn the theory of soldiering and also for the men's recreation away from Boulogne was much felt in Ney's command, and no doubt others. Construction of stone huts is reported by other eyewitnesses. Jean Stanislas Vivien from IV Corps tells us:

My regiment (the 55th), which for a month had been occupying billets stretching from the Pont de Briques to Wimille, was the first of all to draw the line to camp six hundred paces in rear of the Tour d'Ordre, with its left side resting against the town. The site had been well chosen, but the barracks arrangements were flawed and the health of the soldiers suffered as a result.

Instead of raising everything above the ground to protect ourselves from the humidity, pits eighteen feet long by fourteen wide and two feet deep were dug, and it was in these unhealthy pits covered with a straw roof that the army had to spend the winter. The regiments themselves did justice to the worst barracks imaginable, and the following spring the soldiers bribed each other to meet part of the cost of building new dwellings which they erected; their industry did the rest. Labourers who could not be usefully employed would extract rubble and lime stone from the cliffside and carry them to the camp. Others would flush sand out of the sea water, so that it could be more effectively combined with lime, and brought it along as well. A lime kiln was built in each regiment and maintained with combustibles from economies made on firewood. The rebuilding of the barracks was carried out one by one, by company, on a model which offered at the same time elegance, convenience and salubrity. Masons raised the walls; a few camp utensils replaced, in the hands of skilled carpenters, the tools of their trade, and frameworks with joints were substituted for the rafters which, in theory, were simply supported on the right and left of a crosspiece carried by two forks. Straw roofers built roofs that proved impenetrable to the heaviest rains and sea gusts. Carpenters fashioned the wood for doors, windows, cots, and weapon racks. The huts were replaced by charming little

Above and opposite: Fittings from clay pipes from Boulogne. (*Frederick Lemaire*)

houses, which flattered the eye all the more pleasantly, as their walls were whitened both inside and outside.

The space in between the soldiers' and officers' quarters was distributed in gardens, without in any way interfering with the passage of people. The officers' barracks were not strictly subjected to a regular plan; there were some whose interior distribution and furnishings were in no way inferior to the good taste and elegance of town houses.[29]

After being in use for six months, the stone huts needed repairs. It comes as no surprise therefore to discover that men had taken to stealing stone from quarries and the

3330
3331
3338

construction of the Boulogne harbour to repair their huts. To prevent this, Soult ordered on *15 Ventôse An 13* (6 March 1805) that sentries were to be posted to stop men going to the quarry and carrying away stones.[30]

Vigo-Roussillon, an officer of the 32[e] *de Ligne*, in a description he gives of his camp at Camiers tells us: 'Further (behind the barracks and officers' gardens) were the meeting rooms, dance rooms, and for officers and non-commissioned officers there could be found restaurants and cafes with billiards.'[31] It all sounds very pleasant, yet the reality was somewhat different, as we shall see.

Chapter 6
The School of Boulogne

By gathering army corps into a single locale, it allowed entire corps to learn how to manoeuvre as a cohesive whole. It also allowed corps, division and brigade commanders to get to know their colleagues, to build up vital bonds of trust and friendship. The camps allowed conscripts to generals to become proficient in the theory practice of their drills. Bellavoine of the 55ᵉ *de Ligne* reports:

> On the 16th Brumaire, the First Consul reviewed us, accompanied by the generals; After reviewing us, he made us carry out firing drill. The next day, 17th, he wanted the soldiers to experience fatigue; he made us put on our backpacks, at 10 o'clock in the morning sharp, after the soup; he made us march a league and a half from the Camp and for us to carry out our exercises as usual … we each had 30 to 40 shots to fire … we were precisely 10 consecutive hours marching and firing.[1]

A few days later, on *21 Brumaire An 12* (13 November 1803), all the troops at Boulogne and Saint-Omer were reviewed by the first consul. The men were issued 30 rounds of ammunition, and were ordered to wear their *capotes*. After the review the men were to undertake a mock battle.[2] The outcome of the manoeuvres it seems fed into the creation of a distinct programme of training in the following year.

Despite being established in summer 1803, drilling at Boulogne seems to have taken second place to creating the vast camps and carrying out the *Vendémiaire* reforms. Thus, it was not till *Floréal An 12* (May 1804) that General Ney passed the following orders for his IV Corps, which were no doubt broadly similar to those of other corps:

> Generals Dupont, Loison and Partouneaux will give the necessary orders so that the regiments gathered under their commandments take care of the theory and practice of the *école du soldat*, *école du peloton*, *école du bataillon* and deployment in line of battle, as well as the duties and knowledge essential to officers and sous-officiers on campaign.
> To effectively achieve this [illegible] they will establish the work of instruction as follows:
> The recruits of the various classes will be exercised twice a day in the handling of weapons, on fires and walking on Mondays, Tuesdays, Wednesdays, Thursdays and Fridays from six o'clock in the morning until eight o'clock, and from one o'clock in afternoon up to three o'clock. Saturdays and Sundays, are rest days.

The School of Boulogne 59

The Marshal of France in mounted full dress. In the background we see a line battalion on parade led by the grenadier company.

On Mondays and Tuesdays, the *école du peleton* will be instructed for all the men admitted to the 1st class. This exercise will not last beyond three hours, whether it takes place in the morning or in the afternoon. It will be the same with the *école du bataillon* and deployment in line of battle.

Battalion Commanders will monitor this work and order the duration of rest and resumption of education.

On Tuesdays, for the *école du bataillon*, the colonels will be present (at) this instruction […] The regiments will manoeuvre together, separately or by brigade depending on the progress made […] Fridays, exercise and manoeuvre by (company?) for officers and sous-officers in order to accustom them to estimate the distance of the intervals, either marching in line or column, or in wheeling, such as prescribes the regulations on developments.

Saturdays will be instruction in the theory of the duties of officers and sous-officers both in the *école du peleton*, *école du bataillon* and evolutions in line, as well as their duties on campaign and on the attack and the defence of a post, of an entrenchment, redoubt, etc.

Adjutant-Commandants and heads of the divisions staff will go to attend theoretical instruction and report to their generals in division.

Sunday, *Grande Parade*. The armament inspection, equipment and clothing, the contents of the *havresac*, registers of orders and men's account books on the mass of linen and shoes.

The men detained at the custody of the camp, disciplinary or police room, between the chores they have to do at the camp, will exercise every day wearing the *bonnet de police* with the recruits of the 2nd class.

Whenever soldiers will take up arms, either for exercise or manoeuvres, they will wear their the havresac.

The recruits will be (illegible) by corporals on the instruction and (illegible) duty of a sentry, how to recognize a troop, rounds and patrols, or by day or at night, as well as on all parts Armament, equipment, various drum calls, knowledge of their officers, companies' and (their superior), etc.

The code of details and military sentences will be read at the head of the companies assembled unarmed on the camp front of the camp every Sunday, immediately after the morning soup.

The army order will indicate the day that manoeuvres will start. He will mention it when the bodies must perform the fire exercise and shoot.

The generals of division will monitor the execution of these provisions and report to the general-in-chief of progress they will have noticed, [as also] they will make him know the officers who have deployed the most zeal and knowledge in their state and will have contributed to maintaining the right reputation that the French infantry has acquired as the first in the world.

Officers who neglect their duties will also be noted. I like to believe that the generals will not notice anywhere and that they will commit them to redouble their activity and zeal to justify the choice and the confidence of the government.[3]

The School of Boulogne

Grenadier officer in full dress c.1805. Bearskins were used only on special occaisions, If they were issued. Most grenadiers in the line never had such an item of headdress.

We also note that in addition to the daily training regime, large-scale manoeuvres occupied the summer of 1804. General Marchand writes on *26 Prairial An 13* (15 June 1804):

> Yesterday we were under arms from three in the morning until six in the evening. Our whole army was gathered and we did what is called the little war. […] Artillery, cavalry, infantry, everything was there. […] We have marched and manoeuvred for about two leagues across country which was almost entirely covered with wheat, which we crossed and re-crossed throughout the day. You can only imagine the pitiful state of this beautiful harvest after our exploits. We were 12,000 men and we walked through all of this for 15 hours, with horses, cannon and caissons, not to mention the curious who, however, were not very numerous.[4]

One of those witnessing the evolutions of VI Corps that took place later in the year was Soult.[5] IV Corps was reviewed and put through its paces a short time later during *Thermidor* (August), with Soult writing that: 'Colonel Pouget of the 26e légère puts his regiment through drill with celerity and exactness […] It is one of the best regiments in the Camp.'[6] Yet Soult had to 'kick' his officers at times for failing to carry out their duties: *28 Pluviose An 12* (18 February 1804) Soult noted 'several officers were wearing civilian clothing of the affluent middle class' rather 'than their regular uniforms, which is strictly forbidden', commenting 'officers spent too much time at billiards and neglected the training of their men'. Soult was clearly not happy with the officer corps, and reminded his officers that 'the military coat is very honourable to wear, and officers must always remember their duty and position or they will be arrested'.[7] His words went unheeded as Soult had to issue a reminder *20 Germinal* (10 April 1804) to ensure officers and men dressed in a military manner and not wear civilian clothing.[8] This speaks ill of the officer corps in overseeing their men. No doubt the trials and tribulations Soult faced were common across the army.

Endless Drilling

Judging by archive records, upon joining a war battalion, after a few days' instruction, the most able conscripts were selected from their comrades and became first-class recruits, those that showed moderate ability formed the second class and the less-able conscripts were formed into a third class. To recognise their aptitude and ability at drill, the first-class recruits were only drilled once a day, twice on Mondays and Fridays, while those in the second and third classes undertook three intensive drill training sessions every day. In order to encourage third-class recruits to make progress, they were deprived of 'the honour of doing service', i.e., not allowed to stand guard, or they were not allowed to partake in the military activities of the regiment. As further incentive, the third class were assigned to conduct all regimental chores, 'without the same preventing them from attending drill', until they were sufficiently well drilled to move up to second class.[9] Being on constant fatigue duties either made the men 'knuckle down' to learning their trade or drove them to desert.

The guiding purpose of constant drill training – much as it is in the modern-day armed forces – was to make the conscript into an automaton: no time to think exists in the heat of battle and soldiers had to load and fire their weapons automatically and obey commands instantly.

The regimental standing orders of the 64ᵉ *de Ligne* offer us a snapshot of a regiment's daily life at Boulogne. On *30 Vendémiaire An 13* (22 October 1804), the regiment was ordered to ensure the drummers and band were able to carry out the '*école du soldat et du peleton*'. The colonel was ordered to issue them cartridges to learn firing drill by 12 movements. A few days later, on *3 Brumaire An 13* (25 October 1804), the 64ᵉ and the brigaded 40ᵉ *de Ligne* were to undertake brigade-level manoeuvres and firing drills. A day later, *4 Brumaire An 13* (26 October 1804), the brigade were to engage in embarkation drills with the fleet.[10] A trooper of the 11ᵉ *Dragons* recalls such drills:

> Dear brother and dear sister,
> You will no doubt be surprised to find me […] billeted on a gunboat and not in town. For a very long time I had expected to do this chore. I arrived in the port on 25 Ventose and I'm sure I'll only stay there for 3 months. You must realise that here we do not enjoy all the pleasures of life, on the contrary we are very badly off. I await the end of my 3 months with great impatience. Since my arrival, I have already been on the high seas for 24 hours […] We go up there on barges which are very weak buildings. Every day at the rising tide, about 500 men embark on this kind of vessel, who go

Fusilier of 8e *de Ligne* as he appeared at Austerlitz. Tens of thousands of French soldiers were dressed in this manner at the battle. (*A. S. K. Brown Library*)

Grenadiers of the 8e *de Ligne* as they appeared at the time of Austerlitz according to the regiment's paperwork in a period image dated to 1808. The 8e was one of the handful of regiments in the epoch to issue bearskins to its grenadiers. (*A. S. K. Brown Library*)

2 or 3 hours out to sea, it is hardly possible for us to go further since the English are there who form a strong and considerable line to oppose the invasion. It often happens that we let loose a few cannon shots, but without much effect or damage. They don't dare approach to bombard the city as they did in the past, since there

The School of Boulogne 65

Fusilier of line infantry wearing his *chapeau* and greatcoat. As part of the planning process for the invasion of England, General Daru was ordered to make 60,000 *capotes* on 29 May 1803 as a strategic reserve. Days later, on 14 June 1803, Bonaparte ordered all troops at the Channel coast to be issued *capotes*, and General Dejean was ordered to procure 80,000 and 120,000 pairs of shoes by September of that year. Of the regiments at the Camp of Boulogne or on service in north Italy that had not yet received *capotes*, corps commands were reminded on 29 June 1804 to complete the production and issue of these garments. Regarding both the 1804 and 1806 model *capote*, no colour was specified, although archive documents suggest grey.

are terrible forts defending it […] I vomited without being very sick because the sea was very calm, I was not very agitated in my barge. One is very ill only when the sea is very angry and one stays there for a few days.[11]

On *5 Brumaire An 13* (27 October 1804), the division – 17ᵉ *Légère*, 34ᵉ, 40ᵉ, 64ᵉ and 88ᵉ *de Ligne* – were to undertake a route march, and *General de Division* Jean Lannes, head of V Corps, ordered each regimental colonel to ensure they had their *capotes* secured to their *havresacs*. On completion of the route march, the division was to take part in a mock battle, commencing on *9 Brumaire An 13* (31 October 1804). The men were issued 20 rounds of ammunition and told to take a day's rations with them.

Drill did not return to the camp until the first glimmers of spring 1805. On *13 Ventôse An 13* (4 March 1805) Lannes reviewed V Corps, the men to wear *grande tenue* – full dress – and following the inspection were to undertake brigade-level manoeuvres, which were to include the advance, attack, and covering a retreat. Concerning the training of the 64ᵉ *de Ligne*, on 20 *Ventôse An 13* (11 March 1805) the regiment was ordered to assemble on the parade ground behind the men of the 1st class, who were to undertake the *école de peleton* without arms; the others were to be trained in the *école du soldat* with arms. A week later (*26 Ventôse*) the brigade comprising the 64ᵉ and 88ᵉ *de Ligne* was reviewed. The feedback to the colonels was that some men still lacked precision in the *école du soldat* and were to perfect the 1st and 2nd lessons. The company commanders were reminded to take better care in teaching the men how to roll and place their *capotes* on the *havresac*. Drill was once more uppermost in General Suchet's mind as the month of Germinal began. On *4 Germinal An 13* (25 March 1805), he ordered regiments to drill the men and work to prefect the third and fourth lessons of the first part of the *école du soldat*. These were the principles of marching and oblique marching; really basic stuff. It makes us wonder as to efficiency of the division overall by this date? Was this reflective of the corps and army as a whole? Without more research, that is a question we cannot answer. Certainly, it seems training over the winter had literally ground to a halt. On *18 Germinal*, training was to move on to the third and fourth lessons from the second part of the *école du soldat:* firing the musket in 12 movements and directed firing. We assume the intervening weeks had covered the remainder of the first part and the first elements of the second: clearly a specific timetable of training was in place.

General Suchet ordered that the men in the 2nd class were to be reviewed in their training progress on *8 Floréal An 13* (28 April 1805), as were the men in the 1st class, both to be 'exercised in the 1st lesson of the 1st part of the *école du soldat*, i.e., the formation of a regiment in battle order. Suchet was eager that the men were drilled twice a day in his division. Suchet reviewed his division on *1 Prairial An 13* (21 May 1805), the regiment's drill and barracks were to be inspected, the men were to be issued 20 rounds each for evolutions carried out that involved them firing their muskets. On *9 Prairial An 13* (29 May 1805) Suchet ordered that the second lessons from the *école de peleton* were to be the day's, training, which comprised loading the musket in 12 movements, independent fire, directed fire, firing by platoon, and firing to the rear.

The School of Boulogne 67

Drawn in summer 1806, we see the drummers of the 95e *de Ligne* no doubt as they were dressed at Austerlitz. Their appearance was perhaps typical of the army.

As summer progressed, we see the level of training moved on from company level to larger formations. The 64ᵉ and other regiments in its division was ordered on *16 Prairial An 13* (5 June 1805) to exercise the men of the 1st class in the second lesson of the *école de peleton* i.e., loading and firing by 12 movements and independently, and upon completion, to be tested in their execution of the first to fifth lessons of the *école du bataillon*, i.e., opening ranks, firing as a battalion and the charge, wheeling left and right. The men in the 2nd class were to be trained in the same lessons from 1700 to 1900hrs. What is notable is that so far regimental, brigade and division training had not been conducted.

Suchet gave instructions that on *8 Messidor An 13* (27 June 1805) the division was to be assembled 'to execute the *école de la Ligne*, the men and *sous-officiers* will wear full dress; there will be 14 files per peleton'. As summer wore on, the men drilled at company level, but we hear nothing of mock battles or even regimental level drill.[12] But was this necessary? The tactical unit was the company: did a private soldier need to know the minutia of how a battalion moved? No. What mattered was that the officers, guides and *sous-officiers* knew how to manoeuvre their company, as a battalion was in essence a grouping of companies. It was more important that the men could fire their muskets and operate as a cohesive tactical unit rather than worry about how a brigade passed a stream. That was the necessary knowledge of the company commander, battalion commander and brigade commander: this level of training was taught in the classroom and using wooden markers to show deployment. Further, it is unlikely sufficient space existed to actually deploy a brigade into a single location without taking out hedges, walls and fences to practice such movements.

Chapter 7

Daily Life

Outside of drilling, maintenance of their hut must have been a constant preoccupation of the men in their 'down time' as it was in their best interest to do so. We have to imagine the men were as efficient at drill as at DIY. Outside of the day job of learning to be a soldier, the men found their freedoms extremely curtailed, as Ney decreed in autumn 1803:

> The general-in-chief warns the troops are limited in their movements to no more than 300 *toises* out of their camp.
>
> No soldier will be able to move away beyond these limits without a written permission given by the captains for *sous-officiers* and soldiers and by battalion commanders for the officers.
>
> It is forbidden to be absent from the camp during the night.
>
> In no case may more than five permissions be granted for *sous-officiers* and soldiers, per company, to be absent at any one time.
>
> Those who have obtained the first permissions must always have returned before it is issued to others.
>
> The camp police guard will arrest any soldier or *sous-officier* who would be found outside the limits of the camps without permission in writing and will be returned to their regiment.
>
> At the break of day, the drums of the regiments that are camped will beat *La Diane*, and at the sunset they will sound the retreat.
>
> Additional calls will be made as following the morning after one hour after the *Diane*, one at ten o'clock before eating the soup, one at one o'clock afternoon to receive and hear the orders of the general and that of the division, one at four o'clock, for the soup.[1]

In addition, there were three parades per day; one for half an hour after reveille for roll call, one at midday when they had to fall in under arms and with their knapsacks, and the other after the last watch was posted. Rather than a 'hearty breakfast', which we like to imagine a soldier had, the reality was that the men were given a light meal of coffee and bread (*Odroneaux*) around an hour after *La Diane* had been sounded and this was felt to be more beneficial than a large meal. In barracks food was prepared in the kitchen allocated to the company; soldiers were forbidden to prepare food in their barracks. Food was purchased by company by a corporal, the *fourrier*, and men on fatigue duties carried it back to the barracks. Both meals, morning and evening, were some form

Officers of the 95e *de Ligne* drawn in summer 1806. We note the *voltigeur* officer with chamois collar to his coat. No *voltigeur* in the line had these distinctions at Austerlitz. This was an innovation of summer 1806, or in several cases from February 1808.

of soup made from beef, pork or mutton and vegetables; beef usually being reserved for the evening meal. Bread and biscuit (hard tack) was initially obtained from local bakeries, but increasingly became baked by the battalion so as to be self-sufficient. We look at food in more detail in the next chapter.

The first main meal was eaten at 1000 – in theory as no doubt in practice this was incredibly divergent – before the main guard mounting and drill of the day; the evening meal was served before the posting of the evening guard and it was carried out to the men by men on fatigue duties.

Every morning after the first parade the surgeon major or other medical officer would visit the sick in the infirmary, accompanied by the lieutenant colonel, and also inspect the kitchens. Those men who had been detailed off on defaulters or fatigues would carry out their tasks under the close scrutiny of the adjutant.

A second meal was eaten between 1600 and 1700. We look at the soldier's ration later in this chapter. Lights out was at 2200.

How the men used their 'leisure time' is illuminated by the archaeological finds from excavations at the camps: a distraction for soldiers was chewing or smoking tobacco, as we see from contemporary engravings and the recovery of the pipes themselves from the camp of VI Corps.[2] Tobacco was relatively cheap, set at 10 cents per pound in 1793, and pipes cost 2.40 centimes each. Some months earlier, on *28 Vendémiaire An 13* (20 October 1804), an order was issued stating 'the use of the pipe must be not only authorised, but directly provoked by distributing to the soldier's tobacco to chew or smoke'.[3] In their spare time, as well as tending their gardens, they also played dice, board games – dice and board game counters being recovered archaeologically – and cards. Judging by the rate of syphilis and other sexually transmitted diseases, there was access to prostitutes. We also notice a spike in births in the towns and villages around the camp, as men found 'a girl' and settled down to life in the camps.[4]

As well as gaming – gambling – men smoked, read – at least the *sous-officiers* – drank, and no doubt made their way into the local villages or towns to spend their meagre wages on wine, women and food. Outside of this, the men had other duties to fulfil.

Most of the regiments in Soult's corps had a military band attached to them. Seeking to utilise these musicians for functions other than formal parades, Soult organised on *19 Prairial An 12* (8 June 1804) a military mass with massed bands in the Cathedral of Boulogne. This would comprise 'the mass of *Veni Creator Spiritus* and a *Te Deum Laudamus*', after which the announcement would be made of Napoléon proclaimed emperor of the French. Staff officers, senior officers, divisional and brigade officers were to attend. After the mass the the light infantry of the 1st Division, the massed grenadiers of the 1st and 4th Divisions, six pieces of artillery and all the cavalry would parade through the town.[5]

To mark the *fête* of *18 Brumaire An 13* (9 November 1804) Soult ordered that at daybreak the entire corps would be assembled and fire a salvo to commence the day's festivities. At 1000 the troops selected for the parade would march to Boulogne to participate in 'a grand mass'. After the mass 'giving eternal thanks' for the *coup*, at 1100 the troops were to parade through the streets of the town. At the culmination of the parade, the entire corps was to be assembled and the cross of the Legion of Honour would be distributed. At 2000 close of day would be marked by another volley of musketry and artillery.

Lannes' V Corps undertook a similar ceremony, and in preparation for the parade he ordered on 14 *Brumaire* (5 November) that the regiments in his corps were to ensure that every man had a *capote*, check the conditions of those that existed, and to ensure that they had been repaired with all haste. The bands and drummers of each division were to be united for the parade, and Lannes' chief of staff reported in an order dated *16 Brumaire An 13* (7 November 1804) that Lannes would be presented with the 'eagle of the legion of honour'.[6] The first distribution had been made on 16 August.

As well as drilling, the men were to assist in the building of sea defences as well as road building and repairing bridges. While so working the men were to be issued with *sabots* (clogs), *pantalons de toile* (linen overall trousers), a linen smock to be worn over their *gilet or veste* (sleeved waistcoat) and a *capote* to preserve their *habit* (dress coat) from damage.[7] Detachments from the 43ᵉ and 55ᵉ *de la Ligne* were allocated to this task on *7 Nivôse An 12* (29 December 1803).[8] Likewise, detachments from the 46ᵉ and 57ᵉ *de la Ligne* were sent to build sea defences at Boulogne.[9] The cavalry was immune from such duties, so too the artillery.

Keeping discipline was of primary concern for all corps commanders. Boredom, homesickness and damp living conditions fostered desertion and ill-discipline. None of the barracks had chimneys, so must have been especially cold and damp come autumn and winter: one eyewitness lamented 'in these unhealthy pits, covered with a straw roof, the army had to spend the winter'.[10]

Grenadier of the 95e *de Ligne* wearing bearskin in summer 1806. No doubt he wore a *chapeau* in battle: certainly the grenadiers of the 64e did not have bearskins with them at Austerlitz. Note also the use of linen gaiters and overall trousers on campaign. These were an innovation of the 1802 regulations.

It comes as no surprise therefore to find that Lannes issued an order on *20 Brumaire An 13* (11 November 1804) that informed colonels that the *gagistes* – men employed by regiments as musicians – were to come under military law and discipline, as their ill-discipline was 'infecting' the soldiers, especially the newly arrived conscripts. Therefore, Lannes additionally ordered that any *gagistes* fostering desertion or setting a bad example would be removed from the army.[11] It seems some men were more than happy to copy this 'bad behaviour', as our later chapters will explore. It was not just new conscripts who deserted, as Bellavoine of the 55ᵉ *de Ligne* tells us from a year earlier:

16 Frimaire 13 [...] the 2nd Battalion was put under arms to hear the trial of a young man who deserted on the 9th and was tried at noon; he was sentenced to 7 years' in irons and his hair cut off on pain of desertion; nevertheless after eight years of good service, this was appalling in the eyes of us who are Soldiers. This is where feeling must judge with reason in such a reckless matter as this.[12]

Clearly for a soldier with such a length of service to desert suggests conditions were far from ideal. Indeed, Bellavoine admits that he was not immune to the harsh conditions 'being alone in the barracks, I picture, before my eyes, the state I was in [...] wet to the bone, and my effects spoiled by the rain and more'.[13] Rain and damp was a perennial problem. Bellavoine notes on *17 Frimaire* 'the Seine must be very high in Paris. The rain has not stopped here for ten days.'[14]

To try and combat cold and damp, Lannes ordered on *23 Brumaire An 13* (14 November 1804) that colonels were to ensure the men had at least two pairs of shoes in good condition, and to ensure that shoes needing repairs were fixed promptly. He passed orders that company commanders were to ensure that the men cleaned their shoes, which were 'to be well waxed' to make them waterproof. Lannes also urged the company commanders that 'as the bad weather arrives to ensure the men to have a good *capote*'. To preserve the men's shoes from damp and mud, Colonel Joubert of the 64ᵉ authorised a gratuity issue of clogs to every man on Christmas Day 1804. The clogs were to be worn around camp and on fatigues to 'preserve the shoes from rotting'.[15] This suggests the ground was exceptionally muddy and constantly wet, to the point that shoes simply fell to pieces.

As well as ensuring his men had dry feet and a warm *capote*, Lannes also made sure that the men under his command washed both themselves and their shirts. In an order of *12 Frimaire An 13* (3 December 1804) each ordinary was to send a man from the camp to arrange with a washer woman to clean the shirts, beddings, underpants and other items of linen. *Sous-officiers* were allowed to use the battalion or corps washerwomen.[16] The fact that such an order was necessary rather suggests that men did not change their nethergarments with any degree of frequency, wash them or themselves. The order clearly went unheeded: or if it was obeyed the men clearly did not get into the habit of being hygienic.

By spring 1805, men had been living in their huts for over 18 months. Living conditions were clearly bad as on *7 Ventôse An 13* (26 February 1805) General Suchet issued the following orders:

> the disease of scabies multiplies considerably in the regiments. The way to avoid that is of the greatest cleanliness. The *sous-officiers* must ensure that the soldier washes his hands and face every day, he must comb his hair every day, and changes his shirt every Sunday. Their huts are to be cleaned very thoroughly.[17]

Clearly lice had become of almost endemic proportions for such an order to be issued. It also tells us the men did not change their shirts and seldom washed. It seems the men had

We see, left to right, a musician of the 95e *de Ligne*, a man clearly of African origin, his uniform marked out with sky blue facings. We see grenadiers with scarlet epaulettes and *chapeaux*, fusiliers and *voltigeurs*. Of interest, the use of white gaiters and long, ankle-length *pantalons* – presumably made from nankin for walking out dress as the figure does not carry his weapons. We note a chevron on the upper arm denoting the rank of *fourrier*. The drum major in a sombre blue *surtout* with no lace embellishment which is no doubt a campaign garment. The band master has gold trefoils to mark out his rank.

become accustomed to not washing or cleaning, as on *14 Ventôse An 13* (5 March 1805) the officers and *sous-officiers* of the 3rd Division of V Corps were reminded to ensure the men changed their shirts and had them washed, to ensure the barracks were swept, and the soldiers washed and shaved. Furthermore, Suchet ordered that 'the company commanders will assign a barrack to place the men who are suffering from scabies who will be taken there by their regiment's surgeon and confined to the ambulance'. Clearly isolation was seen as the best way of preventing the spread of the disease. No doubt the problems Suchet faced were common accross the various camps.

As March progressed on *19 Ventôse* (10 March 1805), living conditions were still clearly fairly insanitary and Lannes ordered regimental surgeons to check the men for lice on a Sunday and Thursday, to make sure the men cleaned themselves, and their clothing, and to identify men suffering from scabies and make recommendations for their treatment. A double issue of fire wood was authorised to the isolation barracks and the Minister of War was asked to allocate additional funds for treatment.[18] Lannes' corps was not alone: Ney had passed similar orders on *6 Pluvoise An 13* (25 January 1805).[19]

Living in wooden huts with straw roofs was always going to be dangerous when lighting was by oil lamp or candle. An order dated *8 Ventôse An 13* (27 February 1805) tells us that on the previous night fire had broken out in the huts of the 88ᵉ *de Ligne*. Several huts were destroyed and:

Sapeur of the 94e *de Ligne*. Contrary to expectation, his uniform is very sombre.

> consequently, we order that all the *sous-officiers* and corporals are to ensure that all lights are extinguished in the barracks of their company half an hour after the rotation of the guard, which will always be a ¼ hour after lights out has been beaten. it is forbidden for the *sous-officiers* and soldiers to smoke during the day or at night in the barracks. Half an hour after the last evening rotation of the guard, the police guard will be patrolling the whole of the regimental camps to ensure that the lights and fires are extinguished, both in the barracks of the troops and in the kitchens.[20]

We wonder how much of the camp of the 88ᵉ *de Ligne* was destroyed.

The dangers of fire prompted the following order of *18 Ventose An 13* (9 March 1805): 'It is ordered for the regimental police companies to patrol the camp for half an hour after the beaten retreat so that they ensure all lights in the barracks of the troops are extinguished.'

Then as now, the armed forces like giving soldiers mindless tasks, simply to keep them occupied. Keeping boredom away was perhaps behind one of Gabriel Suchet's orders that many ex-forces readers will perhaps remember as a duty conducted on 'jankers'.

In April 1805 the men in the brigade were instructed after morning drill training at 1400hrs to whiten the stone edging around their barracks. We find subsequent orders for the men to keep the edging 'nice and white'.[21] Suchet did not issue white paint, so clearly the men had to use their 'blanco' for this purpose, which they obtained from the Napoléonic NAAFI – the *vivandières*' cart. An analogy here can be made to the writings of Second World War soldier Spike Milligan. He comments in his war diaries about being forced to use toothpaste to whiten webbing 'to keep it nice and white whilst his teeth went nice and black'. One gets the feeling here that Suchet may have overlooked the supply and demand issues of 'blanco' to keep both the stones 'nice and white' and the men's equipment 'nice and white'.

Women and Children

Women serving the French Army were a beneficial feature that dated back to 1657.[22] There were two classes of women who served the army: *blanchisseuses*, who were the washerwomen, and *vivandières*, who ran the canteen and *sous-officiers*' mess. During the 1st Empire these women were organised according to the decree of 30 April 1793. At the urging of Lazare Carnot, all the 'useless women' were banned from the French army. The number of washerwomen was fixed (four per battalion) but the number of *vivandières* was not.[23] An Order of the Day of the *Armée du Nord*, also dated 30 April 1793, restricted the number of women per battalion to six and four per cavalry regiment. Each 'lawful' woman wishing to continue to serve as a *vivandière* or *blanchisseuse* had to present themselves and a letter to the commanding officer of the regiment to which they were attached within 24 hours to prove they had a right to remain with their regiment or be dismissed.[24] A General Order of 15 August 1793 issued to all commanding officers expressed 'surprise' at the illegal number of women with the army, especially officers' wives in barracks and cantonments. This was repeated on 1 September 1793, ordering the expulsion 'of women from the army'. Furthermore, the General in Chief reminded officers and generals that having their wives (and other women) '*à la suite*' was illegal, and that they should be sent home; those officers who did not comply were to be made an example of. Similarly, those women who were illegally serving the army and who refused to quit their units were to be arrested by the Gendarmerie.[25] The 1793 law was modified in 1800, when the First Consul informed unit commanders that the number of women was limited to four per battalion and two per cavalry squadron, regardless of their function. This was repeated by the Regulation of 8 June 1809, and indeed it remained in force until 1832![26] The presence of women in camp was always going to be a 'temptation' for the soldiers young and old alike. Despite the best efforts of the camp guards, the number of women in the camps had grown exponentially – many 'washerwomen' were more than likely providing 'additional services' to the soldiers. On *8 Germinal An 13* (29 March 1805), acting on guidance from General Suchet, the colonel of the 64^e *de Ligne* ordered 'it is forbidden for laundresses of the regiment to cross the line between their barracks and the kitchens of the troop …' Presumably the women were cooking

Officer of mounted gendarmes in full dress. Hundreds of gendarmes were employed in bringing back deserters to the Camp of Boulogne.

as well as 'doing the laundry'. One assumes the men were also forbidden from doing so, as on *14 Germinal An 13* (4 April 1805) Corporal Macon of the 2nd Company, 2nd Battalion 64ᵉ *de Ligne*, was convicted of doing just that, clearly with amorous intentions. He was stripped of his rank as punishment.[27]

The camps, as well as including women, had children around them. One mother named Thérèse, described as 'an employee of the army' and married to a corporal of the 69ᵉ *de Ligne*, gave birth to a daughter, Lucie Bertin, who was born in Étaples in November 1803. Anne Sautiaux, described as 'following the army', was the wife of a military butcher and gave birth to a daughter in Étaples in 1804. Marie Anne Legrand gave birth to a boy, Jean-Louis, in summer 1805. We know nothing of her profession, but the father was Jean-Louis Gagnier, a chasseur with the 9ᵉ *Légère*. They were unmarried. Likewise, Marie Madeleine Peudecoeur gave birth to a daughter, Marie Marguerite Chopin. The father was a corporal in the 32ᵉ *de Ligne*. Were these women prostitutes, employees in the camp, or young women who had taken a shine to a soldier and found herself pregnant? We cannot say for certain.[28]

Concerned by the number of women in camp beyond the regulation allocations, on *29 Germinal An 13* (19 April 1805) General Suchet ordered that only the regulation number of *vivandières* and washerwomen was to be tolerated: those without 'patents' were to remove themselves or to be removed from camp by the Gendarmes on or before *2 Floréal An 13* (22 April 1805). Those remaining, who had authorisation to remain with the army, were to move their lodgings to each regiment's '*petit etat major*'. The right of the women to mess with the officers and eat with them was rescinded. The following day, the *vivandières* and laundresses who did not have authorisation to be with the army, were rounded up by the camp guards, had their head shaved to mark them out as prostitutes and were forcibly removed.[29] Enforcing the regulation was twofold: to keep discipline and to reduce the chance of men catching 'the clap'. However, this attempt to prevent the men catching sexually transmitted diseases was utterly ineffective.

Cooking and Heating

Archive documents tell us that by early winter 1804 it seems that local wood resources had been exhausted in building the invasion flotilla, and in feeding the cooking fires of the camp. Archaeology confirms this.[30]

So scarce was wood come winter 1804 that on *5 Nivôse An 13* (26 December 1804) private Jourdaine of the 64ᵉ *de Ligne* was convicted of stealing wood from the gardens of the Château LaSagniere, close to the regiment's camp. His commanding officer, *General de Brigade* Roger Valhubert, made an example of him, and ordered 'extraordinary patrols' be established to stop men leaving camp to find wood or to desert. Freezing men had clearly taken desperate acts to keep warm.[31] To overcome the lack of wood, the army began using other sources of fuel. Lannes passed orders to ensure that each company had 375kg of wood or 8 '*ectogramme*'[32] of charcoal supplied for heating on *8 Frimaire* (29 November 1804). As well as importing charcoal, coal was imported – at vast cost from Alsace – to the camps. Coal meant a technological change in the way the men cooked. Lannes recommended that a ratio of 24kg of wood to 18kg of charcoal or 37 *'briquettes de houille'* – cobbs of hard coal – was to be used. In the total absence of wood, 36kg of charcoal and 75 pieces of hard coal were to be issued a day. Ideally a ratio of ¼ wood to ¾ *charbon de terre* – soft coal, like shale – or hard lump coal was to be used.[33]

Meat cannot be roasted over coal without it tasting appalling: the men's cooking equipment made for wood fires was totally unsuitable for the hotter coal and would melt, or at least the solder could. It meant the men needed cast iron cooking pots and other vessels, and the coal had to be burnt with a draught via a chimney, and the fire contained in a range or similar with a raised grill in which to place the utensils.[34] At Boulogne, archaeology shows that each company had its own kitchen, with a masonry chimney. Archaeological recovered finds show the men ate from earthenware plates, but no evidence for cooking utensils have been recovered.[35] We do note in regimental records the purchase of iron cooking ranges and grills.[36]

Food and Rations

Talking about cooking, we need to look at what was being cooked. Soldiers in the French army, in theory at least, were paid professionals, as we noted earlier. Out of his weekly wage, the army took pay money as 'stoppages', as we discussed before, to pay for a soldier's clothing and equipment, which meant the final lump sum passing to the soldier was little more than a few sous a week. One of these 'stoppages' was the 'ordinary' (*Masse Ordinaire*), which was used to pay for the men's rations. At the start of the epoch, eight men in the same company were grouped into an ordinary, which was not necessarily the same group as the squad. The ordinary slept, ate, cooked, lived, and drilled together. Each was headed by a corporal or long-serving soldier. Each ordinary was issued a *gamelle* (pan), *grand bidon* (liquid container) and *marmite* (field cauldron). Each *gamelle* was stamped with the ordinary's number, which was checked off against the mess list maintained by the cook house corporal when the meal had been prepared.

Regardless of what the regulations said, it seems undeniable that the ordinary would be lucky to have these when the camps were first established. A report from autumn 1803 tells us that for immediate needs 6,851 *marmites* were needed, along with 3,352 *gamelles*, 9,721 *grand bidons*, 62,756 *petit bidons* and 33,724 leather *banderoles de petit bidon*. Of the items in use, the report starkly informed Berthier, the Minister of War, 'they are of bad manufacture … and generally the iron is badly soldered, and the *bidons* and other items are very weak' and moreover did not hold liquid.[37] Clearly, the men had to improvise: the archaeological excavations carried out at the camps show that men had to use ceramic cooking and storage vessels in camp. How these items fared on campaign we cannot say. Then as now, army issue was not always ideal, and a degree of improvisation and substitution had to take place.

The company captain would appoint a *chef d'ordinaire*, who was often a corporal, who was required to be able to read and write, and understand the new metric system

Mounted gendarme in full dress, c.1805.

of weights and measures. Each ordinary possessed a register (the French army adored paperwork. Lots of little men running around with lots of bits of paper even on campaign made the army either a bureaucratic nightmare or dream depending on one's viewpoint!). In the register the chief was to record all expenses, from the purchase of groceries to laundry expenses. Each man was to contribute the value of one shirt per week to the fund. The chief would write the expenses in the registers and sign it, recording the names of the men in the ordinary, and the name of those who accompanied him on his chores. The chief were paid by the *caporal-fourrier* (in essence, the sergeant major's clerk). Every fifteen days the captain inspected the books to ensure fair play, that the men were not being defrauded out of food and the chef was not spending the money on drink. To ensure food was being purchased, the company sergeant major visited the butchers and bakers recorded in the register to double check the accuracy of the records, to ensure the records were accurate and to satisfy himself the ordinary was not in debt.

Historian Anthony L. Dawson tells us that the French Army ration *c.*1800 consisted of bread, meat, wine or beer and lard to the following proportions:

Bread (made from 3 parts rye flour to 1 part wheat): 750g (to last two days)
Fresh Meat (theoretically beef): 300g
Salted Meat (beef or bacon): 250g
Biscuit (in lieu of bread): 550g
Wine: 1 litre

Each member of the ordinary combined their ration into a single cook pot, to produce a stew. Each *peleton* cooked and slept where it lived: archaeology shows that at the camp of Boulogne, the men also defecated in the same place as they lived, ate, cooked and slept. In *Thermidor An 12* (July 1803), Bonaparte estimated that per year, combined the three major camps would consume 18,000 cattle, 195,061.357 litres of brandy (343,260 pints!), 843,800kg of rice and 56,240kg of beans and pulses as well as 1.2 million hard tack biscuits, 50,000 litres of wine and 3 million loaves.[38] This placed a huge and impossible strain on what could be supplied locally. It meant soldier and civilian slowly starved. By autumn, the army had 2,626 steers, 454 cows, and 1,513 sheep for immediate needs for meat.[39] In addition, the army commissariat had obtained 5.7 million kg of flour to bake bread, 1.2 million rations of biscuit, 38,167kg of rice, 187,064kg peas and beans, and 126,025kg of salt, 207,559 litres of brandy, 47,088 litres of wine, and 12,050 litres of cider.[40] Army consumption raised prices beyond the reach of the poorest in society.[41]

These quantities may seem huge, but the 'average' non-active male requires approximately 2,000 calories per day, with a recommended daily allowance of 250g carbohydrate, 70g protein, and 66–100g of fats. Therefore, unless the soldier was able to supplement the ration – if he received it in full – with his own purchase of food, as Dawson points out:

hunger would have been a common experience for the soldiers of Napoléon's army: they had a calorific deficiency between 500 and 1,000 calories. They would have

Officer of 1e *Dragons* in full dress, c.1805.

been below optimal weight and more prone to disease and infection due to reduced immune systems from a lack of essential micronutrients […] Such a low calorific diet and low carbohydrate diet would lead to weight loss through depletion of lean muscle mass and also through dehydration […] In order for French soldiers to survive any length of time on campaign they would have been forced, largely through hunger, to forage.[42]

Men had to 'fend for themselves'. Despite being paid professionals, a soldier was lucky to have 3 to 5 sous a week pocket money, being paid 25 cents every five days.[43] If the men received the money, they had some 'cash' to buy food and drink. General Marchand wrote that 'a pound of bread is worth seven sous, or 35 centimes […] a pound of meat is almost twice as expensive. Happy is the soldier who can afford a beer a week', which 'cost 3 sous in Boulogne in February 1804'.[44] From the highest to the lowest, food was a constant worry. About food, or the lack of it, Brun-Lavainne, a musician of the 46ᵉ, writes:

> Food, according to the regulations, consisted of a portion of ammunition bread weighing three quarters of a kilogram. It was insufficient for me considering that on the heights where the camp was situated the air was very sharp and gave me a devouring appetite. In the morning, we had the ration of brandy to wash down our dry bread. At ten o'clock, dinner consisted of soup and an imperceptible piece of hard meat to which were added muscles, offal and other culinary amenities from the butchers, in their facetious language, called chittlings. Such was our daily treat, or rather that of our dogs who had the best part of it. Everybody was murmuring, but our leaders didn't worry about it, and the general opinion was that they got along with the suppliers. The fact is that not only were the officers, of course, much better fed, but the sergeants major and quartermasters always had choice cuts of meat in abundance, while, to appease our hunger, we were often reduced to pick up shells by the sea or gather salads in the fields.[45]

Aware that the men were on a starvation diet, on *26 Ventose An 13* (17 March 1804) General of Division Suchet gave orders that the ground between the second row of barracks and the kitchens was to be cultivated as a garden. Each plot was to be laid out on a model uniform pattern; the edge marked with stones. The purpose was twofold: the men could grow food to supplement their rations and in tending the garden it helped prevent boredom.[46] Major Dellard, of the 46ᵉ *de Ligne* in Soult's IV Corps, notes:

> The area behind the second row of barracks was subsequently filled with very beautiful gardens, which the companies cultivated and from which they obtained a large quantity of vegetables for their soup.[47]

These gardens have been identified by archaeology in the excavated camps of VI Corps, and they were a common-sense response to the lack of rations, but what is surprising is the late date of their creation. One solution to the lack of food was to go fishing:

Officer of the 8e *Dragons* in full dress, c.1805.

mutton is sold for 20 sols per pound and the same is true of other objects, except fish [...] which are very cheap. The price of fish is different because of its quality. We find ourselves at moment herring fishing, we catch considerable quantities of them [...] a pound of fish sells at 2 sols.[48]

Trooper Rondey, of the 11ᵉ *Dragons*, writes 'goods and everything else are exorbitantly expensive ... Most of its [Boulogne (ed)] inhabitants make immense and rapid fortunes.'[49]

So scarce was food by early spring 1805 that theft was resorted to. General Gabriel Suchet, who commanded the 3rd Division of Lannes' V Corps, sentenced a young drummer of the 64ᵉ who had been caught poaching for game with his carbine, and ordered that the night time patrols be stepped up in an order dated *3 Pluviôse An 13* (23 January 1805). It was not an isolated incident: a *chasseur* from the 25ᵉ *Légère* had been arrested for stealing meat on *26 Nivôse An14* (16 January 1805) in VI Corps.[50] Lack of food and warmth were driving men to desperate measures.

As Dawson makes out, malnourished soldiers cannot fight illness, and gathering tens of thousands of men together made outbreaks of illness inevitable. Contaminated ground water from overflowing latrines would encourage typhoid fever and typhus. It was literally a death sentence to be conscripted: if you did not starve, you got sick, and if you managed to get to the battlefield the march or bullet would kill you in time. Baron Larrey, in refusing to acknowledge the cause of scurvy – which had been proved to the world as directly due to Vitamin C deficiency – as anything other than a lack of fresh bread condemned thousands of young men to their death.

Chapter 8

I Corps

Yet what were the practical realities of clothing, feeding and training the army? Did the regulations hold up? How was this put into practice? The 1804 and 1805 inspections cover training in great detail. Every regiment was put through its paces in the field, the *sous-officiers* were examined in their theory and practice of the regulations, as were the officers. This was all neatly written down by the inspecting officers and offers us a wealth of details about the Grande Armée weeks before the campaign began. We rely on an Order of Battle dated *1 Vendémiaire An 14* (23 September 1805) for details of regimental allocation.[1]

Led by Marshall Bernadotte, the former Minister for War, the staff work of the corps was in the highly capable hands of *General de Division* Victor Léopold Berthier, one of the foremost staff officers at the time, and younger brother to the more famous Louis Alexandre Berthier. Much has been said about Bernadotte being incompetent, and for some authors he was considered a traitor. Yet behind the bluster of de Seeger and others who had an axe to grind in writing their memoires, the truth is that Bernadotte was a capable field commander, whose reputation, like that of Emmanuel de Grouchy, has been blackened by those seeking to find a scapegoat for the failings of the commander in chief, Emperor Napoléon.

1e Division

The division was led by *General de Division* Olivier Macoux Rivaud de la Raffinière, a veteran of Marengo. His brigade commanders were *General de Brigade* Patchod, commanding the 8e and 45e *de Ligne*, and *General de Brigade* Dumoulin, commanding the 54e *de Ligne*. The staff work was handled by Adjutant-Commandant Rousseau. The Division had a squadron from the 5e *Chasseurs* attached to it.[2]

8e *de Ligne*

The regiment was inspected on *8 Vendémiaire An 13* (27 September 1804) at Verdun. The 8e had bearskins for its grenadiers as 8,053fr 40 was spent between 8 December 1802 and 27 September 1804. In addition, 1,719Fr had been spent on lace, both gold and worsted, and grenadiers' distinctions – again we are ignorant of the number of epaulettes purchased. The regiment's clothing in September 1804 was condemned as entirely bad, yet the inspector noted the regularity of clothing was very good, one of the 'the most marvellous in our armies'. Of the 2,246 *habits* in service, 722 were to be written off and 1,397 were to be issued as replacements![3]

Trooper of the 5e or 7e *Dragons* wearing the undress *surtout*, c.1805. Archive documents confirm the 5e *Dragons'* *surtouts* were exactly as shown here, totally green and devoid of regimental distinctions.

Officer of 26e *Dragons* in full dress, c.1805.

Inspected again on *30 Thermidor An 13* (18 August 1805), General Schauenberg noted that the officers' dress was 'very good, very regular in its conformity to the regulation', that of the '*sous-officiers* and men was very good and generally very regular with great uniformity'. However, behind this superficial appearance all the broadcloth and clothing supplied since 1802 was of a very bad sort, and in most circumstances would have been rejected by the Council of Administration as not of the required standard, he noted, but the regiment had no option but to use low grade materials as it had been impossible to source cloth of the required standard. This says a lot about the economic reality of France, already being unable to supply it armies. The situation was only going to get worse, especially so with the continental blockade. Schauenberg, perhaps optimistically, ordered that within the next three months the cloth merchants and suppliers were to replace all the items they had supplied. He remarked 'the *habits, vestes, culottes*, gaiters and shoes are all extremely badly made'. Another point of contention was that *fourriers* were not wearing their corporal's stripes. The regiment was armed with a motley collection of muskets. Of the 2,141 muskets, 1,750 were in good condition, 391 were model 1763 or 1777 and 109 were Hanoverian muskets! All these non-regulation firearms were to be replaced at the earliest convenience. The regimental band was costing more than the regulated allowance from the officers pay per month and thus needed reforming. This over-generous compulsory deduction from the pay was no doubt not questioned by the officers, who lived in fear of the colonel.

About the regiment's manoeuvres, its battalion level drills were noted as very good, the *sous-officiers* were good at their jobs, knew their different drills well and were good at practical instruction. This had been achieved, Schauenberg noted, because the regiment's discipline was harsh, and the colonel's severity had rendered the officers and *sous-officiers* totally servile, mute automatons, and he was too heavy handed in doling out punishment. The inspector noted that this 'was not the way of the French!'[4]

45ᵉ *de Ligne*

Inspected on *4 Vendémiaire An 13* (23 September 1804), the regiment was well dressed and the inspector noted the major had organised the production of *capotes* for 896 men. Alarmingly, the inspector reported that most of the clothing was tatty and in need of repairs, even newly issued clothing! Since 1802 the regiment had issued 1,120 brand-new *habits* to 1,786 men. Of the 1786 *habits* in use, 1,110 were in good condition, 120 needed repairs and 556 needed total replacement as life expired. The depot held 80 brand-new *habits*, 50 *vestes*, 4 *bonnets de police*, 600 musket slings, 547 shirts, 49 black stocks, 545 pairs of socks, 277 pairs of grey linen gaiters, 428 *sacs a distribution*, 108 *havresacs* and 1,701 cockades. The major reported that the corporals and old soldiers were all to receive new *habits*, and their old clothing handed to new conscripts – ergo it was better to give the new issue to men who knew how to care for and maintain clothing, and to give old, tatty items to new entrants who had no idea how to care for clothing and equipment. The regimental band was costing more than the regulated allowance from the officers pay per month and thus needed reforming.

Officer of 27e *Dragons* in full dress, *c.*1805.

A perusal of the regiment's accounts notes some 2,880fr had been spent buying grenadiers bearskins, with a further 1,440fr spent buying bearskins for the 3ᵉ battalion by the time of the next inspection – clearly all battalions had grenadiers swaggering in bearskins and no doubt fringed scarlet epaulettes. Yet these men were not serving with the parent regiment and were part of the *Grenadiers Réunis*.[5]

Reviewed on *8 Fructidor An 13* (5 September 1805), the dress of the regiment was noted as good, but 50per cent of the clothing was still worn out. Of the 1,856 *habits* in use, 1,076 needed repairs and 180 total replacement. Also needing repair were 994 *vestes*, 1,080 *chapeaux*, 1,700 *bonnets de police*, 687 *gibernes* and 17 sets of drummers' equipment. Needed were 404 pairs of *culottes*, 250 *vestes* and 350 *chapeaux*, but stores held just 89 pairs of *culottes* ready to issue and 33 *chapeaux*. The men marched to war dressed in uniforms that were falling to pieces. The regiment's muskets were all 1777 model and 'very old' and in need of urgent replacement. The *sous-officiers* and men were wearing their *chapeaux* at 'jaunty angles' and not in accordance with the regulations, and the *fourriers* were ordered to sew on their corporals' stripes. Despite being in camp, kit cleaning was not high on the men's priority, and the regiment's major was ordered to ensure that the men whitened the *porte-giberne* and musket slings 'according to the regulation'.[6]

54ᵉ *de Ligne*

Reviewed on *14 Vendémiaire An 13* (6 October 1804), the major reported the regiment comprised three battalions, some 2,198 men. The other ranks' drill was described as 'passable'. The men were lodged with the townsfolk of Osnabrück and, thanks to Marshal Bernadotte, food was excellent, cheap and plentiful, the inspector noted. The regiment's accounts record that since June 1803, 1,023 *habits* had been made and issued alongside 1,023 *vestes*, 200 pairs of *culottes*, 1,778 *chapeaux* and 13 sets of *sapeur* equipment, which we assume includes bearskins. Some 2,014 muskets were in use, of which 710 were 1777 model and needed repairs. Due to shortages of muskets, these old muskets had to be kept in service.[7]

Inspected on *12 Fructidor An 13* (30 August 1805) in Osnabrück, the regiment had 83 officers under arms and 1,982 other ranks. The Inspector noted 53 muskets needed to be replaced as they were of non-French calibre. The eight-man strong regimental band was costing more than the regulated allowance from the officers' pay per month and thus needed reforming. One assumes their uniform was ostentatious, but alas we have no records that tell us how it looked. The primary concern for the inspector was the poor state of the regiment's clothing: of 2,180 *habits*, 1,090 needed repairs, every single one of the 2,180 pairs of *culottes* needed total replacement, 1,090 *chapeaux* needed repairs, 839 *bonnets de police* needed repairs and 1,090 replacing, 409 *gibernes* and belts needed attention, as did 420 *baudriers*. For immediate needs, stores held 710 brand-new *habits*, 643 *vestes*, 25 pairs of *culottes*, 1,129 *chapeaux* and 529 *bonnets de police*.[8] As insufficient numbers of items existed to replace all the worn-out items, clearly men marched to war in clothing well past its best.

2ᵉ Division

The division was led by *General de Division* Drouet, future *Comte d'Erlon*, with his staff work being handled by Adjutant-Commandant Luthier. *General de Brigade* François Werlé led the 27ᵉ *Légère*, and *General de Brigade* Bernard-Georges-François Frère led the 94ᵉ and 95ᵉ *de Ligne*.[9]

27ᵉ *Légère*

Reviewed on *5 Vendémiaire An 13* (14 October 1804), General Rivaud, who inspected the regiment, tells us the regiment had 83 officers present, 2,181 other ranks, of which 8 men formed the regimental band, the *voltigeur* companies had 6 *cornets*, and the regimental school had 19 *enfant de troupe*. About the *sous-officiers*' abilities, Rivaud remarked that 'they lack skill and precision in acting as guides' and 'lacked skill in dressing their companies' as well as 'keeping the lines straight' on manoeuvres. At the time of the review, no man had yet received the new regulation *schako*, 2,318 *chapeaux* were in use, and the *voltigeur cornets* had no instruments and carried drums. Despite this, the *voltigeurs* had chamois collars to their *habits*, as 39m 94 of chamois broadcloth had been utilised for this purpose. Rivaud ordered that the regiment was to obtain 6 *cornets* and authorise the replacement of the *chapeaux*.[10]

Inspected again on *19 Thermidor An 13* (1 August 1805), days before the campaign opened, General Schauenbourg remarked that regimental clothing was good, but finances were badly administered. Discipline was good, but Schauenbourg recommended the dismissal of 56 men from the regiment for bad conduct. He added that the men were well dressed, but the *havresac* was worn too low and interfered with the *giberne*. The men had still not received their *schakos*, 706 *chapeaux* being delivered since the previous review. The *carabinier* companies did not have bearskins, and not a single pair of epaulettes was recorded, but they may have been counted with the *habits*.[11]

94ᵉ *de Ligne*

Reviewed on *16 Thermidor An 13* (4 August 1805), the regiment had 83 officers and 1,943 other ranks, of which 8 were the regimental band and 7 were enfants de troupe. The regiment was quartered around Hanover, with officers and men lodged with the townsfolk.

The inspector noted a great regularity in the dress of the men, which was highly commendable, and the clothing in use was generally considered to be in good condition. The equipment was noted as being in excellent condition, perfectly well maintained and very uniform in appearance. The inspector did note, however, the regiment had 1,100 1777 model muskets in use, which were to be changed as soon as was possible for the An IX model. General Schauenbourg noted in his report that despite the good and regular appearance of the *sous-officiers* and men, the regimental tailor needed to cut the

Trooper of 27e *Dragons* in full dress, c.1805.

Squadron commander of the 10e *Chasseurs*, in full dress, c.1805.

clothing with greater accuracy according to the regulations as indicated on *1 Vendémiaire An10* (23 September 1801). The master gaiter maker and shoe maker also had to be more thorough in their understanding of this regulation. The master leather worker was ordered to adjust all the straps of the *havresac* as they hung too low on the men's backs. In the previous year, 6,000fr had been received to reimburse the regiment for its expense in repairing clothing and that 5,950fr 60 had been spent making new clothing, with a further 1,789fr 20 spent on repairs to old clothing. The regimental accounts record 22,914fr 80 being spent in the previous 36 months on broadcloth, serge, linen and tricot and that 200 *capotes* costing 3,100fr were made for the *sous-officiers*. It is interesting to note that despite the huge expenditure on clothing, just 112 *habits* had been made and issued, along with 137 *vestes*, 2,130 pairs of tricot *culottes*, 60 *chapeaux* and 81 *bonnets de police*. Of the 2,092 *habits* in use, 964 needed repairs, and 1,016 were write offs, with a minimum of 1,054 to be replaced: 50 per cent of the *habits* were 'knackered', likewise 1,174 *chapeaux* out of 2,130 were to be replaced, as were 1,085 *bonnets de police* out of 2,130 and every single pair of *culottes*. We doubt these replacements appeared before the regiment left its cantonments! By winter 1805 the regiment was surely in little more than rags. The depot was virtually empty, holding no clothing or equipment, but it did contain 982m 50 of white broadcloth, 167m 50 white tricot, 5,360m 82 white serge and 291m 60 of linen. In the list of the regiment's weapons, we note that the 13 *sapeurs* with the unit were armed with An XI light cavalry musketoons.[12]

On *6 Vendémiaire An 14* (28 September 1805) the regiment's major began the process of forming *voltigeur* companies in all three battalions.[13] The process was completed in Munich on *26 Vendémiaire* (18 October 1805) but no clothing or weapons were issued.[14] By 1807 these men did not have yellow or chamois collars, but were armed with sabres.[15] Every man wore a *chapeau* – no bearskins are listed – and on 3 December 1807 the regiment was authorised to replace its *chapeaux* with *schakos* costing 10fr 70 apiece.[16]

95ᵉ *de Ligne*

Inspected on *25 Thermidor An 13* (13 August 1805), General Schauenbourg reported the regiment mustered 2,486 officers and men, of which 80 had joined since the last review, 25 had died, 22 had deserted, and 20 had never come back from leave. The regiment was at Lüneburg, lodged in barracks, each able to accommodate 112 men. The unit had recently arrived from Saint-Omer, where they had been under canvas. Drill was considered to be good, however, larger-level battalion manoeuvres were far from ideal. Discipline 'without any exaggeration was very good' and 'the clothing of the officers was very good, very correct and very regular', and of the men 'was very regular and well sewn'. However, 'the commanders of the companies had to pay more particular attention to the regulations with the cut of the clothing and headdress, particularly the grenadiers', reported the inspector. Despite initial praise, the clothing in use was 'showing its age'. For example, of the 2,366 *habits* in use, 833 needed immediate replacement and 538 needed urgent repairs; just 67 new items being issued since the last inspection. The men were wearing 2,366 *chapeaux*, of

Trooper of 10e *Chasseurs* in full dress, *c.*1805. The sabretache is non-regulation, but attested by archive documents. In the background we see the elite company with scarlet *culottes hongroise*.

Colonel of the 1e *Hussard* in full dress, *c.*1805.

which 636 needed immediate replacement. Armament wise, General Gassendi reported that of the 2,255 muskets, 961 had to be written off as beyond repair, a further 225 had to be replaced as they were of the 1760 model: he gave orders for the arsenals at Mayence (Mainz), Metz and Strasbourg to send 'with all speed' the required number of firearms.[17]

1ᵉ Light Cavalry Division

Allocated to the cavalry reserve, the division was led by the son of the victor of Valmy, François Étienne de Kellerman. Distinguished at Marengo, he would prove himself to be one of the ablest commanders of cavalry in the French Army for 15 years, ending his career at Waterloo. The 2ᵉ and 5ᵉ *Hussard* were led by *General de Brigade* Piraud, and the 4ᵉ *Hussard* and 5ᵉ *Chasseurs* by *General de Brigade* Marisy. The staff work was handled by Adjutant-Commandant Noizet.[18]

2ᵉ *Hussard*

Dressed in chestnut brown *pelisses* and *dolmans* with *bleu celeste* facings, with similar colour *culottes hongroise*, the 2ᵉ *Hussard* had a highly distinctive uniform. Inspected on *21 Thermidor An 13* (9 August 1805), the regiment mustered 772 men and had 522 horses, but needed an additional 63. Clothing in use comprised:[19]

Item	In Good Repair	In Need of Repair	To be written off	Total	Total made since 23 September 1803
Habits			Nill		
Dolmans	617		2	619	183
Pelisses	482	130	60	672	198
Surtouts	377	291	47	715	273
Manteaux	393	197	124	623	204
Gilets	504	47	9	560	148
Stable coats			Nil		
Culottes Hongroise	388	13	266	607	346
Stable trousers	51	80	581	682	19
Underwear	388	4	277	667	576
Barrel sashes	465	6	3	474	7
Schakos a poil	73		2	75	13
Schakos a flamme	508	36	47	301	2
Bonnets de police	291	94	378	703	18
Adjutants *redingote*	2			2	1

Clearly the regiment had the elite company in fur-covered *schakos*, and the rest with the old *schako* with the coloured wing as shown by Hoffmann. In the eighteen months prior to the inspection, some 748m 69 of blue – presumably *bleu celeste*? – broadcloth had been

Trooper of the 1e *Hussard* in full dress, *c.*1805.

used, 1,065m 17 green broadcloth to make *manteaux*, 877m 48 brown broadcloth, 362m *treillis*, 650m flannel, 20m 80 brown tricot, 486m 91 white serge, and 2,162m 58 linen. Rather than stable coats, the regiment used smocks made from linen, 42 being made and 17 issued. In terms of armament, the regiment had 726 carbines, 518 pairs of pistols and 818 sabres. The carbines, however, 'were very heavy, inappropriate for the army of cavalry'. We assume these were not the hussar pattern and not taken into the field.

5ᵉ *Hussard*

Dressed in white and *bleu de ciel* with yellow lace and trim, the uniform of the 5ᵉ *Hussard* was one of the most elegant of the epoch. Sadly, between 1802 and 1808 we have no inspection returns for the regiment.[20]

4ᵉ *Hussard*

The regiment's archive is sporadic for inspection returns during the course of the Empire: the 1804, 1805 and 1808 inspection returns are missing.[21]

5ᵉ *Chasseurs*

Reviewed on *15 Thermidor An 13* (3 August 1805), shortly before it departed for the Austerlitz campaign, the regiment accounts record that 864fr had been spent buying colpacks for the elite company, 2,546fr 35 had gone towards repairing clothing and 1,167fr 30 had been allocated to making new items. The regiment was wearing:[22]

Item	In Good Repair	In Need of Repair	To be written off	Total	Total made since last inspection
Habits					
Dolmans		350	162	512	
Surtouts	276		41	317	276
Manteaux	302	138	57	497	
Gilets in broadcloth	469	102	202	773	212
Gilets d'ecurie	272	97	414	773	167
Culottes hongroise			773	773	128
Stable trousers			773	773	31
Colpacks	77	7	16	100	
Schakos	346	150	177	673	89
Bonnets de police	167		606	773	469

Brand new and ready to be issued were 790 pairs of stable trousers, which were hastily issued to ensure the men had at least one pair of legwear in good condition. The inspector ordered *dolmans* suppressing and authorised 202 new *surtouts*, 808 pairs each of *culottes hongroise* and stable trousers, 404 *gilets d'ecurie* and 202 white *gilets* to be made.

Chapter 9

III Corps

The corps weas led by Marshal Louis Nicholas Davout. This was his first major command. The author has been unable to find anything from his pen or his staff officers can be located concerning his corps in the French Army Archives. This does not mean a more diligent researcher may find something of course.

1ᵉ Division

Commanded by *General de Division* Bisson, the Division was under Lannes' orders during the battle. The 1st Brigade – the 13ᵉ *Légère* – was commanded by *General de Brigade* Demont, the 2nd Brigade, comprising the 17ᵉ and 30ᵉ de Ligne, by *General de Brigade* Jean Louis Debilly. Lastly, the 3rd Brigade, mustering the 51ᵉ and 61ᵉ *de Ligne*, was led by *General de Brigade* Georges-Henri Eppler.

13ᵉ *Légère*

Reviewed on *11 Vendémiaire An 13* (3 October 1804) by *General of Brigade* LaMartilliere, the men's clothing came in for some critique: of the 2,024 *habits* in use, 874 needed replacing and 353 total replacement, or give or take 50 per cent. Every single pair of *pantalons* had to be replaced as they were 'worn out'. The men all wore *schakos*, but 961 had to be replaced as they were damaged beyond repair and 200 needed repairs. We wonder what exactly the men had been doing with their headdress to damage it so badly less than a year since it was issued? Despite having six *voltigeur cornets*, they had no instruments and carried drums. However, 10m 80 of chamois broadcloth had been used to make collars of *voltigeur habits*. Less than half of the *carabinier*s had bearskins: just 40 were in use for 84 men in 1st battalion, with a 40 brand-new examples in stores with 49 *schakos*. The regiment unusually – perhaps copying the *garde impériale* – used three sizes of buttons on their *habits*, stores holding 329 dozen large regimental buttons, 245 dozen small regimental buttons and 288 dozen medium regimental buttons. LaMartilliere ordered the production of 1,100 *habits*, 2,200 pairs of *pantalons*, and 1,100 *schakos*, and 6 horns were to be purchased.[1]

Inspected again on *9 Thermidor An14* (28 July 1805) at Gand by LaMartilleire, he noted that 130 muskets, 130 bayonets and 30 sabres needed immediate replacement as they were damaged beyond economic repair. Regimental accounts report 50,632fr spent on 'clothing for the sea and clogs'. Does this mean 'bathing costumes' or are we missing something in translation? Looking at the men's clothing, a matter of weeks before leaving

Colonel of 3e *Hussard* in full dress, c.1805.

III Corps 103

Trooper of 3e *Hussard* in full dress, *c*.1805. The number on the *portmanteaux* is an error to be ignored.

camp, of the 2,148 *habits* in use, 1,214 were '*hors de service*', i.e., totally worn out, and 365 needed immediate repairs, 1,428 *vestes* needed replacing and 1,197 pairs of *pantalons*, 266 *schako*s, 572 *gibernes*, 523 *giberne* belts, 253 *baudriers*, 395 musket slings and 6 drums all needed replacing. Yet for immediate needs stores held just 483 *habits*, 451 vestes, 2,311 pairs of *pantalons* and 13 *schakos*, leaving 64 *habits*, 204 *vestes*, 60 pairs of *pantalons*, and 36 *schakos* to make up the shortfall. It is incredibly unlikely that the 'knackered' clothing was replaced before the regiment hit the road to Vienna. For whatever reason, just 13 bearskins were issued – for the *sapeurs*? – to the *carabinier*s, leaving 27 in stores, with a further 24 being ordered to be purchased. The officers, *sous-officiers,* corporals and *fourriers* of the *voltigeur* companies were all issued An XI light cavalry *mousquetons*.[2]

17ᵉ *de Ligne*

Inspected on *18 Vendémiaire An 13* (8 October 1804) by *General of Brigade* Peionville in Brussels, he reported the regiment's administration was in 'chaos'. Clothing was little better. Of 2,610 *habits*, 952 needed repairs and 375 total replacement. Every single pair of *culottes* had to be replaced, so too 1,305 *chapeaux*.[3]

Given a shake-down inspection on *9 Thermidor An 13* (28 July 1805) by General Belliard, he noted drill was good, discipline very good, and the regiment's manoeuvres were good, but had room for improvement. About the men's clothing, he noted that, despite an issue of *habits* being made three days before the inspection, 967 still needed to be repaired and 710 replaced, yet stores held just 202 to make up the shortfall. In addition, 1,021 *chapeaux* were needed, just 44 being in store. No grenadiers' bearskins are reported and no *sapeurs*' equipment. Belliard ordered the immediate production of 1,305 *habits* and *vestes*, 2,610 pairs of *culotte*s and 128 *gibernes*. We doubt the men with worn-out clothing in the two war battalions received any before they left their cantonments for Vienna. We do note, however, that 36 of the 72 drummers were armed with An XI light cavalry *mousquetons* and *gibernes*, as were the 8 regimental bandsmen.[4]

30ᵉ *de Ligne*

Reviewed on *20 Vendémiaire An 13* (12 October 1804) by General Franceschi, the regiment's clothing was in a sorry state. Of the 1,916 *habits* in use, 525 needed repairs, and 487 were life expired, a total of 981 examples. Every single pair of *culottes* needed replacing, along with 981 *vestes* and *chapeaux*. Over the past year, regimental accounts tell us 318 *habits* were issued, 122 repairs and 227 remained in stores to be issued. Quite clearly more needed to be made to allow every man to have a serviceable garment. No bearskins were listed in use or in store, or any *sapeurs*' equipment.[5]

Inspected again on *8 Thermidor An 14* (27 July 1805) by General Tigny at Aix-la-Chapelle, he reports that 74 men had joined the regiment, 43 had died, 12 had deserted and 15 were missing. The *sous-officiers* needed to pay more attention to their lessons in theory and practice, he reported, the officers to pay particular care to their instruction.

Officer of 4e *Hussard* in full dress, *c*.1805.

Clearly, the *sous-officiers* were not all that was hoped of them in their education and in giving and obeying orders. Reflecting the failing 'and ignorance' of the *sous-officiers*, officers' battalion-level drill was totally lacking, but company-level manoeuvres were quickly and strictly executed. Not being able to operate at higher organisational level beyond a company was a major failing with the 30ᵉ – was this resolved in time? We shall never know, but we suspect the 30ᵉ was one of the weaker regiments at Austerlitz in performing its given orders. Discipline was 'good and well observed' but the men were merely 'passable' in their appearance and physique. The men's turnout was 'good but it lacked uniformity'.

Clothing wise, of the 1,858 *habits* in use, 981 needed to be replaced and every single pair of *culottes*: stores held just 120 brand-new *habits* and 11 needing repairs and 93 pairs of *culottes*. It seems doubtful if every man had received their new clothing before the regiment left their cantonments to go to war. In terms of armament, 9 sergeants and sergeant majors had a An XI model light cavalry mousqueton, so too did 27 corporals and *fourriers* and every drummer had a *giberne* and *mousqueton*. No grenadiers' bearskins are listed; we assume they wore *chapeaux* and their epaulettes were counted with their *habit*.[6]

Regimental accounts tell us 177fr 30 was spent dyeing white broadcloth and serge *bleu de ciel* for the uniform of the band, drummers and *sapeurs*.[7] The *sapeurs* presumably had bearskins. Rousselot suggests that the drummers and band were dressed in scarlet-faced *bleu de ciel*, and sapeurs wore the inverse of this.[8] Is this correct?

The regimental archive holds some clues, however. In 1803 to 1804 for the production of 818 *habits*, 166m 90 of scarlet broadcloth was used. Each habit needed 0m 15 of scarlet broadcloth, or 122m 7 in total. The remaining 44m 2 was sufficient to make 26 scarlet *habits*. In 1804 to 1805, to make 790 *habits*, 138m 81 of scarlet broadcloth was used, of which the *habits* required 118m 5 of cloth, leaving 20m 31, sufficient for 11 *habits*. To make 64 *habits* – 6 for the band, 52 for the drummers, 6 for the *sapeurs* – would take 96m of cloth. Potentially, assuming no scarlet cloth was used for repairs or on the collar of the *veste* of grenadiers, 37 scarlet *habits* may have existed with *bleu de ciel* facings, insufficient for all drummers, if – and a big if – this cloth was used to make garments over a two-year period and not used elsewhere. It seems more reasonable that the *habits* were dark blue.

51ᵉ *de Ligne*

The regiment was inspected on *14 Vendémiaire An 13* (3 October 1804), when it mustered 60 officers and 1,529 men in the two war battalions, which included an eight-strong band. In terms of drill, the corporals and *fourriers* were 'generally very poor … the sergeants mediocre' in their theoretical knowledge and practical instructions. Clothing was 'well sewn and very regular', with the regimental accounts showing that 37,600fr was spent buying the men *capotes* as well as linen *pantalons de route*. A further 44,500fr had been spent on smocks and shoes.[9]

Reviewed on *12 Thermidor An 13* (31 July 1805), the inspector noted 45,600fr had been spent on shoes, smocks, linen *pantalons du route* and *capotes*. The men's arms drill

Trooper of 4e *Hussard* in full dress, *c.*1805. The number on the *portmanteaux* is an error to be ignored.

was passable, but he noted many of them still had to learn how to carry their muskets correctly. Clothing wise, of the 2,099 *habits* in use, 877 needed replacement, and every single pair of *culottes* also needed replacing. For immediate needs stores held 2,000 brand-new pairs of *culottes* and 307 *habits*, which would solve some of the shortages; even so, some men marched to war in worn out clothing. We note the regiment's 62 drummers were issued with An XI light cavalry *mousquetons* and infantry *gibernes*.[10]

61ᵉ *de Ligne*

Inspected on 16 *Vendémiaire An 13* (8 October 1804) the inspector noted the men's turnout was 'very uniform and good', and regimental discipline 'very good'. Clothing needed attention: 790 *habits* needed repairs, so too 1,065 *vestes*, 508 *habits* were worn out and needed total replacement, as did 1,468 pairs of *culottes* and 1,881 *chapeaux*. To meet these needs, stores held 579 brand-new *habits*, 303 *vestes*, 562 pairs of *culottes* and 61 *chapeaux*. The inspector also noted 44 An XI light cavalry *mousquetons*, accompanied by *gibernes* and belts, were issued to the band and drummers.[11]

Reviewed on *4 Fructidor An 13* (22 August 1805), the inspector noted the men were all 'active and very animated' but were of medium height and small, weak, stature. The dress of the men was 'good thanks to the surveillance of the Officers'. The regiment had a band of eight men – one bandsman was sick in hospital. The regimental accounts tell us 48,020fr had been spent on an unknown number of *capotes* and smocks. Looking in detail at the clothing, of the 2,052 *habits*, 420 needed repairs and 530 total replacement, as did 400 pairs of *culottes*, 708 *vestes*, and 1,030 *chapeaux*. For immediate issues, 85 *habits*, 250 *vestes* and 635 pairs of *culottes* existed in store, so men clearly went to war in tatty and worn-out clothing. Stores held 46 black *baudriers* that had been recently taken from service.[12]

2ᵉ Division

Commanded by Louis Friant, the 1st Brigade, comprising the 15ᵉ *Légère* and 33ᵉ *de ligne*, was led by Etienne Heudelet de Bierre. Pierre Charles Lochet led the 48ᵉ and 111ᵉ *de Ligne*, which formed the 2nd Brigade, while the 3rd Brigade, comprising the 108ᵉ *de ligne*, was commanded by *General de Brigade* Grandeau.

15ᵉ *Légère*

Given a shake-down inspection on *20 Vendémiaire An 13* (12 October 1804), the men's dress was 'was very good with a high degree of uniformity' and 'the uniforms were very good and conformed exactly to the cloth samples' that had been sent by the War Ministry to ensure that every regiment wore cloth of the same quality and colour. However, the inspector continued that 'with use, it is obvious the broadcloth and tricot is a very low quality and has worn badly, which means the clothing does not last to the required length

Officer of the 5e *Hussard* in full dress, *c.*1805.

of service'. Reflecting quality control issues, of the 1,381 *habits*, 88 needed repairs despite being only 6 months old. The *voltigeur* companies had 6 horns issued to the *cornets*, and 13 sets of *sapeurs*' equipment were in use, yet no bearskins and no chamois broadcloth had been obtained to make *voltigeur* uniforms.[13]

Inspected again on *14 Thermidor An 13* (2 August 1805), the regiment had 59 officers, 1,189 other ranks which included the 8-man band, and 19 *enfants de troupe*. The men's turnout was still considered good, and very little of the clothing needed to be replaced, except 866 *bonnets de police*, and nothing needed to be repaired. We note 19 sets of *sapeurs*' equipment now existed, 18 examples of which were in stores – clearly these were parade items only and not taken on campaign! No chamois broadcloth existed and every man still wore a *chapeau* rather than a *schako* – so much for the 1801 regulation introducing these items. Armament wise, 954 infantry muskets were in use, and 337 An XI light cavalry *mousquetons*. Of these, 7 were issued to the band, 15 to sergeants and sergeant majors, 19 to corporals and *fourriers*, and 246 to presumably *voltigeur*s. Also issued were 24 *carabines rayé*, i.e., rifles.[14]

33ᵉ *de Ligne*

Inspected on *10 Thermidor An 13* (29 July 1805) by General Rey, the regiment had 2,131 others ranks under arms in three battalions, 1,800 forming the two war battalions. The regiment's battalion and higher-level formation movements were considered 'very bad', and it was suggested the officers and *sous-officiers* be formed into classes to acquaint them with theory and practice of the 1792 regulation. We cannot say how effective this training was before the regiment hit the road to Vienna. The men's turnout was good, but was made according to different models, and headdress was not uniform. A lot of the clothing needed repairs or total replacement. Of 2,060 *habits* in service, 709 needed repairs, and 217 total replacement, 1,226 *vestes* needed total replacement, every single pair of *culottes* and 1,226 *chapeaux*. We suspect men marched to war wearing their battered and worn-out clothing. General Rey noted that 90 An XI light cavalry *mousquetons* were in use: 14 with the staff, 6 with grenadiers, 36 with fusiliers, and 34 with drummers in the war battalions.[15]

48ᵉ *de Ligne*

Inspected on *5 Brumaire An 13* (27 October 1804), the men's clothing was in poor condition: of 2,200 *habits* in use, 950 needed repairs and 398 were fit only for the rag merchant, along with every single pair of *culottes*. In the previous year, the regimental workmen had made and issued 2,429 *habits* and repaired a further 1,120, and had 57 in stock to be issued. For the *habits* to be so damaged, being less than a year old, the materials used must have been low grade and the men fairly careless with them. The *sapeurs* were issued with 13 aprons and we assume bearskins, though none are mentioned, nor are axes.[16]

Trooper of 5e *Hussard* in full dress, *c.*1805. The number on the *portmanteaux* is an error to be ignored.

Inspected again on *10 Thermidor An 13* (30 July 1805) by General Mouton, the men's turnout was considered good and nothing needed repairs or replacing. The regimental stores were overflowing with brand-new clothing: 147 *habits*, 138 *vestes*, 458 pairs of *culottes*, 98 *bonnets de police* and 139 *chapeaux*. No grenadiers' bearskins are mentioned. We note that the 54 drummers were issued *gibernes*, belts and An XI light cavalry *mousquetons*, as were 22 fusiliers: we cannot explain why.[17] These men were certainly not *voltigeur*s, as the 48^e only began the process to form *voltigeur* companies on 23 October 1805.[18] Officers were only appointed to the *voltigeur* companies on 31 December 1805.[19] Certainly these men lacked any distinctions as such at the Battle of Austerlitz, nor Jena, because as late as December 1807 not an inch of chamois cloth existed, nor a single bearskin, the drummers still had *mousquetons* and half the men had *chapeaux*.[20]

111e *de Ligne*

Reviewed on *19 Vendémiaire An 13* (11 October 1804), the inspector noted that the regiment had 62 officers and 1,173 men in the two war battalions The men's clothing was fairly shabby: 488 *habits* needed total replacement out of 2,260, and 452 needed repairs. Every pair of *culottes* needed replacing.[21]

Inspected again on *3 Thermidor An 13* (22 July 1805), the regiment mustered 62 officers and 1,894 men in the two war battalions, which included the six-man regimental band. The men's clothing was, however, in deplorable condition. Of 2,188 *habits*, 668 had to be replaced as life expired and 800 needed repairs, likewise 1,113 *vestes*, 2,227 pairs of *culottes*, and 1,113 *chapeaux* were needed. It is doubtful if the men received their new clothing before they left their cantonments: stores held 78 *habits*, 54 *vestes* and 90 pairs of *culottes*, far short of the numbers needed. In terms of armament, 10 An XI light cavalry *mousquetons* were issued to the staff – no doubt 6 to the band – and the 36 drummers in the war battalions were also allocated these weapons along with *gibernes* and belts.[22]

The regiment's *voltigeur* companies were formed on *1 Brumaire An 14* (23 October 1805).[23] They had not received their chamois facings as late as 23 November 1807.[24]

108e *de Ligne*

Reviewed on *18 Vendémiaire An 13* (18 October 1804), regimental accounts reveal that 45,569fr had been spent on smocks, shoes, linen *pantalons de route* and *capotes*. The men's clothing was overall in good condition, but needed repairs: 351 *habits*, 349 *vestes* and 106 pairs of *culottes* needed repairs and 1,408 *chapeaux* total replacement. The major was ordered to be keep a closer eye on the production of uniforms to ensure it matched the regulations.[25]

Inspected once more on *15 Thermidor An 13* (3 August 1805), a lot of the clothing needed repairing: 136 *habits*, 675 *vestes*, 914 *bonnets de police*, with new items needed 265 *habits*, 229 *vestes*, 1,854 pairs of *culottes* out of 2,037 in use, and 1,434 *chapeaux*. For immediate needs, stores had just 102 *chapeaux*, so they clearly set off on the road to Vienna

Officer of the 6e *Hussard* in full dress, *c*.1805.

Trooper of 6e *Hussard* in full dress, *c.*1805. The number on the *portmanteaux* is an error to be ignored.

in clothing that had 'seen better days'. We note 61 An XI light cavalry *mousquetons* were in use, 53 with the drummers, and 8 more with fusiliers.²⁶ The drummers still had these firearms on 30 November 1807, by which time the *voltigeurs* had still not received any distinctions, and the regiment was in the process of adopting *schakos*.²⁷

1ᵉ *Dragons*

The regiment was attached to the division, according to Chief of Staff Belliard.

Inspected on *19 Vendémiaire An 13* (11 October 1804), the regiment mustered 590 other ranks who were wearing 843 *habits*, of which 450 needed repairs, 946 *surtouts*, of which 419 needed repairs and 133 total replacement, and the elite company had 107 bearskins. We note a huge shortfall in harness; 404 *housses* and 296 pairs of *chaperons* for 478 horses, which had just 337 saddles! The *manteaux* the inspector noted were made from *blanc picquer de bleu* broadcloth.²⁸ This cloth was made from a mix of 7 white threads to 1 blue, giving a very light shade of blue.

Reviewed on *19 Thermidor An 13* (7 August 1805), since the previous inspection 181 *habits* had been made, but despite these 189 needed repairs and 175 total replacement. We note 787 *surtouts* were in use, of which just 10 were in good condition – all brand new and issued since the last inspection: were these for trumpeters? Of these, 489 needed repairs and the remainder were 'worn out'. Also, 707 pairs of *culottes de peaux* and 150 helmets had been purchased. Furthermore, 250 pairs of boots, 530 *housses* and 700 sets of *chaperons* now existed. The men were issued 807 dragoon muskets and 1,011 pairs of pistols, 830 sabres and, for some odd reason, 844 bayonets.²⁹

3ᵉ Division

The division was led by *General de Division* Gudin. The 1st Brigade, comprising the 12ᵉ and 21ᵉ *de Ligne*, was led by *General de Brigade* Petit, and the 2nd Brigade by *General de Brigade* Gauthier. *General de Brigade* George Kister commanded the 21ᵉ *Légère*.

21e *Légère*

Inspected on *19 Vendémiaire An 13* (11 October 1804), the regiment's major reported that over the previous year, 69 men had died and 111 had deserted, 74 had been sent home from hospital, and 302 men were sick. In terms of clothing and equipment, the regiment had 13 *sapeurs* and every one of the 1,084 men in the two war battalions had a *schako*, and the 6 *voltigeur cornets* were issued horns. We note 10m 80 of chamois broadcloth had been used for *voltigeur* distinctions, 1,588 *capote*s were in service and 1,762 linen smocks. The men had both black twill gaiters as well as natural linen gaiters.³⁰

Reviewed again on *4 Thermidor An 13* (23 July 1805), the war battalions mustered 1,220 *sous-officiers* and men. The major reported 80 men had died, 69 had deserted, 211 had been discharged, 9 had been discharged from hospital and two musicians were on leave. The men of the 3rd battalion were mostly 'convalescing' and most of the recruits were of 'a bad disposition'. Since the previous review, the major noted 547fr 43 had been spent replacing headdress, but despite this of the 1,537 *schakos* in service, 50 per cent needed replacing, of the 1,537 *habits*, 1,276 needed replacement – of these 645 needed repairs – and every single pair of *pantalons* needed replacement. Did these items get replaced before the regiment left on campaign? Certainly, some did, as stores held 525 brand-new *habits*, 448 *vestes*, 602 pairs of *pantalons*, 368 *schakos*, 282 *capotes* and 346 smocks for immediate needs. The *capotes* – 225 being issued over the course of the year prior to the inspection and 121 being repaired – were dark blue. Armament wise, the *voltigeurs* were issued 288 dragoon muskets, while 20 An XI light cavalry *mousquetons* were issued to the 13 *sapeurs*, four were issued to grenadier *sous-officiers* and 36 to the drummers and *cornets* in the war battalions. The officers and *sous-officiers* of the *voltigeur* companies were issued 27 *carabine rayé* (rifles). Sabres were issued to the *voltigeurs*, carabiniers and nearly all the *chasseurs* – 947 sabres issued to 690 men.[31]

12ᵉ *de Ligne*

Reviewed on *8 Vendémiaire An 13* (30 September 1804), the 12ᵉ *de Ligne* mustered 63 officers and 1,493 men in the war battalions. This included the eight-strong regimental band and 128 grenadiers. A further 33 men were sick in hospital, and the inspector tells us 44 men had died of disease in the last year, 128 had deserted and 68 had been discharged as unfit for further service following a spell in the regimental hospital. The 3rd battalion mustered 23 officers and 273 other ranks, which included 15 *enfant de troupe*. Garrisoned at Mézières, the men were housed under canvas, as well as permanent barracks and other buildings in the citadel. The various places of accommodation were well maintained by the corporal of the Ordinary, reported the inspector. However, he noted with alarm to the colonel, that the men's clothing was extremely shabby: of 1,876 *habits*, 1,146 needed repairs, likewise 1,146 *vestes*, 1,158 *bonnets de police* and 417 *chapeaux*, with 1,961 pairs of *culottes* needed, 981 *chapeaux*, and 981 *habits*. For immediate needs stores held 90 *chapeaux* and 25 *bonnets de police*. The grenadier companies had 14 *sapeurs*.[32]

Reviewed once more on *24 Thermidor An 13* (12 August 1805), the inspection report tells us the two war battalions mustered 64 officers and 1,751 men, with a further 30 men sick in hospital. Since the previous inspection, 39 men had died of disease, and 34 had deserted. The men were now lodged in the citadel but their accommodation 'had been very badly kept' and needed considerable expense to repair it. Officers were still under canvas. The men had new beds, blankets and mattresses. The inspecting general noted the clothing was old, and the buff equipment and brass work was dirty and had not been cleaned for some time. The men's *chapeaux* were all entirely bad, the inspector remarked, 'the dimensions were not regulation' being 'much too large' and badly worn. The *sous-officiers* were admonished for wearing non-regulation red and gold epaulettes with gold bullion crescents and fringing. The regiment was further admonished for having two *fifres* per company: the men were ordered to return to their company and their duties taken on by *enfant de troupe*, who were aged 14. When we look in detail at the regiment's clothing, out of 1,816 *habits*, just 235 were in good condition, 730 needed repairs and 861 total replacement, the same for the *vestes*, and every single pair of *culottes* had to be replaced. The regiment still had 14 *sapeurs*, the 8-strong regimental band were issued *gibernes* and An XI light cavalry *mousqueton*, as were the 36 drummers in the war battalions.[33] The grenadiers were issued 275 bearskins and fringed scarlet epaulettes.[34] The 12ᵉ was one of the few regiments we know that had its grenadiers and *sapeurs* in bearskins.

21ᵉ *de Ligne*

The regimental paper for the 21ᵉ *de Ligne* is incomplete, like a number of other regiments' archives. The sole remaining document that informs us about the dress of the regiment is dated *1 Thermidor An 13* (20 July 1805), about the regiment's turnout. The inspector noted the *chapeaux* were all misshapen and needed replacement. The inspector ordered them to be worn across the shoulders, as the men were wearing them improperly 'front to back'. Of the 2,537 *habits* in service, 611 needed immediate replacement, so too the same number of *vestes*, 558 pairs of *culottes*, 313 *gibernes* and 316 *giberne* belts. We note that the regiment was issued 64 light cavalry *mousquetons*: 8 were issued to the band, 20 to grenadiers – *sapeurs*? – and 36 to the drummers along with *gibernes* and belts. As the regiment had 72 drummers, one wonders as to why only 50 per cent were armed with firearms?[35]

25ᵉ *de Ligne*

Reviewed on *16 Brumaire An 13* (28 October 1804), the inspector noted that the regiment's discipline was good and that the men were very regular in their dress, but some *sous-officiers* were rather negligent in their clothing and appearance. Of the regiment's 2,094 *habits* in use that day, 769 needed urgent repairs and 91 needed total replacement, along with 947 *vestes*, every single pair of *culottes*, 1070 *chapeaux* and 963 *bonnets de police*.[36]

Reviewed on *13 Thermidor An 13* (1 August 1805), the men's uniforms were mostly in good condition: of the 1,977 *habits* in service, 500 needed repairs. We note 291 had been issued since the last review, 209 brand-new examples were in stores and 500 had been repaired, as were 912 brand-new pairs of *culottes*, 425 *chapeaux* and 240 *vestes*. The equipment was in excellent repair, noted the inspector. The drummers were issued 44 An XI light cavalry *mousquetons*.[37]

85ᵉ *de Ligne*

Reviewed on *25 Messidor An 13* (14 July 1805), the regiment was at Sarrelibre, the barracks were commodious, well maintained, and the furniture and fittings 'all passed muster', to use a modern military turn of phrase. The *sous-officiers* wore enormous cravats and not the regulation stock, which were to be adopted forthwith, but, the inspector noted, had turned out their men immaculately. All ranks were ordered to cut their queues to regulation length. The inspector noted that of the regiment's 1,916 *habits* in use, 615 needed to be repaired as a matter of urgency and 499 needed replacing. Every single pair of *culottes* had to be replaced immediately, along with 496 *vestes*, 530 *chapeaux* and 1,388 *bonnets de police*. To meet this shortfall, the regiment's depot had 523 brand-new *habits*, 517 *vestes* and 1,498 pairs of *culottes*. Only 40 of the regiment's drummers were armed with light cavalry *mousquetons*.[38]

3ᵉ Light Cavalry Division

The division was led by *General de Brigade* Viallanes, with the future General Montbrun as one of his two aides-de-camp.

1ᵉ *Chasseurs*

On *10 Vendémiaire An 13* (2 October 1804) the regiment was inspected at Gand. The men were wearing 583 dolmans, of which just 35 were in good repair, with 548 to be written off after the inspection. Every man was wearing a brand-new *surtout*, and the elite company had 100 colpacks. The regiment possessed some 613 carbines, and yet had no shoulder belts to carry them. The regiment also had 586 pistols and 614 sabres for 720 men, so clearly over 100 men, presumably those in the depot, had no weapons at all. The regiment was also recorded as having 14 *enfant de troupe* as cadet trumpeters.[39] Some ten months later the regiment was inspected on *3 Thermidor An 13* (22 July 1805), when 646 *surtouts* were in use and the 35 *dolmans* that remained in use were ordered to be removed from service.[40]

7ᵉ *Hussard*

The 7ᵉ *Hussard* were inspected on *8 Thermidor An 13* (27 July 1805). The men were issued 808 *dolmans*, of which 156 needed repairs and 139 total replacement, 808 *surtouts*, 808 *pelisses* – 229 to be written off – 507 linen smocks, 808 barrel sashes – 385 to be written off – and the elite company had 64 *schakos a poil*. Given the amount of clothing to be written off as life expired, it is odd to find not a single scrap of clothing in the depot. What the men were wearing was literally everything the regiment possessed. The men were issued sabretaches, 86 being in stores.[41] The unit must have presented a poor appearance before the campaign began: we guess it was dressed uniformly in *surtouts*, which we imagine are in fact *Kinskis*.

2ᵉ *Chasseurs*

Inspected on *9 Thermidor An 13* (28 July 1805), the regiment was dressed in 542 *surtouts* – 300 needed repairs and 280 to be written off – with the elite company wearing

80 colpacks. To make good the defective clothing, the depot held 287m 83 of green broadcloth, 131m 32 of white broadcloth, 50m 2 of scarlet broadcloth as well as 61 new *surtouts*, 79 *vestes*, 244 stable coats, 198 pairs of *culottes hongroise*, 118 pairs of stable trousers, 5 colpacks, 104 *schakos* and 50 *bonnets de police*.[42] The uniforms may have been repaired before it left on campaign.

12ᵉ *Chasseurs*

Reviewed on *2 Vendémiaire An 13* (24 September 1804), the regiment had 41 officers and 760 other ranks. Some 503 *dolmans* were in use, just a single example being in good condition, as well as 486 *surtouts*: clearly it was a case of either/or as insufficient existed for every man to have a *dolman* and a *surtout*. We note only the elite company and *sous-officiers* had *culottes hongroise* – 148 examples – with everyone else wearing *pantalons à cheval*, even in parade dress. The elite company had 100 colpacks. The trumpeters were dressed in blue as 25m 62 of bleu celeste broadcloth had been used to make their clothing.[43] We suppose a *bleu celeste dolman* with crimson collar and cuffs.

Reviewed again on *9 Thermidor An 13* (28 July 1805), we note 413 *surtouts* had been issued since the last review along with 4 *manteaux*, 258 stable coats, 22 *vestes*, 489 pairs of *culottes hongroise*, 458 pairs of stable trousers and 206 pairs of *pantalons à cheval*. We also note that some 19m 28 of *bleu celeste* broadcloth had been used to make new trumpeters' clothing. Just 36 plumes were issued.[44]

4ᵉ *Dragons* Division

Led by *General de Division* Antoine Louis Bourcier – the Inspector General of Dragoons no less and one of the most competent cavalry men in the army – the division comprised three brigades: Louise Michel Antoine Sahuc led the 1st Brigade, which comprised the 15ᵉ and 17ᵉ *Dragons*; the 2nd Brigade was led by Claude Joseph La Planche and comprised the 18ᵉ and 19ᵉ *Dragons*; and the 3rd Brigade, comprising the 25ᵉ and 27ᵉ *Dragons*, was led by *General de Brigade* Verdière.

15ᵉ *Dragons*

Reviewed on *15 Vendémiaire An 13* (7 October 1804), the regiment was in cantonments at Versailles. The regiment musted 553 other ranks with 427 troop horses, and needed a further 132 mounts. We note 16 horses had died of disease over the previous year, as had 37 men. A further 200 men had deserted and 31 were officially AWOL. The barracks were described as good, well kept, and food for both men and horses was described as 'good and issued regularly according to the regulation'. The men were well drilled with new clothing in good condition. The elite company had no bearskins, and despite the regiment's best efforts, men still had clothing and equipment that needed repairs or total replacement. Stores had issued 250 pairs of shoes, 269 *havresacs*, 256 pairs of gaiters and 256 *sacs a distribution* to the foot company.[45]

Inspected on *20 Thermidor An 13* (8 August 1805), the unit was based at Laon. The war squadrons mustered 586 other ranks. Over the previous year, 12 men had died, 29 had deserted and 22 were AWOL. The regiment had 355 horses, 6 had died over the previous year and 43 had been disposed of, meaning 181 horses were needed. The men were placed in barracks in the citadel of Laon, which were in bad condition, the inspector noted, and it would be preferable to lodge the men with the townsfolk. The stables were clean and well kept, food for men and horses being 'generally good'. The men's dress was remarked as being particularly good, and we further note the elite company had 106 bearskins, the men had both a *habit* and a *surtout*, and the *manteaux* were made from *blanc picque de bleu* broadcloth. Also in service were 587 plumes for 592 helmets, every single one of which needed repairs, and 72 men had no headdress beyond their *bonnet de police*. The horses were equipped with *housses* and *chaperons*. The dismounted company were provided with 678 *havresacs*.[46]

17ᵉ *Dragons*

Inspected at Laon in early autumn 1803, the regiment mustered 730 other ranks, of which 155 were dismounted and 549 allocated to the mounted contingent, for whom 442 horses existed. Four officers' mounts and 98 troop horses were needed as a priority. A further 328 men were needed to bring the regiment up to strength. The men were well dressed, but the inspector noted the shade of *rose* (pink) used for the regiment's facings did not match the government's sample in terms of colour, quality of material and cost. The elite company was issued with 147 bearskins, one remained in stores and the unit's *manteaux* were made from *blanc picque de bleu* broadcloth.[47]

Reviewed again on *20 Thermidor An 13* (8 August 1805), the barracks were in poor condition and needed repairs, so too the beds and blankets, the inspector tells us, and the townsfolk had been asked to supply these. We note the dismounted contingent had 500 *capotes* and 439 *havresacs*, and wore black gaiters and shoes. The mounted contingent had 456 *blanc picque de bleu manteaux* and the elite company had 107 bearskins. The trumpeters were armed with light cavalry *mousquetons*, as were the drummers, who were also issued *gibernes*.[48]

18ᵉ *Dragons*

Formed in Metz in 1744, it became the 18ᵉ *Dragons* in 1791 and was with the Grande Armée from 1805. Inspected on *4 Vendémiaire An 13* (26 September 1804), 67 bearskins were in service for the elite company. The men were wearing 503 *habits* and 716 *surtouts*.[49] By *17 Thermidor An 13* (5 August 1805), 133 bearskins were in use. The foot company had 500 *capotes*, 449 pairs of *pantalons de toile*, and only 225 *sacs a peau*. Unusually, the men's waistcoats were green rather than regulation white, some 292m 74 of green broadcloth being used for this purpose. We also note 520 linen smocks in service. The trumpeters were armed with 17 light cavalry *mousquetons*.[50]

Officer of the 7e *Hussard* in full dress, *c.*1805.

19ᵉ *Dragons*

Created with the decree of 27 February 1793, the regiment's yellow facings made it highly distinctive. Inspected in October 1804, we note 502 *habits* were in service, 625 *surtouts* and 164 linen smocks, along with 105 bearskins and 600 plumes.[51] By August 1805, the 14 trumpeters were issued light cavalry *mousquetons*. We note 411 smocks in use, and 600 plumes.[52] Reviewed on 17 December 1807, 338 smocks had been lost on campaign, and just one bearskin was in service with the trumpet major, while 88 were in stores needing repair.[53]

25ᵉ *Dragons*

Created on *1 Vendémiaire An 12* (23 September 1803) from the 16ᵉ *régiment de Cavalerie*. Reviewed *on 24 Vendémiaire An 13* (16 October 1804), the elite company had 73 bearskins – just 15 being made since 1803 – and the process had begun to reclothe the regiment as dragoons. We note 130 new *habits* had been made since September 1803, 329 *surtouts*, 3 *manteaux*, 186 *vestes*, 193 stable coats and 687 pairs of *culottes de peau*. The inspector noted 'everything is good, the blue *habits* are to be dyed green'. As could be expected from these comments, all the new clothing was green, as 1,185m 08 green broadcloth, 25m 10 aurore broadcloth, 507m 87 aurore serge and 538m 83 green tricot had been used. The green broadcloth seems to have been dyed to colour as 695fr had been spent dyeing broadcloth and serge green. Presumably the trumpeters had worn rose *habits* faced in blue, which were replaced – we assume – with aurore faced in green. The men's footwear was still the heavy cavalry *botte forte*. We also must note 415 men were still dressed in their blue *cavalerie habits*, likewise 44 blue *surtouts* were in use. Likewise, of 412 *housses*, 323 were blue, and of the 409 pairs of *chaperons*, 328 were blue. Trumpeters, we guess, were wearing crimson faced in blue. Of the leather work in service, 300 out of 522 sabre belts were dragoon model, and of the 428 *gibernes* and belts, 201 were dragoon model. The sabres were all *cavalerie* model.[54]

Inspected on *21 Thermidor An 13* (15 August 1805), 544 *habits* were in use – all brand new and green – and just 138 *surtouts* – presumably for *sous-officiers* and trumpeters. Also in use were 79 bearskins and the foot company had 205 *havresacs* issued, 212 pairs of shoes and 218 pairs of black gaiters. Both mounted and dismounted men had *blanc picque de bleu manteaux*.[55]

27ᵉ *Dragons*

Reviewed on *1 Sansculottides An 13* (21 September 1804), General Grouchy noted that the formation of the regiment had been entrusted to him by General Augereau. The 392 men on parade were all clad in blue *habits* with crimson facings, while the elite company had 86 bearskins, along with 523 helmets of the dragoon type having been delivered, but not issued. The regiment was clearly a hybrid of dragoons and *cavalerie* in appearance.[56]

Trooper of 7e *Hussard* in full dress, *c*.1805. The number on the *portmanteaux* is an error to be ignored.

Inspected on *5 Thermidor An 13* (24 July 1805), regiment accounts show the process of converting the regiment to dragoons was a costly enterprise. Since 1804 39,976fr 62 had been spent making new clothing, 4,077fr 61 was spent on materials, 3,487fr 15 on repairing clothing and equipment in use that could be adapted for continued service, 3,745fr 45 had been spent equipping new entrants, 3,800fr on gratuity for *sous-officiers* promoted to officers, and 325fr 20 was spent on lace and other distinctions for the elite company. Since the last inspection 415 dragoon *habits* had been made and issued, and 471 green *surtouts*. The regiment had changed its footwear from the rigid *bottes forte* to *bottes a la écuyer*, 506 pairs being in use. We also note nine new trumpets had been issued and the foot company had eight drums, yet we find no specific clothing for the foot companies in use. Having been a cavalry regiment, the men in theory that remained in ranks were good riders and swordsmen and were not the 'jack of all trades' soldiers that true dragoons were. This excellence in equitation is reflected in the inspection of 1805, whereby the équitation is described as good and well executed. We suppose all bar a hard-core cadre of old cavalry troopers remained to act as instructors. The inspector noted the men were all 'a little small for dragoons', the former *cavalerie* troopers being sent to the *cuirassiers*, but added the regiment's discipline was 'good, just and severe!'[57]

Chapter 10

IV Corps

The corps was commanded by Marshal Nicholas Soult, an excellent staff officer and field commander, who has left us hundreds of documents about his corps, its training and march to Austerlitz as well as his own account of the battle: alas we do not have the space in this book to present a translation of these documents.¹ Soult's chief of staff was General de Division Salligny – who has also left us an account of the battle, which again contradicts later writers.² Two of Soult's *aides-de-camp* in the campaign were Auguste Petiet and Saint-Chamans, who served the marshal until 1815.

1ᵉ Division

The division was commanded by *General de Division* Louis-Vincent-Joseph Le Blond de Saint-Hilaire. The 10ᵉ *Légère* formed the 1st Brigade, commanded by Charles Antoine Morand; the 2nd Brigade, comprising the 14ᵉ and 36ᵉ *de Ligne*, by Paul Thiébault, a gifted *General de Brigade* who had served under Massena; and the 3rd Brigade, the 43ᵉ and 55ᵉ *de Ligne* and the single battalion of the *Tirailleurs du Po* by General *de Brigade* Louis-Prix Varé. The brigade was seconded to Vandamme for the Battle of Austerlitz.³

10ᵉ *Légère*

Reviewed on *19 Vendémiaire An 13* (11 October) 1804, the two war battalions mustered 63 officers and 1,632 other ranks, which included 2 master workmen and the 8-man regimental band. The inspector noted the regiment needed to refresh its knowledge of the 1792 regulation for clothing, and was not proficient at the *école du peleton*. The major was instructed to establish classes to educate the *sous-officiers* and men in the various regulations. About the appearance of the men, the inspector was aghast that the *sous-officiers* had cropped their hair short, and the inspector reminded the regiment's colonel that the band was to cost no more than one day's pay per officer per year. The colonel and other officers were 'chewed out' for having 'embroidered epaulettes indistinguishable from a general', and for having 'ordered the officers to cut their hair in the style *a la titus*'. Compounding this crime, the colonel had ordered his officers to wear non-regulation épées. The colonel was also reminded that light infantry officers had silver appointments and not gold. The inspector also remarked that the cut of the regiment's clothing was of several models, none of which accorded to the regulations, so we are left to wonder as to what exactly what was being worn. Again, the inspector noted the *schakos* in use were not of regulation model. None of these issues should exist, reported the inspector,

Officer of the 8e *Hussard* in full dress, c.1805.

none other than General Suchet. Perhaps not surprisingly, when we look in detail at the clothing, of 2,226 *habits*, 586 needed repairs and 775 total replacement. Also needing replacement were 1,360 *vestes*, every pair of *culottes* was to be replaced with 2,226 pairs of *pantalons*, 803 *bonnets de police* were needed and 803 *schakos*. Suchet added that the master tailor would be sent model items to copy to ensure what he made was according to the regulation and the *sous-officiers' bonnets de police* and other non-regulation items, which included silver- and red-fringed epaulettes, were to be suppressed immediately as well as those of the *chasseurs*.[4]

Reviewed again on *30 Thermidor An 13* (29 July 1805), the inspector noted that the *sous-officiers* were still attending regimental schools to learn the school of the platoon, which obviously impacted on the men's training. Despite orders being passed to make over 1,200 *habits*, just 116 had been issued, along with 84 *vestes* and 445 *schakos*. This left 1,236 *habits* and *vestes*, 1,419 pairs of *culottes* and 396 *schakos* to be renewed in 6 weeks before the regiment left cantonments. Stores were ordered to issue 103 *habits* and *vestes*, 460 pairs of *pantalons* and 147 *schakos*. This still left a large shortfall. The *voltigeur* companies had no distinctions, but the six *cornets* were armed with six An XI light cavalry *mousquetons*, as were the eight-strong regimental band, who were also issued with *gibernes* and belts.[5]

14e *de Ligne*

General Legrand inspected the regiment on *25 Vendémiaire An 13* (17 October 1804), when it mustered 2,167 men and 95 officers, of which we find an 8-strong regimental band, 51 drummers and 25 *enfant de troupe*. In addition, 28 men were sick in hospital, 36 had died over the previous year, and 200 had deserted. The first battalion was garrisoned at Maastricht and the second in Brussels, the lodgings being considered good. The men's drill was considered competent, but their clothing was in poor shape: of the 1,606 *habits* in service, 796 needed repairs, and 554 total replacement, as did 549 *vestes*, and 963 pairs of *culottes*, with a further 1,000 pairs also needing repairs. We note 1,564 *capotes* were issued, and 3,808m of broadcloth of unknown colour had been used to make them. Also in use were 1,600 linen smocks and 1,600 pairs of linen *pantalons de route*.[6]

Reviewed on *2 Thermidor An 13* (21 July 1805) at Maastricht, the regiment mustered 1,403 other ranks and 35 officers in the two war battalions, 403 men and 30 officers in the 3rd battalion and 20 officers and 260 men in the 4th battalion. In hospital were 59 men. In the previous year, 163 conscripts had joined the regiment and 184 had left, which included 23 who died from illness and 39 deserters. The barracks were in good condition and clean, while food was considered 'excellent'. With the regiment being stationed in the Netherlands, it had many non-French-speaking conscripts, and an interpreter was employed: despite this, the drill was considered very good. The regiment's clothing was still in poor condition: of 1,997 *habits* in use, 1,250 needed replacing or repairs, or 62 per cent, the same number of *vestes* needed replacing, 2,239 pairs of *culottes*, as did 1,250 *bonnets de police* and *chapeaux*. Immediately to hand were 492 *habits*, 421 *vestes*,

Trooper of 8e *Hussard* in full dress, c.1805. The number on the *portmanteaux* is an error to be ignored.

128 pairs of *culottes* and 456 *chapeaux*: clearly some men marched to Austerlitz in worn-out uniforms. In terms of armament, 15 An XI light cavalry *mousquetons* were with the staff – 7 *mousquetons* and infantry *gibernes* were with the band – along with 16 sabres, 34 *mousquetons* were with fusiliers, and 34 with the drummers in the two war battalions.[7]

36ᵉ *de Ligne*

General Rey reviewed the regiment on *10 Vendémiaire An 13* (2 October 1804). The war battalions mustered 1,854 men, which included 7 musicians, and was overseen by 66 officers. Since the previous year, the regiment had gained 604 conscripts, but had lost 75 men who had died from disease, and 84 had deserted. Indeed, at the time of the inspection, 39 men were sick in hospital. Based at Mons, the barracks were considered 'in the most part good, but needed repairs', the beds, blankets and mattresses were considered to be in good condition, and the rations 'good'. General Rey noted that the regiment's drill was good and satisfactory, but noted regimental money had been spent on cloth, epaulettes and gorgets for the officers, which by rights were private purchase, some 17,734fr 32. The men's clothing was in good condition, with just 88 *habits* needing to be replaced, for which purpose stores held 62.[8]

Inspected again by General Rey on *10 Thermidor An 13* (29 July 1805), the war battalions mustered 62 officers and 1,826 other ranks, which included the 7-strong regimental band. Since the previous inspection, 16 men had died, 18 deserted and 134 discharged. The men carried out their orders promptly, Rey remarked, but the regiment's drill at battalion level was very weak. Regimental accounts tell us that 33,282fr 49 had been spent on bearskins for the grenadiers, whom we also assume had fringed epaulettes. The regiment's clothing, despite not being cut in the regulation manner, was entirely satisfactory with nothing needing repairs or replacement. However, 1,115 *gibernes* out of 2,236 needed repairs and 112 total replacement, as did 1,646 musket slings. In terms of armament, the regiment's 54 drummers were all armed with An XI light cavalry *mousquetons* and equipped with infantry *gibernes*. Seven fusiliers were so armed, as were six grenadiers and a sergeant major.[9]

43ᵉ *de Ligne*

Drawn up in review at Bethune on *30 Vendémiaire An 13* (22 October 1804), the regiment's major was instructed to ensure that the men wore their *chapeau* according to regulations, and noted the *habits* and *vestes* did not match the model issued by the War Ministry. In addition, the officers and adjutants needed to be better schooled in the 1791 drill regulation and 1792 *police* regulations. Regimental accounts reported 9,600fr had been spent on the production of 1,600 *capotes*, and 27,500fr had been used to make smocks, *capotes*, and *pantalons de route* for new entrants to the regiment and 130fr 75 on paper for cartridges and flints for target practice. Of the 2,456 *habits* in use, 981 needed immediate replacement and every pair of *culottes*.[10]

Officer of the 9e *Hussard* in full dress, c.1805. The leopard skin *schabraque* would not be worn in battle or even taken on campaign.

Inspected again on *21 Thermidor An 13* (21 August 1805), the men's dress was 'passable'. Of the 2,242 *habits,* 277 needed immediate replacement and 840 urgent repairs, 2,261 pairs of *culottes* needed immediate replacement, while 894 *chapeaux* needed repair and 896 total replacement. It is unlikely the men received these and marched to war in clothing well past its best. Armament wise, 83 An XI light cavalry *mousquetons* were issued. Thirty-one were issued to *sous-officiers* and 52 to the band and drummers. We note 600 sabres were issued to grenadiers and *sous-officiers*.[11]

55ᵉ *de Ligne*

The regiment was inspected on *2 Vendémiaire An 13* (24 September 1804). The regiment had 1939 men under arms. They were wearing 1,928 *habits*, of which 680 needed repairs, 45 were to be written off. The inspecting officer authorised 1,027 to be replaced, along with 1,027 vestes and 1,939 new pairs of tricot *pantalons*, despite only 105 pairs being life expired! No mention is made of grenadier bearskins or *sapeurs'* equipment, ergo we suppose they did not exist, likewise fringed epaulettes, yet we find 2,363fr had been spent on *sous-officiers'* lace and distinctions, which surely includes non-regulation epaulettes.[12]

Inspected on *6 Brumaire An 13* (20 August 1805), the report reveals that 16 light cavalry carbines were issued to the regimental staff, and 54 to the drummers, along with *gibernes* and belts. Further, the drummers had 54 sabres and the grenadiers 179. Since the last inspection the depot had made 1,029 *habits* and repaired a further 1,040 examples. Despite these efforts, nearly 50 per cent of the *habits* in use, 1,059 out of 2,118, needed to be replaced and 600 needed repairs. Likewise, the regiment's *vestes* were in terrible condition, 918 needed repairs and 1,360 total replacement, every single pair of *culottes*, 2,118 examples, needed to be replaced, 390 *chapeaux* needed repairs and 1,090 needed replacing, likewise 200 *bonnets de police* needed repairs and 800 needed replacing. The regiment's clothing was in terrible condition even before it left Lille for Austria.[13]

Tirailleurs du Po

Reviewed on *21 Vendémiaire An 13* (13 October 1804) at the Camp d'Ostrowe, the battalion mustered 758 men: since 1803 16 men had died and 242 had deserted. The inspector noted that the unit had 'very short gaiters', were wearing Piedmontese-issue clothing, adding the men had cut their queues off. He ordered the adoption of French model uniforms. We note the men had 839 smocks and 858 pairs of *pantalons de route*, and that cloth in stores was blue, white and scarlet broadcloth, and blue tricot.[14]

Inspected again on *24 Messidor An 13* (13 July 1805), the single battalion of light infantry mustered 878 men. Since 1804, 1 *enfant de troupe* and 15 men had died, and 65 men had gone AWOL. In addition, 86 men were sick in hospital, the captain commandant reported. Why is revealed in the inspector's notes: 'The men are barracked on very wet ground [the roofs of the] barracks are covered with earth, which makes them very damp. It is better to build new barracks than to try and repair them.' From this I imagine the huts to have had a turf roof rather than straw. As could be expected, the bedding was totally worn out and the beds and others items in a similar sorry condition. The ordinary was anywhere from 12 to 16 men, bread cost 3 sous per day per man. This left just 2 sous for meat and vegetables. Wet, cold, hungry men do not make good soldiers. As could easily be anticipated, all was not happy, the inspector noted: the majority of the *sous-officiers* could not speak a word of French, and translators had to be employed to teach them their duties and words of commands. This was 'very inconvenient', the inspector noted. The young and old soldiers 'could not support the fatigues of war' remarked the inspector, but the rest of the men were robust and could become good soldiers. The clothing was well made and in good condition, he added. Over the previous year 804 *capote*s had been purchased for 12,683fr, and sabre belts costing 3,416fr and bearskins costing 1,926fr had been obtained for the elite company. Six officers and 18 drummers were armed with light cavalry *mousquetons*.[15] Presumably they were dressed as French light infantry.

2ᵉ Division

General de Division Dominique Joseph Rene Vandamme had gained the reputation during the Revolution for his bluff talking and capable command abilities. For good reason he was known as the '*enfant terrible*'. The 24ᵉ *Légère* formed the 1st Brigade commanded by Joseph François Ignace Maximilien Schiner; the 2nd Brigade, comprising the 4ᵉ and 28ᵉ *de Ligne*, by Claude François Ferey, and the 3rd Brigade, the 46ᵉ and 57ᵉ *de Ligne*, by Jacques Lazare Savettier de Candras.

24ᵉ *Légère*

Reviewed on *1 Vendémiaire An 13* (23 September 1804), the inspector noted that the weapons were clean and the uniforms were well sewn and conformed to the models sent by the war minister, even if the cloth used was very low grade. Interestingly, every man wore a *chapeau*, although 1,614 *schakos* were ready to be issued. We also note 3m 98 chamois broadcloth had been used to make *voltigeurs*' clothing.[16]

Inspected on *10 Thermidor An 13* (29 July 1805), the major reported 38 men had died, 282 men had deserted – the same number of desertions was reported a year earlier – and 37 had been discharged from hospital as unfit to return to ranks. We note the regiment now had 13 *sapeurs* issued aprons, axes and axe belts, and we remark just 244 *schakos* had been issued, meaning 80 per cent of the 2,045 men under arms were wearing *chapeaux*. Since the previous inspection the 6m 85 chamois broadcloth had been used and 64 bearskins were in use. *Voltigeur*s were issued 221 sabres and infantry muskets, although the corporals, *sous-officiers* and officers were armed with An XI light cavalry *mousquetons*, as were the *drummers*, *cornets* and *sapeurs*, some 107 *mousquetons* being issued.[17]

Trooper of the 9e *Hussard* in full dress, c.1805. The number on the *portmanteaux* is an error to be ignored.

Officer of the 10e *Hussard* in full dress, c.1805.

4ᵉ de Ligne

Inspected on *2 Vendémiaire An 13* (23 September 1804) at Nancy, discipline was good and drill was satisfactory, reported the inspector. Over the previous year, 30 men had died and 137 had deserted. Regimental accounts report 28,800fr had been spent on linen *pantalons de route, redingotes* and smocks. Since the previous inspection in 1802, 2,321 habits had been made, while some 896 needed repairs and 1,198 total replacement. The same pattern was repeated for most items of clothing and equipment. Of interest, the 4ᵉ *de Ligne* had *sapeurs'* aprons, yet they had not a single bearskin for grenadiers or *sapeurs*. Some 1,154fr 92 had been spent on distinctions – presumably this includes epaulettes for grenadiers. In addition, 11,3600fr had been spent on equipping the regiment with *redingotes* and a further 28,800fr on buying linen overalls and smocks. Since 1802, 600 *habits* in the depot had been issued, 123 had been repaired, 3,797 *habits* had been made and 287 new examples were in the depot, along with 419 *vestes manche*, 2 pairs of *culottes*, 800 *chapeaux*, 110 *bonnets de police*, 200 *gibernes*, 400 *porte-gibernes* and 34 musket slings.[18]

The regiment was inspected less than a year later on *28 Messidor An 13* (17 July 1805) when it was still in Nancy. The inspector reported that 22 men had died since the last inspection and 42 had deserted, but despite this the war battalions mustered 1,575 men. Since the previous review, 993 *habits* had been made, but this still left a further 1,199 to be replaced and 116 needing repairs. Of the 896 *habits* that needed repair, at the time of the 1804 inspection, only 90 had been – clearly rather than repair the *habits* they were simply written off as life expired and beyond economic repair. Even at peace, it clearly demonstrates the very high attrition rate of clothing. The inspecting officer noted it was urgent that the regiment received new stocks of clothing. By summer 1805 not an inch of chamois cloth existed for *voltigeurs'* distinctions, but perhaps destined for drummers were 96 An XI *mousquetons* that had been delivered since September 1804. In addition, 1,418fr had been spent buying 1,773 pairs of *sabots* and 2,519fr 69 on lace for *sous-officiers* and other distinctions, presumably epaulettes, drummers' lace etc. Again, no mention of bearskins is made. Discipline in the regiment was perfect, reported the inspector. The 1st and 2nd battalions were well trained but the 3rd, being mostly new entrants, needed more training to make them proficient.[19]

A document of *1 Brumaire An 14* (23 October 1805) tells us that the major had given orders to disband 2ᵉ company of 1st battalion and 2ᵉ company of 2nd battalion, and to form them as *voltigeurs*.[20] The major, in a letter of *10 Nivôse An 14* (31 December 1805), enquired when the effects for the *voltigeurs* would be received in the depot so that they could be passed to the war battalions.[21] The major commanding the depot wrote to the colonel on 2 January 1806 informing him that the War Ministry had authorised the formation of *voltigeur* companies in war battalions and materials would be received at end of the campaign.[22]

28ᵉ de Ligne

Inspected on *1 Vendémiaire An 13* (23 September 1804), the officers came in for criticism for wearing non-regulation leather equipment and *chapeaux* again of non-regulation form and way. The *corporal-fourriers* were ordered to sew on their corporal stripes and the major was ordered to ensure the men's clothing was made according to the model provided by the war minister, and provided copious notes on how the uniform should appear and should be worn. Nothing existed for grenadiers: every man was dressed with a *habit, veste, culottes* and *chapeau*.[23]

Reviewed again on *15 Thermidor An 13* (3 August 1805), we note the 8-man regimental band, the drum major and drum corporal were armed with 10 light cavalry *mousquetons*, 36 of the 80 drummers were likewise armed, and 34 fusiliers. Of the 2,160 *habits* in service, 1,402 had been issued since 23 September 1804, with 292 needing repair and 125 to be replaced. Overall, the regiment's clothing was in good condition.[24]

46ᵉ de Ligne

Reviewed on *5 Sansculottides An 13* (22 September 1804) at Lille by General Schauenbourg, regimental accounts note 9,600fr had been spent buying *capote*s. We also note 1,413fr 28 was spent buying 13 axes with cases, aprons and bearskins for the *sapeurs*. These were the sole bearskins the regiment possessed. To the general chagrin of the inspector, the regiment had abolished the queue, the blue broadcloth used to make the *habits* was very low quality, and the *habits* themselves were badly made. Of the 1,950 *habits* in use, 1,186 had been issued for less than a year, yet despite this fact 586 needed urgent repairs and 492 total replacing. Likewise, 410 *vestes* needed repairs and 492 replacing, 732 pairs of *culottes* needed replacing and 1,287 *chapeaux*. The regiment's leather work was in very poor condition. Of 1,879 *gibernes* in service, 871 needed urgent repairs and 622 were fit only for scrap. The *giberne* belts were in a better state. Of the 1,879 in service, 169 needed repairs and 266 replacing. To make up the shortfall, depot held stocks of brand-new clothing and equipment, namely 42 *habits*, 62 *vestes*, 248 pairs of *culottes*, 30 *chapeaux*, 85 *bonnets de police*, 24 *gibernes*, 26 *porte-gibernes*, 93 muskets slings and 21 *baudriers*.[25]

Reviewed again on *27 Thermidor An 13* (15 August 1805) at Lille, regimental accounts note 1,314fr 40 had been spent on buying clogs for the 1st and 2nd battalions. The regiment's clothing was still in poor condition. Of the 492 *habits* that needed replacing 11 months earlier, just 58 had been issued. Of the 1,992 *habits* in use, 1,467 were life expired: in basic terms, 73 per cent of the regiment's *habits* were falling to pieces and desperately needed replacing. Again, of the 1,992 pairs of *culottes* in use, 1,808 pairs had to be replaced – 90 per cent of the regiment's *culottes* were fit only for the rag merchant to take away! Every single *bonnet de police* had to be replaced and 1,370 chapeaux – or 68 per cent of all in use – had to be replaced. Equipment was still in terrible condition: 4,360 *gibernes* and belts had to be replaced urgently. The 3rd battalion had been clothed like new, but the war battalions were in rags! Depot held virtually nothing for immediate

Trooper of 10e *Hussard* in full dress, *c*.1805. The number on the *portmanteaux* is an error to be ignored.

issue: 65 new *habits* and 132 needing repairs, 82 pairs of *culottes* and 24 *chapeaux*. Armament wise, the band were issued 10 *sabre briquets* and belts, 10 *gibernes* and belts and 10 light cavalry *mousquetons*. The drummers were likewise issued 54 *sabre briquets* and *baudriers*, 54 *gibernes* and belts and 54 *mousquetons*.[26]

57ᵉ *de Ligne*

The regiment was reviewed on *4 Vendémiaire An 13* (26 September 1804). The inspector noted the regiment's *habits* overall were badly cut, made from low-grade materials and badly sewn, meaning nearly all had to be replaced. Of 2,051 *habits* in use, 157 needed repairs and 854 immediate replacement; we note the inspector authorised 1,131 *habits* be made along with 1,131 vestes, 2,261 pairs of *culottes* as a matter of urgency, 1,131 *chapeaux* and 1,131 *bonnets de police*. For immediate issue, depot held 212 brand-new *habits*, 216 *vestes*, 193 pairs of *culottes*, 465 *chapeaux* and 38 *bonnets de police*. Also issued were 764 new pairs of grey linen gaiters and just 148 pairs black tricot gaiters. In the period since 1803, 1,445fr had been spent in distinctions for *sous-officiers* and other ranks; we assume this included grenadiers' epaulettes.[27]

Inspected on *6 Fructidor An 13* (24 August 1805) at Lille, the inspector recorded that 2,055fr 95 had been spent on lace for *sous-officiers* and other distinctions. In addition, 5,184fr had been spent on the purchase of 216 bearskins for the grenadiers, costing 24fr each. The grenadiers alone were issued sabres, 190 men excluding their *sous-officiers* and drummers, 14 grenadiers were armed with light cavalry *mousquetons* – the *sapeurs* we wonder? – and every drummer was issued a *giberne* and belt, sabre and light cavalry *mousqueton*. Likewise, the band had 10 *gibernes* with belts, 10 *sabre briquets* and *baudriers* and were likewise armed with *mousquetons*. The regiment had a total of 77 *mousquetons*. Since the previous inspection 1,027 *habits* had been made, 644 *vestes*, 975 pairs of *culottes*, 1,168 *chapeaux* and 532 *bonnets de police* – far below what the regiment needed. Indeed, some 1,224 *habits* needed repairs and 452 total replacement out of 2,316 in use. Likewise, 666 vestes needed repairs and 592 replacing, 416 pairs of *culottes* needed to be repaired and 1,587 had to be replaced as a matter of urgency. For immediate use the depot held 25 brand-new *habits* and 310 undergoing repairs, 335 brand-new *vestes* accompanied by 1,198 pairs of *culottes*, 178 *chapeaux*, 106 *bonnets de police*, 12 *gibernes* and belts, 141 musket slings, and 1 drum carriage and sabre belt. The inspector noted 'discipline was severe and paternal'.[28] Not a word was spoken about the band or drummers. We wonder if the worn-out clothing was replaced before the regiment marched to destiny at Austerlitz?

3ᵉ Division

General de Division Claude Juste Alexandre Legrand led the division, his son performing the function of senior aide-de-camp. Pierre Hugues Victoire Merle led the 1st Brigade, the 26ᵉ *Légère* and the single battalions of the *Tirailleurs Corse*. The 3ᵉ *de Ligne* formed the 2nd Brigade headed by *General de Brigade* Brouard, with the 3rd Brigade formed by the 18ᵉ and 75ᵉ *de Ligne* headed by *General de Brigade* Victor Levasseur.

26e *Légère*

Inspected on *4 Vendémiaire An 13* (26 September 1804) at Sedan, the inspector tells us the regimental depot had processed 1,400 men to the war battalions, but 10 of these had died and 286 had deserted with a further 52 missing. He added that every man was wearing a *chapeau*, but no distinctions existed for *voltigeurs* or *carabiniers*.[29]

Moving on to *5 Thermidor An 13* (24 July 1805), 2,235 *schakos* were ordered and 781 *habits* and *vestes manche* had been made for new entrants to the regiment. Nothing is reported for *carabiniers* or *voltigeurs*. We do note 74 light cavalry *mousquetons* were in use: 48 with the drummers and *cornets*, 14 with *voltigeurs*, 1 with a *fourrier*, 1 with a sergeant and 10 with the band. Also in service with the *voltigeurs* were 27 *carabines rayé* (rifles): 9 with the officers and 18 with the *sous-officiers*. Clearly officers had *gibernes* issued.[30]

Tirailleurs du Corses

No archive papers for the unit's clothing and equipment can be located at the time of writing.[31]

3ᵉ *de Ligne*

The depot of the regiment was reviewed on *3 Brumaire An 13* (25 October 1804), when the regiment was housed in the former convent of Notre-Dame at Meaux. However, the convent buildings could only accommodate 400 men, and over 2,000 were present, as many rooms and buildings needed repairs. The depot had processed 773 into the war battalions, but had lost 242 men as deserters and 39 had died. The report details the regiment had 164 new bearskins, 40 needing repairs, and 38 that were to be written off, making 242. Some 46 were scheduled to be obtained as replacements. The inspector tore the colonel off a strip: men were lacking *habits* and *vestes* on parade when sufficient numbers existed in the depot to make up the shortfall – depot held 86 brand-new *habits* and 34 brand-new *vestes*; many muskets had no musket slings; the grenadiers' epaulettes were worn on the back of the shoulder and not the top; the men's *gibernes* were worn either too high or too low; overall the regiment lacked uniformity. Of the regiment's 2,524 *habits*, 626 needed repairs and 666 total replacement, likewise, 524 *vestes manche* needed repairs and 531 total replacement. Also in desperate need of replacement were 1,664 out of the 2,524 *chapeaux*, and 1,441 of the 2,524 *bonnets de police*. We also note 16 sets of *sapeurs'* equipment were in use and missing were over 1,000 musket slings. Since 1803 some 1,167 *habits* had been issued, 1,693 *vestes manche*, 2,508 pairs of *culottes*, 1,333 *chapeaux*, 849 *bonnets de police*, 117 *gibernes*, 56 *porte-gibernes*, 12 musket slings and 4 *baudriers*.[32]

Inspected on *18 Thermidor An 13* (6 August 1805), the regiment was at Longwy, near to Luxembourg: the barracks were well kept, clean and the furniture and bedding was in good condition. Clearly the unit had been moved to find better lodgings. Days before the campaign began, a huge amount of clothing needed repairs or replacing: of 2,488 *habits* in use, 254 needed repairs and 1,100 needed to be replaced, as did 1,244 *vestes*, and 867 *chapeaux*. Notably, 238 men lacked a *giberne* and belt. To make up some of the shortfall, depot held 19 brand-new *habits*, 24 *vestes*, 112 pairs of *culottes* and 137 *bonnets de police*, as well as 110 *habits* that were waiting disposal accompanied by the same number of *vestes*. Because of the regiment's harsh discipline, its drill was, we are told, impeccable, but its clothing was well past is best.[33]

18ᵉ *de Ligne*

Drawn up in review on *26 Vendémiaire An 13* (18 October 1804), regimental accounts report 33,369fr 30 had been spent making 1,600 *capotes*, 1,254 pairs of *pantalons de route*, 1,588 smocks and buying shoes. We note that every man had a pompom for their *chapeaux*.[34]

Still quartered in Paris at the time of the next review on *3 Thermidor An 13* (22 July 1805), the bulk of the regiment's clothing needed urgent attention: of 1,842 *habits*, 978 needed immediate replacement and 114 had no *habit*, likewise every pair of *culottes*, and 978 *chapeaux*. We doubt this happened before the regiment headed to Austria as stores held just 4 *habits* waiting to be issued, 120 *vestes*, 4 pairs of *culottes* and 25 *chapeaux* for immediate needs. We do note that since 1804 70 *pompoms de grenadier* had been issued, 1,347 *pompoms de fusilier*, 52 sword knots for grenadiers and 87 pairs of epaulettes for grenadiers. No bearskins existed, we note.[35]

75ᵉ *de Ligne*

Reviewed on *4 Brumaire An 13* (26 October 1804) at Quesnoy, the inspector noted the men were well dressed, but barely had a uniform appearance. It was important, he ordered, that the *sous-officiers* and older soldiers teach the new conscripts how to care for and clean their clothing and equipment. He said this was a disgrace, ranting that 'it appears to me that not a single buckle or any buff work has ever been cleaned … nor have the soldiers and *sous-officiers* paid attention to the buttons on their uniforms …' The buff work was all very old and needed cleaning and repairs. We also find that 286 non-French muskets were in use and had to be replaced immediately, and a further 64 of the 1777 model were to be written off. The *sous-officiers* came under critique again for being negligent in their dress, and the *fourriers* did not wear their corporal's stripes. The men's clothing and equipment was in terrible shape: of 2,237 *habits*, 1,592 were new, but 474 examples needed repairs and 645 total replacement. Of the 2,261 pairs of *culottes*, 524 needed repairs and 907 total replacement. We note 729 *chapeaux* needed repairs and 465 replacing, and 400 *gibernes* and belts needed repairs. For immediate needs, stores held 253 brand-new *habits* and 17 needing repairs. Likewise, 69 *vestes* had been repaired, 241 were waiting to be issued and 3 needed repairing. Depot also held 326 brand-new pairs of *culottes* and 311 *chapeaux*, 218 *gibernes* with belts and 7 musket slings.[36]

The 1st and 2nd battalions were reviewed at Quesnoy on *27 Thermidor An 13* (15 August 1805). Since the last inspection the inspector noted that the regiment's accommodation had been repaired and was clean, but the bedding was still in appalling condition, and the food was little better. The dress of the regiment was noted as good and very regular, adding that all the recently made items of clothing 'was exactly of the model'. However, a lot of the clothing was still in poor condition. Of the 2,349 *habits*, 1,161 had been issued new since 1804, yet 520 needed to be written off and 668 needed urgent repairs! This means that 50 per cent of the regiment's *habits* were either 'knackered' or close to being so. The inspector ordered the production of 1,233 *habits*. The *vestes manche* were in worse condition; some 964 needed urgent repairs and 306 total replacement, resulting in 1,233 new items being ordered, which more than likely never arrived before the regiment left its quarters. Some 550 pairs of *culottes* were needed, 114 *chapeaux* and 877 *bonnets de police* as well as 120 *gibernes* and belts. So close to departing for the 1805 campaign, we wonder if the regiment was re-dressed or did it go to war wearing rags?[37]

4ᵉ Light Cavalry Division

The division was led by General de Brigade Pierre Margaron, former colonel of the 1ᵉ *Cuirassiers*, with the son of Second Consul Cambacérès acting as Adjutant-Commandant, along with the son of General Humbert in the same capacity.

8ᵉ *Hussard*

Inspected on *9 Fructidor An 13* (27 August 1805) at Lille, the regiment mustered 508 men, and days before the campaign began needed 195 horses, some 73 being lost over the previous year, along with 12 men who died from disease and 6 who went AWOL. The barracks and stables were all considered good and clean, with food being of good quality and frequently distributed, reported the major. We note for the 508 men, all had a *dolman*, *pelisse*, *manteau*, and *surtout*, as well as white *veste* and a pair of *culottes hongroise*. Just six stable coats were issued, all scheduled for replacement. A hundred colpacks were in use, and everyone else had a *schako*. For immediate needs to replace the worn-out clothing, stores held 177 *dolmans*, 3 *pelisses*, 332 *surtouts*, 5 *manteaux* and 527 *gilets*, as well as 791 pairs of *culottes hongroise*. Stores report the use of 1,593m 53 green broadcloth for *manteaux*, *dolmans*, and *pelisses*, 893m 34 scarlet broadcloth for *culottes hongroise* and 175m 08 heavy weight green broadcloth. The unit was armed with 749 *mousquetons* – 10 with the trumpeters – 700 bayonets, 751 sabres and 324 pairs of pistols.[38]

11ᵉ *Chasseurs*

The regiment was inspected on *16 Vendemiaire An 13* (8 October 1804) and mustered 713 other ranks. Every man had a *dolman*, and 694 men had a *surtout*, while just 472 *manteaux* were in use, alongside 639 *schakos* and 74 colpacks. A lot of the clothing was in poor condition, with 644 *surtouts* needing to be immediately replaced along with 168 *manteaux* and 360 white *gilets*. Of the dolmans, 690 needed repairs and 23 replacing;

all bar six were over 18 months old. The *dolman* we suppose were being phased out in 1804 as no new ones were authorised for production. The depot held 399 new unissued *surtouts*, 53 *manteaux*, 305 *gilets*, 36 stable coats, 100 pairs of Hungarian breeches, 90 pairs of stable trousers, 36 colpacks, 100 *bonnets de police*, 174 waistbelts, 62 *gibernes* with belts as well as 34 saddle blankets and 26 sheepskin *schabraques*.[39]

The regiment was inspected on *29 Thermidor An 13* (17 August 1805), when every one of the 684 men on parade was wearing a brand-new *habit*, while the elite company had 75 colpacks.[40]

16e *Chasseurs*

Inspected on *2 Vendémiaire An 13* (23 September 1804), the regiment's clothing, even at a time of peace, was in very poor condition. The regiment had 671 *dolmans*, all of which were scheduled for replacement. Likewise, it had 590 *surtouts* in use, 440 being scheduled for replacement as *hors de service*. Indeed, most of the clothing was listed as *hors de service*: 302 out of 456 *manteaux*, 547 out of 647 white *gilets*, every single one of the 500 *gilets d'ecurie* and pairs of *caleçons*, 585 pairs of stable trousers, the 695 pairs of *culottes hongroise*, and 511 of the 623 *schakos a flamme* were also on the list for replacement. The clothing must have been in tatters! Yet sat in the *dépôt*, brand new and unissued, were 201 *dolmans*, 89 *manteaux*, 628 new white *gilets*, 544 *gilets d'ecurie*, 16 pairs of *caleçons*, 24 pairs of *culottes hongroise*, 626 pairs of stable trousers, and 34 '*cordons du fil*' with 42 sets in use that we assume to be *schako* cords. Five plumes were in store with 192 in service, which we assume were the regulation black, 142 *schakos* and 450 *bonnets de police*. One wonders why all this new kit was not issued to make up for the acute issues facing the rank and file's clothing?[41]

Reviewed on *3 Fructidor An 13* (19 August 1805), the war squadrons mustered 348 men. We note 175 *dolmans* were in service and all brand new, while 511 *surtouts* were in use, all bar 8 being indeed to immediate replacement. Also in service were 450 *manteaux*, 647 white waistcoats, 64 colpacks, and 584 *schakos*. Two types of *schako* were in use, 186 of the 1801 issue were in stores with 114 sets of cords and 36 *schakos a flamme*. We also remark that 5 *pelisses* were in use: with the trumpeters?[42]

26e *Chasseurs*

The regiment was raised in 1802 from the *Piedmontese Chasseurs à Cheval*. Inspected in October 1804, every man was issued a *dolman*, and just 65 *surtouts* were in service, all needing repairs. The elite company had 64 colpacks. Stores held 619 brand-new *surtouts* waiting to be issued in accordance with the decree of *1 Vendémiaire An XI*, which removed *dolmans* from service for *chasseur* regiments.[43] Reviewed on *12 Thermidor An 13* (31 July 1805, every one of the 554 men on parade was wearing a *surtout*, and the elite company was wearing 100 colpacks. We assume only the elite company troopers carried carbines as only 80 *banderole porte mousquetons* were issued for 481 firearms![44]

3ᵉ Dragoon Division

The division was led by General de Beaumont. The 1st Brigade comprising the 5ᵉ and 8ᵉ *Dragons* was led by Charles Joseph Boyé; the 2nd Brigade, which was composed of the 9ᵉ and 12ᵉ *Dragons*, by Nicolas Joseph Scalfort; and the 3rd Brigade, the 16ᵉ and 21ᵉ *Dragons*, by Édouard Jean Baptiste Milhaud, who ended his career at Waterloo leading the IV Cavalry Corps.

5ᵉ *Dragons*

Formed in 1668, the regiment was with the Grande Armée in 1805. On *19 Brumaire An 14* (10 November 1805) every man had a *habit* and a *surtout*, 806 of each being in use, and the elite company had 106 bearskins. We also note 518 *blanc picque de bleu manteaux* were in service accompanied by 413 pairs of green *pantalons à cheval* reinforced with leather. Some 504 *housses* were in service, with 549 *chaperons*. The inspector ordered 217 *habits* to be made, which required 440m 50 of green broadcloth, 49m of scarlet broadcloth and 7m 22 of white broadcloth. Sixty *manteaux* were to be made, lined in scarlet serge, and 433 *surtouts*, which were entirely green. The trumpeters were all armed with light cavalry *mousquetons*, as were nine dragoons who were potentially *sapeurs*. Fifty-six tools were in use.[45] The elite company wore bearskins, and had white *contre-epaulettes* and *aiguilettes* on the right shoulder.

8ᵉ *Dragons*

Created on 1 March 1674, the regiment was reviewed on *8 Vendémiaire An 13* (30 September 1804). The men were issued a *habit*, *surtout*, *veste*, a *blanc picque de bleu manteaux* as well as a pair of *culottes de peau* and stable trousers and stable coat. The elite company had 143 bearskins and scarlet plumes. The horses were equipped with *chaperons* and *housses*. Part of the regiment was dismounted, and these men were issued 260 *havresacs*, two pairs of shoes and a pair of black twill gaiters.[46]

Reviewed again on *20 Thermidor An 13* (8 August 1805), the regiment had 8 trumpeters and 12 drummers, as well as drum major and a trumpet major. We note 503 men were mounted and 305 dismounted. Just 84 bearskins were in use, and we note 300 pairs of leather wrist gloves and 400 pairs of gauntlets were in service. As before, men had both a *habit* and *surtout*, and the *manteaux* were *blanc picque de bleu* rather than green. The drummers and trumpeters were issued 16 light cavalry *mousquetons*.[47]

9ᵉ *Dragons*

Inspected on *15 Vendémiaire An 13* (4 October 1804), the inspector noted the regiment's clothing was well made and in good condition, but the master tailor, it was felt, should spend more time studying the regulation. Regimental accounts report 20,5140fr had been spent on shoes, smocks and *capotes* for the dismounted company, and 284fr 45 had been spent on lace for *sous-officiers* and other distinctions for the rank and file. Since 4 July 1803, 500 *capote*s had been made, 561 smocks, 60 bearskins – making 119 in use – and 551 *havresacs*. We also note the depot had produced for the foot companies 403 pairs of tricot *pantalons*, 388m 39 of linen had been used making grey gaiters and 204 pairs of black worsted gaiters had been made, with 203 pairs issued. Depot had also issued 590 plumes but we are ignorant of their colour.[48]

Reviewed on *10 Thermidor An 13* (29 July 1805), the inspector remarked that the regiment's clothing was generally good, and the materials used were of good quality. The regiment had a dismounted squadron. The regiment's account lists 371fr 25 had been spent on *capotes*, smocks and shoes and 284fr 45 had been spent on lace for *sous-officiers* and other distinctions. The regiment had a mix of leg wear in use: 341 pairs of linen overalls had been issued to the foot company, some 1,007m 82 of linen being used for this purpose, alongside 652 pairs of stable trousers. Some 388m 39 of linen had been used to make gaiters for the foot companies – 606 pairs of grey linen gaiters were issued and 28 pairs of black tricot gaiters, yet just 107 pairs of shoes were issued and 114 pairs had been lodged in stores. Lace in depot included 18m 68 27mm wide white worsted lace for corporals' stripes, 309m 48 60mm wide lace for *housses*, 69m 20 35mm white worsted lace for *portmanteaux*, and 79m 60 10mm wide white worsted lace for numbers on the *housses* and *portmanteaux*. In theory the numbers were to be cut from white cloth; clearly the 9^e used lace. For the foot company, two drums and carriages were in use and 12 light cavalry carbines were issued to trumpeters along with 8 pairs of pistols and 20 sabres – clearly a mix of firearms were in use, but we assume trumpeters had *gibernes* and belts. Despite the 1801 regulation, the regiment marched to war retaining its sheepskin *demi-schabraques* – some 453 in use – along with 453 *housses* and 540 round *portmanteaux*.[49]

About the regiment's training, the inspector noted that most men could manoeuvre, and that the basics of equitation were understood – how competent the men actually were would soon be discovered, the inspector remarked! The regiment had been inspected by Prince Murat, who had been satisfied, but the inspector warned that the officers and *sous-officiers* needed to be on their guard to ensure the men carried out their duties, cared for their horses – a great number were being injured by the ignorance of the men and corporals – and overall the men needed more training in all duties. The biggest failing was that most men simply could not ride with any degree of proficiency.[50] Damning words indeed.

12^e *Dragons*

Formed in Maastricht in 1675, the regiment was reviewed on *5 Fructidor An 13* (23 August 1805). The first surprise is that 11m 08 of blue broadcloth had been used to make trumpeters' clothing and over 73m remained in stores. We note 611 *habits* were in use, 687 *surtouts* and just 398 *blanc picque de bleu manteaux*. No bearskins were reported for the elite company. The horse equipment included *housses* and *chaperons*.[51]

16ᵉ Dragons

Created as the 16ᵉ *régiment des Dragons* in 1791 from various 'free corps', the regiment was inspected at Soissons in early autumn 1803. The regiment's major noted that since the last review in 1802, the regiment had received 320 conscripts, bringing it up to 658 men, but added 18 men had died and 138 had deserted, with 29 horses having died, meaning 158 horses were needed to mount the regiment. Just 373 troops horses were in service, and 56 for the officers. The inspector noted that the men were based in the citadel, but many of the barracks were in very poor condition, many rooms could not be occupied and the men had to lodge in corridors or any room they could find. The beds were likewise in bad condition, most of the rooms lacked the bread shelf, chairs and tables: every scrap of wood the regiment could obtain for heating and cooking had been burned and we suspect this had been the fate of the furniture. Being cold and damp perhaps explains the number of men deserting. Bread was available and of good condition, the inspector noted, so too the forage for the horses. Regimental accounts reported 37,250fr had been spent making *capotes*, and we note the elite company had 101 bearskins. The horses were equipped with 354 sheepskin *schabraques*, and just 12 pairs of *chaperons* were used by the trumpeters. The *manteaux* were made from regulation *blanc picque de bleu* broadcloth.[52]

Reviewed on *13 Thermidor An 13* (1 August 1805) still based in Soissons, the regiment mustered 831 men with 421 horses. Due to improvements in the supply of fire wood, beds and blankets, only 10 men had died and 41 deserted. Despite these improvements, the barracks were still considered very bad and damp. Clothing wise, 680 *habits* were in use, 720 *surtouts*, 177 *bearskins*, and 16 sets of *chaperons* were in use along with 338 sheepskin *schabraques*. The 362 *manteaux* in use were all *blanc picquer de bleu*. The 16 trumpeters were armed with light cavalry *mousquetons*.[53]

21ᵉ Dragons

Reviewed on *20 Pluvoise An 11* (9 February 1803), the regiment mustered 427 rank and file and had 339 new *habits* in service. The regiment had no *habits* in use, and was wearing 424 *surtouts*, all brand new, with 36 more in depot accompanied by 60 *manteaux*. Some 391 pairs of stable trousers were in use, with 27 more in the depot, 369 brand-new helmets with 109 more in depot, and 59 bearskins with 16 in depot. The depot also held 1,254 hides to make culotte de peau, 1,227m 40 *blanc picquer de bleu* broadcloth to make *manteaux*, 848m 33 green broadcloth, had used 95m 10 of yellow broadcloth, and held 495m 74 green tricot, 858m 22 white serge, 1,588m 36 yellow serge, 762m 82 linen, 1,492m 35 *treillis*, 689 dozen large buttons and 34m 18 of yellow tricot. Tricot was used either for leg wear or *portmanteaux* – so did trumpeters have yellow *portmanteaux*? The elite company had 59 bearskins in use and a mix of *culottes de peau*: 363 brand-new pairs in depot from sheepskin and 391 pairs made from doe hide – given their ochre colour and costing twice that of sheepskin *culottes*, were these for the elite company and *sous-officiers*? Arguably so. Needed for An 11 were 135 *habits*, 170 *surtouts*, 54 *manteaux*, 105 *vestes*, 270 stable coats, 540 pairs each of *culottes de peau* and stable trousers, 48 helmets and 14 bearskins. Materials authorised for purchase were 37m 80 yellow serge to line *manteaux*, 7m 20 white serge for *gilets*, 199m 80 *treillis* to make stable trousers, 15m 40 *treillis* to line the *portmanteaux*, 5m 40 *treillis* to line 18 repaired *housses* and 2m 55 *treillis* to line 17 pairs of *chaperons*.[54] Due to the vagaries of history the 1804, 1805 and 1808 inspections cannot be located at the time of writing.

Chapter 11

V Corps

Marshal Jean Lannes, one of Napoléon's most able subordinates, led the corps. In the French Army Archives he has left us hundreds of letters and other documents relating to the operation of his corps in the campaign, which sadly we have no space to reproduce here as a direct translation.

1ᵉ Division

Grenadiers Réunis

As part of the build-up of the invasion force of England, on *30 Brumaire An 12* (22 November 1803), Consul Bonaparte decided to organise an infantry reserve corps with a view to landing in England, with grenadier companies from the 9ᵉ, 13ᵉ, 58ᵉ, and 81ᵉ *régiments de La Ligne* and the *carabiniers* from the 2ᵉ, 3ᵉ, 12ᵉ, 15ᵉ, 28ᵉ and 31ᵉ *Légère*. An order of *4 Pluvoise An 12* (25 January 1804) instituted 12 battalions forming 6 regiments grouped into a body of reserve grenadiers. In March 1805, the command was entrusted to General de Division Oudinot and their number was reduced to 5 regiments. The 1st Brigade (9ᵉ, 13ᵉ, 58ᵉ, and 81ᵉ *de Ligne*) was commanded by General LaPlanche, the 2nd Brigade (2ᵉ, 3ᵉ, 28ᵉ and 31ᵉ *Légère*) by General Dupas and the 3rd Brigade (12ᵉ and 15ᵉ *Légère*) by General Ruffin.[1] We do not have inspection returns for all the units involved in this formation.

2e *Légère*

The 607 *carabiniers* of the 2ᵉ *Légère*, which formed the 5th battalion on *17 Vendémiaire An 13* (9 October 1804), were wearing almost brand-new uniforms, every *habit* and *veste manche* was in good condition and the only items in need of replacement were 131 pairs of *pantalons*. The men were issued 300 *schakos* – every single one to be replaced – and 300 bearskins. Stores held a further 75 bearskins and 60 *schakos*. In addition, 14m 76 of white broadcloth was held, along with 585m 48 blue broadcloth, 9m 84 scarlet broadcloth, and 400m 98 of serge.[2]

3ᵉ *Légère*

The 6th battalion, formed from 954 men of the 3ᵉ *Légère*, who on *25 Vendémiaire An 13* (17 October 1804) were wearing 298 *schakos* and 300 bearskins. Just 386 *bonnets de police* were in use, and of the 594 *habits*, 166 needed repairs and 37 replacing. Depot held

Colonel of the 1e *Cuirassiers* in full dress, c.1805.

Trooper of 1e *Cuirassiers* in full dress, *c.*1805.

37 *habits*, 33 *vestes* ready to be disposed of, and 2 new *baudrier*s. In terms of cloth, 2m 22 of white broadcloth was held, along with 124m 70 blue broadcloth, 36m 48 scarlet broadcloth, 386m white tricot, 60m 31 blue serge, and 374m 2 of linen. No small stores were held at all: the shirts and socks the men we wearing were literally all that were to be had.[3]

12ᵉ *Légère*

Reviewed on *12 Vendémiaire An 13* (4 October 1804), we note the battalion mustered 606 other ranks. They were wearing *chapeaux*, everyone being life expired, and furthermore we note 128 *habits* needed to be written off. Rather than *pantalons*, the men had *culottes*, with 399 pairs needing repairs and 71 to be replaced. Light infantry in *chapeaux* as late as 1804 is notable, four years after the *schako* was to be the regulation headdress, and to this end the inspector ordered 606 *schakos* to be made with all haste. No chamois broadcloth existed for the *voltigeurs*' uniform.[4]

15ᵉ *Légère*

Forming the 8th battalion was the 15ᵉ *Légère*, which was reviewed on *8 Fructidor An 12* (26 August 1804). The inspector tells us 'the officers and *sous-officiers* have NO theoretical training' and added 'their instruction in practical application is not regulation'. Reflecting this catastrophic breakdown in training, the 'men can march a little' and battalion level drill, quite obviously, 'had not attained a level of perfection'. Regimental accounts show us 6,000fr was spent buying bearskins for the *carabinier*s in the past year and 7,200fr had been spent in the current financial year on the same items, making 300 in service, alongside 596 *schakos*: clearly *carabiniers* had two types of headdress. Clothing was overall in good shape, but 167 *vestes* needed replacing, 200 *schakos* and every pair of *pantalons*.[5]

28ᵉ *Légère*

The 11st battalion was formed from 600 men of the 28ᵉ *Légère*. Inspected on *16 Vendémiaire An 13* (8 October 1804), we note 366 men had *chapeaux*, the remainder *schakos*, 346 *habits* and *vestes* needed repairs, as did 318 *bonnets de police*. The depot held 2 brand-new unissued *habits*, 2 new *vestes* and 9 pairs of *culottes*, 608 pairs of unissued shoes and remarkably 585 *capote*s in need of repair.[6]

31e *Légère*

The 12th battalion was drawn from 606 of the 31ᵉ *Légère*, who were wearing 606 *schakos* on *7 Vendémiaire An 13* (29 September 1804). Of the *habits*, we note 279 needed repairs, so too 343 *vestes* and 188 pairs of *pantalons* and remarkably 588 of the *schakos*. The men were also issued 597 capotes. Stores held brand-new unissued 7 *habits*, 3 smocks, 2 *vestes*,

Senior officers of the 3e *Cuirassiers* in full dress, *c*.1805.

2 pairs of linen *pantalons*, 10 pairs of blue tricot *pantalons* and 15 *capote*s, and 620 pairs of shoes. The inspecting officer reported that the *schakos* needed to be replaced with the regulation model – so were these in fact mirlitons? Not impossible. The inspector also reported that 303 new *habits*, and *vestes*, as well as 606 pairs of *pantalons*, would be issued in the coming year.[7]

2ᵉ *de Ligne*

The 806 grenadiers and *chasseurs* of 2ᵉ *régiment de Ligne* on *21 Ventôse An 12* (12 March 1804) were uniformly dressed in *chapeaux*. Only the 428 grenadiers carried sabres, and we assume scarlet epaulettes.[8] We cannot be sure which brigade the battalion served with.

9ᵉ *de Ligne*

Reviewed on *1 Vendémiaire An 13* (24 September 1804), the battalion mustered 25 officers and 591 other ranks. The men were all uniformly wearing *chapeaux*, each man carried a sabre. The 252 grenadiers we assume were marked out by their scarlet epaulettes counted with their *habit*.[9]

13ᵉ *de Ligne*

Reviewed on *1 Vendémiaire An 13* (24 September 1804), the battalion mustered 597 officers and men, of which 245 were grenadiers, 262 *chasseurs*, and 12 drummers. Despite

Trumpeters of the 3e *Cuirassiers* adopted scarlet *habits* faced in blue in summer 1805, which this illustration captures well.

being designated grenadiers, every man in the unit wore a *chapeau*. Only 130 *habits* were in serviceable condition, 138 needed repairs and 338 immediate replacement.[10]

58e *de Ligne*

The 606 grenadiers of the 58e *de Ligne* formed the 4th battalion, which had on *7 Vendémiaire An 13* (29 September 1804) 391 *chapeaux*, 300 *schakos* as well as 302 bearskins. Clearly some men had two forms of headdress. In addition, the men had 600 pairs of linen *pantalons de route*, 600 white linen *gilets* – as well as 606 sleeved *vestes* made from tricot – and 599 *capotes*.[11]

Colonel of 3e *Cuirassiers* in full dress, *c.*1805.

81ᵉ *de Ligne*

Reviewed on *1 Vendémiaire An 13* (24 September 1804), the battalion mustered 582 officers and men, of which 243 were grenadiers, 262 *chasseurs,* and 12 drummers. Despite being designated grenadiers, every man in the unit wore a *chapeau*.[12]

Comment

On 5 December 1808 the process began to reorganise and break up Oudinot's grenadiers. Those companies whose parent regiments were assigned to Bernadotte's and Davout's corps were returned. Overall, the division was reduced to a total of 62 companies organised into ten elite battalions. The Decree of 31 March 1809 reorganised the division again, this time into twelve *demi-brigades*, each of 3 battalions. It ceased to exist following Wagram. Despite being grenadiers, very few men actually wore bearskins. Further, no archive reference supports the notion of light blue facings for the drummers, *sapeurs* and cornets traditionally ascribed to this formation. Such assertions are clearly not supported by archive evidence.

2ᵉ Division

The division was led by General de Division Gazan. The 1st Brigade, which comprised the *4ᵉ Légère* and *58ᵉ régiment d'infanterie de la Ligne*, was commanded by *General de Brigade* Graindorge, and the 100ᵉ and 103ᵉ formed the 2nd Brigade led by *General de Brigade* Campana.

4ᵉ *Légère*

Reviewed on *23 Vendémiaire An 13* (15 October 1804), the three battalions mustered 1,716 men. Since the last review a year earlier, 978 men had left the regiment, and 1,015 had joined. The men were noted as being physically weak and malnourished, and the theoretical knowledge of the officers and men of the 1791 regulation and their duties was weak: indeed, over the previous ten months the inspector was at pains to point out to the war minister that 'no instruction had been carried out'. In terms of clothing, 'the majority of the *habits* are in bad condition', reported the inspector.[13]

Inspected on *24 Messidor An 13* (13 July 1805), the three battalions mustered 89 officers and 1,699 other ranks, which included 7 musicians. The men were wearing *schakos*, no bearskins existed for the *carabiniers*. Stores held 1,456m 84 of beige broadcloth to make *capotes*, but no garments had been made, and 4m 69 of chamois broadcloth had been used to make *voltigeurs*' clothing. The *voltigeur* company was wholly armed with 326 light cavalry *mousquetons*. Of the 1702 *habits* in service, 707 needed repairs and 72 immediate replacement; of the 1,903 pairs of *pantalons*, 869 pairs needed repairs and 647 immediate replacement, as did 290 *schakos*, 45 *gibernes* and 54 *baudriers*. For immediate needs stores held 203 *habits*, 201 *vestes*, 118 pairs of *pantalons* and 509 *schakos*.[14]

Colonel of 10e *Cuirassiers* in full dress, *c.*1805.

58ᵉ de Ligne

Reviewed on *22 Vendémiaire An 13* (14 October 1804), the two war battalions mustered 898 men, which included the 7-strong regimental band. Over the previous year, 50 men had died and 64 had deserted. Of the 1,105 men under arms in all three battalions, 371 men needed their *habit* repairing and 314 needed a new one, while 449 men needed a new *chapeau*, and 177 men needed a new *giberne*. Remarkably, given the poor condition of the men's clothing, 1,396 *habits* had been issued over the previous year and 856 *chapeaux*, so we wonder what the men had been doing to render so many 'knackered'? Indeed, regimental records report 653 *habits* had been 'patched up' over the previous year.[15]

Inspected on *7 Thermidor An 13* (25 July 1805), the major noted that the two war battalions mustered 1,065 men, 75 men were in hospital and the band was 7-men strong. The old soldiers were proficient at their drills, remarked the inspector, but the new intake of 430 conscripts and newly promoted officers needed to spend more time on training and learning their theory. The inspector noted that sending 774 men to the elite battalion robbed the regiment of its best *sous-officiers* and men, leaving men of 'bad spirit, short stature and weak constitution'. Of the men under arms, 439 needed a new *habit*, 645 needed a new *veste*, 480 a new pair of *culottes*, 593 a new *chapeau*, and 321 a new *giberne*. For these needs, stores held 56 *habits*: we guess the men marched to war in life-expired and tatty uniforms.[16]

100ᵉ de Ligne

Inspected on *20 Vendémiaire An 13* (12 October 1804), the three battalions mustered 2,374 men, which included an 8-strong regimental band. The inspecting officer noted the regiment was particularly weak in carrying out manoeuvres in line, but the *sous-officiers* were making good progress in improving the regiment's drill. He added that the regiment's clothing was in overall good condition and well sewn and accorded overall to the regulation. The *habits* came in for criticism: 50 per cent needed immediate replacement, some 1,225 examples, despite 1,800 new *habits* being issued over the previous year with a further 329 repaired. Many of the *chapeaux* were deformed, 1,225 new examples being needed, and many of the *culottes* were cut too short at the knee and waist, some 2,449 pairs being needed. Furthermore, the regiment's leather work was in the 'worst condition imaginable', with 126 *gibernes* needing repairs and 1,700 to be replaced with immediate effect. Regimental accounts report 5,112fr 77 was spent buying bearskins for the grenadiers.[17]

Reviewed again on *1 Thermidor An 13* (20 July 1805), the regiment mustered 2,218 men with a further 156 men sick in hospital. For the men under arms, 2,148 *habits* had been issued since the last inspection, along with 2,187 *vestes*, 771 pairs of *culottes*, 994 *chapeaux* and 289 *bonnets de police*. The regiment we note at this date had 8 *sapeurs* commanded by a *sapeur* corporal.[18]

Colonel of 1e *Carabiniers* in full dress, *c*.1805.

103ᵉ de Ligne

Reviewed on *8 Vendémiaire An 13* (30 September 1804), the two war battalions mustered 2,289 men, which included the 8-strong regimental band. The regiment's clothing was in overall bad condition: of 2,387 *habits*, 1,193 needed replacing, every single pair of *culottes* likewise needed to be replaced, as did 50 per cent of the *chapeaux*. We also note 7 *redingotes* were in use by the *adjutant-sous-officiers* and 1963 *capotes* for the other ranks were made from dark blue broadcloth. We also note both black and white stocks were used, and we also note black twill gaiters, linen gaiters and white cotton gaiters were in use as well as pompoms, and grenadiers' epaulettes, for which 37m of scarlet worsted fringing was in stores, and 3m58 in gold bullion. The *bonnets de police* had worsted tassels, stores holding 235 of these. We also note the other ranks had woollen socks and the *sous-officiers* linen stockings.[19]

Inspected again on *4 Thermidor An 13* (23 July 1805), the war battalions mustered 2,205 men. Regimental accounts report 5,184fr had been spent buying grenadier bearskins and 6,975fr on buying ready-made *capotes*. Despite 1,096 brand-new *habits* being issued since October, 904 *habits* needed repairs and 359 immediate replacement, 470 vestes needed replacing and 686 immediate repairs. Also needing repairs were 818 *chapeaux*. Stores held nothing to replace the defective clothing: we assume the men marched to war in clothing that was very much past its best.[20]

3ᵉ Division

Future Marshal Louis Gabriel Suchet led the division, which was attached to Soult's IV Corps, forming a 4th Division on *1 Vendemiaire An 14*.[21] Michel Claparède, who would make his name at Aspern-Essling in 1809, led the 1st Brigade, the 17ᵉ *Légère*. The 2nd Brigade was commanded by Nicolas Léonard Beker and comprised the 34ᵉ and 40ᵉ *de Ligne*, with the 64ᵉ and 88ᵉ *de Ligne* forming the 3rd Brigade headed by Jean-Marie Valhubert, who was mortally wounded at Austerlitz.

17ᵉ Légère

Inspected on *15 Vendemiaire An 13* (7 October 1804) in Strasbourg, the major reported that the regiment mustered three battalions, and 2,612 men, of which 73 were sick. Since the previous year's review, 36 men had died and 353 had deserted. This despite the barracks being clean, in good repair and food plentiful and of good quality. The men were 'a good type' but 'had very weak constitutions'. Despite this the accommodation was very good, so too the blankets, mattresses and food. Clearly the men were heading home for other reasons. The men recruited from the Dordogne in rural south-west France, the inspector noted, 'showed no intelligence and absolutely no spirit for the military'. Basically, being far from home, resenting conscription and with language barriers, the men simply went back to their farms. The inspector ordered the regiment to make

Trooper of 1e *Carabiniers* in full dress, c.1805.

capotes with all urgency. Of the men's *habits*, 2,598 existed, some 1,014 examples needed replacement and 449 repairs. Since 1803, 1,190 *schakos* had been issued, replacing the largely useless *chapeaux*.[22]

Reviewed in Strasbourg on *28 Thermidor An 13* (16 August 1805), the major reported the desertion rate had plummeted: just 100 men had gone AWOL in the preceding year, although 42 men had died, 38 had been discharged from hospital and 186 were currently in hospital out of 2,506 men under arms. The barracks occupied by the regiment were well situated and in good condition, as was the bed and bedding. Rations were plentiful and of good quality.

We note by this date the *carabinier* companies had 244 bearskins, with the *voltigeurs* and *chasseurs* wearing 2606 *schakos*. We assume the *voltigeurs* had chamois facings as the inspector notes 70m of 'scarlet broadcloth and other colours' had been used for facings. In stores were 28 additional bearskins. The clothing was overall in desperately bad condition: of the 2,506 *habits* some 913 needed immediate replacement and 703 repairs. Stores held just 175. The inspector ordered 1,347 *habits* and *vestes* made, 2,698 pairs of *pantalons de tricot* and 898 *schakos* for immediate needs, or 50 per cent of the regiment needed reclothing before the long march to Austerlitz began. Armament wise, the *voltigeurs* were issued 312 sabres and dragoon muskets, with the officers and *sous-officiers* being issued 27 rifles. The drummers, *cornets, fifre* and *sapeurs* were issued 91 An XI light cavalry *mousquetons*.[23] We doubt the men received new clothing before hitting the road to Austria.

34ᵉ *de Ligne*

Inspected on *7 Brumaire An 13* (29 October 1804), the major reported the regiment mustered 2,460 men in three battalions, 57 of whom were sick in hospital. Since October 1803 he reported 55 men had died and 252 had deserted and 60 had been discharged as unfit for further service from hospital. The two war battalions were at camp in Wimereux, near Boulogne, and the two depot battalions were at Mayence, where they were lodged in the citadel. The inspector noted the men were all robust and the grenadiers tall and gave a 'good impression', the men's clothing respected the regulations in all regards, he noted, but added the regiment needed to swap its blackened cow hide leather equipment for buff.[24]

Reviewed again on *24 Thermidor An 13* (12 August 1805), the major reported that desertion rates had more than halved: 89 men going AWOL and 25 men had died. The men were well fed, but had to use their pay to buy sufficient food, as the allocated funds to the ordinary did not cover the inflated prices. The men's clothing was by and large in tatters: of the 2,812 *habits* in existence, 767 needed repairs and 1,175 replacement. Likewise, 767 *vestes* needed repairs and 791 to be replaced, while 914 pairs of c*ulottes* were needed. By the time the regiment arrived at Austerlitz, its uniforms must have been in a very sorry state indeed. We also note 395 *giberne* belts were needed and 475 musket slings in whitened buff to replace blackened cow hide examples. The regiment's 73 drummers were issued An XI light cavalry *mousquetons*, and infantry *gibernes* and belts.²⁵ Despite no bearskins existing, the grenadiers had epaulettes, 2 pairs being in store, along with sword knots and pompoms.²⁶

40ᵉ *de Ligne*

Inspected on *19 Vendémiaire An 13* (11 October 1804), the regiment was based at Orléans. We remark that the officers were chastised for spending more than a day's pay a month on the band's uniforms: sadly, we have no idea how it was dressed. Clothing was in tatters: of 2,219 *habits*, 1,091 were new, 143 needed repairs and 1,128 total replacement. Every single pair of culottes had to be replaced, 940 of the *chapeaux*, and 466 of the *vestes*. Furthermore, over 1,400 *gibernes* needed repair or replacement and over 1,600 *giberne* belts. The clothing was clearly in tatters, as was the vast majority of the leather work.²⁷

Trumpeters of 1e *Carabiniers* in full dress. *c.*1805, wearing reversed colours of scarlet faced with blue. This is possibly the sole image from the epoch showing the dress of the trumpeters prior to the adoption of armour.

Reviewed on *6 Thermidor An 13* (25 July 1805), again by General Thiébault, the men's clothing was still in terrible condition. Of the 2,111 *habits* in use, 1,091 needed immediate repairs and 351 were to be written off, and some 1,055 examples were ordered as replacements. The *vestes* were also in terrible condition, with 1,517 examples out of 2,111 needing repairs. Likewise, the *culottes* were in poor condition: 1,366 pairs needed repairs and the inspector authorised every single one of the 2,111 pairs in use to be replaced with immediate effect. Remarkably, since 1804 1,091 *habits* had been issued – so how had the *habits* become so damaged? Likewise, 1,723 *vestes*, 2,257 pairs of *culottes*, 1,279 *chapeaux* and 1,371 *bonnets de police* had been made and issued. Clearly the men were simply not maintaining their clothing and effects. We wonder if these repairs and new items were issued before the regiment hit the road to Vienna? Concerning drill, the inspector remarked the regiment was still far from proficient, especially battalion level.[28]

64ᵉ *de Ligne*

Inspected on *1 Vendémiaire An 13* (24 September 1804), the two war battalions mustered 1,687 men. Since the previous review some 18 months earlier, 97 men had died and 177 had deserted, with a further 63 men discharged as unfit for service from the regimental hospital. Among the items issued, we note 21 *sapeurs'* aprons, axe and axes cases were in use.[29] Regimental orders suggest the grenadiers and *sapeurs* wore bearskins.[30] Reviewed on *11 Thermidor An 13* (30 July 1805), the regiment mustered 1,382 in the two war battalions. Since the previous inspection, 40 men had died and 42 had deserted. The practical knowledge of the *sous-officiers* was a little better than those in the depot, but they still needed to improve the practical knowledge of their duties. The men's uniform came in for criticism: the men's *habits* did not accord to the model sent from the War Ministry as the tails had vertical pockets rather than horizontal. The *chapeaux* likewise did not accord with the regulation. Of the clothing in use, just 985 *habits* out of 2,076 were in good condition; all the rest, 1,058 examples, needed immediate replacement. In addition, 1,058 *vestes* were needed, 480 pairs of *culottes* and 1,046 *chapeaux*. The regiment had a huge amount of brand-new clothing ready to be issued to meet these needs: 845 *habits*, 923 *vestes*, 1,440 pairs of *culottes* and 904 *chapeaux*. Potentially, the men were all re-dressed before hitting the road to Vienna.[31] The regiment had 96 musketoons issued in November 1804 – clearly some of these had been issued to the 51 drummers present at the time of the inspection.[32]

88ᵉ *de Ligne*

Inspected on *6 Thermidor An 13* (27 August 1805), the war battalions mustered 1,743 men. Since the previous inspection in October 1804, 26 men had died and 59 had deserted. The regiment's clothing was exactly as per the regulations, but the materials used were very low quality. Of the 2,193 *habits* in use across all three battalions, 716 needed immediate repairs and 265 replacing, as did 265 *vestes* and *chapeaux* and 825 *bonnets de police*. No clothing was held in stores to meet these needs, and we suppose men marched to war in tattered and worn-out uniforms. Armament wise, 93 light cavalry *mousquetons* had been issued, 53 to drummers and 40 to fusiliers. Sabres were restricted to *sous-officiers* and grenadiers, and the latter it seems had no bearskins. In addition, the report notes that the *sous-officiers* were well versed in the 1791 regulation. The officers needed to become more proficient in their theory and battalion drill. The regiment's battalion level drill was particularly weak. Discipline in the regiment was good, just but very severe, the inspector noted.[33]

5ᵉ Light Cavalry Division

The division was detached to the reserve. *General de Brigade* Treillhard led the division and also the 9ᵉ and 10ᵉ *Hussard*. The 13ᵉ and 21ᵉ *Chasseurs* were commanded by *General de Brigade* Fauconnet.[34]

9ᵉ *Hussard*

Formed on 2 September 1792 as the *Hussards de la Liberté*, the 2nd squadron became the cadre of the 10ᵉ *Hussard* on 25 March 1793. On 1 May 1794 the first squadron of the *Hussards de la Liberté* became the 7ᵉ *régiment bis de hussards*. The 10ᵉ was renumbered as 9ᵉ on 4 June 1794. Dressed in scarlet *dolmans* with yellow lace and braid, and *bleu celeste pelisse* and *culottes hongroise*, the 9ᵉ was one of the most picturesque regiments of hussars. One of the earliest documents we have for the dress of the regiment is dated *20 Prairial An XI* (9 June 1803). We note the regiment had 624 *dolmans*, 620 *pelisses*, 581 *surtouts*, just 102 barrel sashes, as well as 559 *schakos* with cords. *Dépôt* held yellow basane leather for lining trumpeters' *dolmans* and also red basane leather for lining troopers' *dolmans*. The elite company had 64 colpacks and one was left in *dépôt*.[35]

Inspected on *18 Fructidor An 13* (5 September 1805), the elite company had 100 colpacks, and 629 *schakos* with cords were in use. In addition, 691 *dolmans* were in use, 685 *pelisses*, 343 *surtouts*, 348 barrel sashes – not enough for every man to have one – of which 178 were newly issued, and 680 sabretaches.[36]

10e *Hussard*

The 10ᵉ *Hussard* had been formed in 1793 from the '*Hussard Noirs*', otherwise known as the '*Hussards de la Mort*', organised in the *Département du Nord* as a free corps. The regiment was dressed in light blue and scarlet with white lace. Inspected on *22 Thermidor An 13* (8 August 1805), we find scarlet broadcloth in use and in the depot: 1,177m 55 of *bleu celeste* broadcloth being used, 420m 74 green broadcloth for *manteaux* and 191m 57 scarlet broadcloth being used in the 1803 to 1805 period. The regiment had 566 *dolmans*, 529 *pelisses* and 59 *surtouts* in use, accompanied by 509 green *manteaux*, 557 *gilets*, 647 stable coats, 629 pairs of *culottes hongroise*, and 528 pairs of stable trousers. The elite company had 96 colpacks and the remainder of the regiment wore *schakos*. The colpacks were clearly an innovation after 1803. The depot held 68 new dolmans, 178 having been repaired, 93 *pelisses* in were in depot and 168 had been repaired. Brand new and ready to be issued clothing included 1 *surtout*, 39 *gilets*, 206 *manteaux*, 31 stable coats, 68 pairs of *culottes hongroise*, 107 pairs of stable trousers and 155 *bonnets de police*.[37]

13ᵉ *Chasseurs*

Formed in 1792 from the *Legion des Americains* and the *Legion des Midi* as the 13ᵉ *Chasseurs*. Inspected at Brussels on *26 Vendémiaire An 13* (26 October 1804), the regiment mustered 704 other ranks, 442 in the war squadrons and 234 in the depot. Since the 1803 inspection, 12 men had died and 55 had deserted. Manoeuvres were exactly conforming to the regulation, the inspector noted, and the men's equitation was proficient due to good instruction. The men in depot and the war squadrons were universally wearing *surtouts* and the elite company had 64 colpacks. Of the 657 *surtouts*, 34 needed repairs and 6 total replacement, 691 examples being made and issued since 1803. Remarkably, stores held 347m 67 white broadcloth for *manteaux*, and reported the use of 557m 74 green tricot to make *portmanteaux* for other ranks, and 11m 32 of orange tricot for trumpeters' items. We also note 215 pairs of shoes were issued for stable duties.[38]

Reviewed on *10 Thermidor An 13* (29 July 1805), the war squadrons mustered 307 men, and since the last inspection 13 men had died and 15 had deserted. The depot held 167 men, 44 men were sick in hospital, and 143 men were 'embarked'. The war squadrons had 315 horses and the depot 80, meaning a substantial number of 665 men were dismounted. We note that 664 *surtouts* were in service – of these 127 needed repairs and 56 total replacement – and the elite company had 80 colpacks.[39]

21ᵉ *Chasseurs*

Inspected on *30 Messidor An XI* (19 July 1803), the regiment had 561 *dolmans* in use and 563 *surtouts*, 546 white *gilets* and 568 green *gilets* – these were presumably laced like the *dolman*? The elite company had 64 '*bonnets d'oursin*', which we assume to be colpacks. The depot held 308 aurore *gilets*, along with 259 brand-new green *gilets*, 27 *surtouts*, 139 *manteaux*, 132 white *gilets*, 130 stable coats, 169 pairs of *pantalons basane*, which are non-regulation *pantalons à cheval*, 253 pairs of stable trousers, 39 pairs of linen *pantalons*, 1 colpack, and 65 *schakos*.[40]

Inspected again on *1 Vendémiaire An 13* (23 September 1804), 589 *habits* were in use, although the regiment still had 545 dolmans and not a single *surtout* remained in use! Only white *gilets* existed, 122 new examples being in depot, and just 2 *dolmans* had been made and issued since the previous inspection. Quite clearly over the course of the summer of 1804 the regiment had been re-dressed in *habits*![41]

Inspected on *8 Fructidor An 13* (26 August 1805), the regiment mustered 66 men in the depot, and 461 in the war squadrons, of whom only 320 were mounted. Days before the campaign began, the regiment still needed 182 horses. Since the last review 6 men had died and 16 had deserted. By the time the review was carried out, not a single *dolman* existed, and the regiment was wearing 503 *surtouts* along with 498 white *gilets* and 547 braided aurore waistcoats! Presumably, as only 31 *surtouts* had been issued since 1804, the name *surtout* is actually a reference to '*habit-surtout*', the semi-official name for the short-tailed *habit veste*. The white *gilets* we assume were for everyday wear and the aurore braided examples for full dress parade. The elite company now boasted 88 colpacks, with 12 more brand-new examples in the depot.[42]

2ᵉ Dragoon Division

The division was in the capable hands of 'old scar face', Frédéric Henri Walther, who would become colonel of the *Grenadiers à Cheval de la Garde Imperiale* in new year 1806. He would be joined by his aides-de-camp, Maucomble, Leonard Morin and Junker. The 1st Brigade, the 10ᵉ and 13ᵉ *Dragons*, was led by Horace François Bastien Sébastiani, the 2nd Brigade, which comprised the 22ᵉ and 3ᵉ *Dragons*, by Dominique-Mansuy Roget de Belloquet – with his son as aide-de-camp and future officer of the *Grenadiers à Cheval de la Garde Imperiale* – and the 3rd, which mustered the 6ᵉ and 11ᵉ *Dragons*, by André Joseph Boussart.

3ᵉ *Dragons*

Levied in 1649, the regiment was reviewed on *24 Messidor An 13* (1 August 1805), when it mustered 226 men in the depot and 633 men in the war squadrons, of which 335 were mounted, and an additional 123 horses were needed to bring the squadrons up to strength. Over the past year, 12 men had died and 140 had deserted. In use at the time of the inspection were 894 *habits*, 894 *surtouts*, 894 helmets, 740 green broadcloth *manteaux*, 481 sets of *housses* and *chaperons*. A lot of the clothing was past its best: 418 *habits* needed repair and 190 total replacement, so too 284 *surtouts* needed repair, and 367 total replacement. Every single pair of *culottes de peau* and stable trousers needed to be replaced, so too 89 helmets. Stores held very little to meet immediate needs: 75 *surtouts*, and 142 pairs of *culottes de peau*. We can only assume men marched to war in clothing that was in dire need of replacement. Of the regiment's 24 trumpeters, 8 were armed with light cavalry *mousquetons*.[43] At the time of the 1803 review, 56 bearskins existed for the elite company.[44] These items are notably missing at the 1805 review and in 1807.[45]

6ᵉ *Dragons*

Inspected on *20 Vendémiaire An 13* (12 October 1804) at Creil, the regiment's major reported it mustered 567 men in the war squadrons and 117 in the depot. Over the last year 222 men had gone AWOL and 13 had died. Regimental accounts tell us 3,126fr had been spent buying *gibernes*, 3,518fr on clothing and just over 4,000fr on horseshoes.

Of the men in the war squadrons, every man had a *habit* less than 18 months old, as well as a *surtout*. The elite company had 138 bearskins. In stores were 501 infantry *havresacs* and 8 drums.[46] Reviewed again on *15 Fructidor An 13* (2 September 1805), the mounted contingent mustered 339 men, dépôt held 142 men and the foot company mustered 197 men. Since the last inspection 11 men had died and 34 had deserted. Feed for the horses was noted as being 'mediocre' but that of the men as excellent, 'being above reproach'. In terms of armament, the 8 trumpeters were armed with An XI light cavalry *mousquetons*, a pair of pistols and a sabre, 14 drummers were armed with An XI light cavalry *mousquetons* and *sabre briquettes*. Also in use were 742 *fusils de dragon*, 762 sabres and 540 pairs of pistols.[47]

10ᵉ *Dragons*

Reviewed on *27 Vendémiaire An 13* (19 October 1804), the regiment had 189 dismounted men with 8 drummers and 548 mounted with 4 trumpeters. The dismounted men had black twill gaiters, *havresac* and *capotes*, which like the *manteaux* were made from *blanc picque de bleu* broadcloth. We note 701 *habits* were in use and 739 *surtouts*, 447 *manteaux* and 127 bearskins for the elite company. The horses were equipped with *chaperons* and *housses*. Regimental accounts report 19m 90 of blue broadcloth had been used to clothe the trumpeters and drummers; presumably the facings.[48] By the time of the next review on *9 Thermidor An 13* (28 July 1805), the drummers and trumpeters were issued 16 light cavalry *mousquetons*.[49]

11ᵉ *Dragons*

Formed by a Royal Commission at Tournai in 1674. The paper archive for the regiment is remarkable for its completeness and complexity. The regiment was reviewed on *23 Vendémiaire An 13* (15 October 1804). In the report, the regiment's clothing was described as being 'in good condition and clean thanks to the example set by the *sous-officiers* of the elite company'. Regimental accounts attest to 6,596fr being spent on buying new buff work for the regiment to enable the use of dragoon muskets, and 200fr on lace for *sous-officiers* and other distinctions. The regiment now had 107 bearskins in service, 51 being obtained since July 1803. The regiment had *bottes a la écuyer*, some 425 pairs being in use and 169 being issued since 1803. Depot had used 32m 2 of crimson tricot – for trumpeters' *portmanteaux* we wonder? Further, some 428 pairs of shoes were in use, with 445 in depot, accompanied by 288 pairs of black worsted gaiters. The inspector officially reported that *bonnets de police* were to made from materials reclaimed from old clothing. The regiment had received 840 dragoon muskets and had retained 17 light cavalry carbines, 16 of which were issued to the trumpeters and drummers. The inspector noted that two *sous-officiers* had been sent to the cavalry school to train to be riding masters. The majority of the men were not capable of passing the *Ecole de cavalerie* as laid out in the regulations – i.e. the men could barely sit on a horse. The inspector stressed that equitation was not to be neglected. The regiment's dismounted manoeuvres were excellent, the inspector noted, but added that equitation 'had yet to be perfected'.[50]

Under a year passed until the regiment was inspected again, on 18 August 1805. The biggest surprise was the vast sum of 908fr 60 being spent on dressing the drum major! The mind boggles as to the extravagance of this uniform for such a large sum of money. Further, 516fr had been spent on lace for *sous-officiers* and other distinctions – presumably plumes and the epaulettes for the elite company. The regiment now had 540 linen smocks in use, 540 *capotes*, 540 pairs of black gaiters, the same number of linen overalls and pairs of shoes, and 304 infantry *havresacs*. The elite company had 116 bearskins, and 330 pairs of cloth *chaperons* were in service – four years after they had been officially introduced into service – along with 405 sheepskin *demi-schabraques*. Clearly a mix of *schabraques* and *chaperons* were used. Of interest, the regiment's 22 drummers and trumpeters were armed with 16 light cavalry carbines, 22 sabres and 8 pairs of pistols. We assume the drummers had the light cavalry carbines. A matter of weeks before departing for campaign, the regiment's equitation was simplistic; the men had the basics mastered but nothing else. The regiment's discipline was 'just and severe'.[51] We are left to wonder at the regiment's battlefield performance – one can only hope the men developed a seat – and no doubt saddle sores – when riding to Vienna from Cambrai!

13ᵉ *Dragons*

Formed in the Languedoc in 1676, it became the 'Conde *Dragons*' in 1724, and thence '*Dragons* de Monsieur' in 1774. As the 13ᵉ *Dragon* from 1791 the regiment seemingly adopted the provisions of the 1799 dress regulation to wear *bleu de ciel* with yellow facings. The regimental archives show that during the course of year 12 (1802–03) stores had used of 188m 87 of blue broadcloth and not an inch of green, to make 61 *habits*, 87 *surtouts* and 158 *housses*. We also note the elite company had 56 bearskins. Other materials used included 77m 49 of white broadcloth and 231m 14 white serge.[52] Not an inch of yellow broadcloth existed, so we are left to wonder how the regiment was dressed. Presumably these *bleu de ciel habits* were 'more of the same' of those already in use. Yet, at the time of the 1802 inspection, stores held 201m 10 of green broadcloth and 98m 22 of rose broadcloth.[53] Presumably the non-green uniform was a short-lived innovation as by *29 Vendémiaire An 13* 18 October 1804, the regiment was wearing green habits, 500 being produced since 18 December 1803. On this date the elite company had 125 bearskins.[54] Inspected on *6 Thermidor An 13* (25 July 1805), the elite company and trumpeters had 158 sheepskin *schabraques*, all scheduled for replacement. So too 25 blue habits, no doubt worn by trumpeters and drummers.[55]

22ᵉ *Dragons*

Raised in Piedmont in 1635, it became the *13e Régiment de Cavalerie* in 1791 and the *22ᵉ régiment des Dragons* in September 1803. Reviewed on *16 Vendémiaire An 13*

(8 October 1804), the inspector noted that the clothing and equipment was well made and followed very closely the model examples sent from the Ministry of War. Repairs were needed to items of headdress and buff work. The helmets were *cuirassier* helmets and not dragoon model – therefore the 13ᵉ *Cavalerie* had started the process to convert to *cuirassiers* before disbandment. The inspector further commented that the regiment was not wearing dragoon clothing or equipment, i.e., the blue *habit-longue* of the *cavalerie* regiments. He remarked that some green broad cloth had arrived in the depot, so 'construction' of dragoon uniforms could begin. Out of a matter of economy, it was to decided what old *cavalerie* items could be retained and what had to be changed in addition to the blue *habits*, blue *surtouts*, blue *bonnets de police* and blue stable coats.

The depot held a mix of fabrics, notably 507mm 33 blue broadcloth, 1,026m 65 green broadcloth, 409m 37 white broadcloth, 75m 67 yellow broadcloth, 35m 18 crimson broadcloth, 190m white tricot, 1,750m 94 crimson, white and yellow serge, and 1,215m 30 linen. Also in depot were 208 *habits* needing repairs, 39 brand-new pairs of *culottes de peau*, 157 pairs of stable trousers, 9 *cavalerie modelle chapeaux*, 111 *cuirassier* helmets, 36 *bonnets de police* that were brand new and 36 to be disposed of, 110 new *cuirassier* waistbelts and 108 old *cavalerie* model to be disposed of, accompanied by 267 brand-new *gibernes* with 210 belts. Some 258 *housses* were in use accompanied by 300 pairs of *chaperons* – clearly some men simply had the saddle blanket on show. The inspector authorised the regiment to have 107 bearskins for the elite company, and gave permission for 17 to be made. The regiment as *cavalerie* had carried carbines, which had been replaced with 440 dragoon muskets, yet 483 *cavalerie* sabres were in use and 457 pairs of pistols.[56]

Inspected on *2 Thermidor An 13* (21 July 1805), the inspector remarked that the full dress was very good and very uniform for all ranks, and the same regularity and uniformity could be found for the officers and men in undress. The regiment was now dressed in green *habits* and *surtouts* – only some of the *manteaux* had been changed, and men still mostly wore blue stable coats and *bonnets de police*. The helmets were still *cuirassier* pattern. Leather work was a mix of *cavalerie* and dragoon model – just 110 dragoon sabre belts were in use, yet all the round blue tricot *portmanteaux* had been swapped out for rectangular green examples. For the horses, 447 *housses* were in use accompanied by 447 pairs of *chaperons* – the vast majority of which were blue! With *cuirassier* helmets, blue saddle furniture, dragoon *habits* and *cavalerie* leather work, the regiment was highly distinctive! The regiment was armed with 440 dragoon muskets, 457 pairs of pistols and 476 *cavalerie* sabres. The inspector noted that several pistols were not regulation issue – some 90 examples being too large to fit into the holsters – and many lacked ram rods – making them totally useless.[57]

Chapter 12

The Cavalry Reserve

The cavalry reserve was led by Marshal Joachim Murat, with the staff work in the capable hands of General Belliard, one of the most competent officers of the epoch. He has left us a wealth of fascinating documents, running into the thousands, concerning the cavalry and its operations in the campaign.[1]

The Austerlitz campaign was the first campaign for the *cuirassiers* – it was the baptism of fire for 8 of the 12 regiments. Alongside the *cuirassiers* came the *carabinier* brigade. The 10 regiments were formed into two divisions, with the 1st commanded by General Nansouty.

The division comprised three brigades: the *Carabinier* brigade formed the 1st, commanded by General Joseph Piston; the 2ᵉ and 9ᵉ *Cuirassiers*, the 2nd brigade, was under the orders of General La Houssaye; and the 3ᵉ and 12ᵉ *Cuirassiers*, the 3rd brigade, was commanded by General Saint-Germain. The 2nd Division was led by Jean-Joseph Ange d'Hautpoul. It was subdivided into two brigades, the 1st led by Jean-Baptiste Noirot (1ᵉ and 5ᵉ regiments) and the 2nd by Raymond-Gaspard de Bonardi de Saint-Sulpice, leading the 10ᵉ and 11ᵉ *Cuirassiers*. Among the records of the Heavy Cavalry we find after-action reports by every *cuirassier* regiments' colonel. None of these have ever been published.[2]

1ᵉ *Cuirassiers*

Created on *18 Vendemiaire An 10* (10 October 1801), the regiment was reviewed on *17 Germinal An 10* (7 April 1802), when it had 452 *habits*, of which 181 had been made since 1800.[3] These were without shadow of a doubt *habits-longues*. Reviewed again on *23 Messidor An XI* (12 July 1803), 411 *habits* were in use, every one being made since 1802. These were beyond reasonable doubt *habits de cuirass*.[4] The regiment received from the arsenal of Paris by the end of November 1802 406 *cuirasses* and helmets, and a further 219 examples of each between December 1802 and February 1803. The regiment had 625 *cuirasses* and helmets.[5]

Inspected on *7 Thermidor An 13* (26 July 1805), the regiment had a mix of *habits* and *surtouts* in use. The *habits* were described as 'cut short'.[6]

2ᵉ *Cuirassiers*

Becoming the 2ᵉ *Cavalerie-curaissier* on *20 Vendémiaire An 11* (12 October 1802), the regiment was reviewed on *20 Thermidor An 12* (8 August 1803). It had 356 brand-new

170 Napoleon's Army at Austerlitz

Company officer of the *Grenadiers à Pied* in full dress, *c.*1805.

The Cavalry Reserve 171

Private of *Grenadiers à Pied* in full dress, c.1805. The parade uniforms were left behind in Paris when the regiment marched to war.

habits in use, all issued since the review of 30 January 1802. No doubt these were *habits a revers*. Some 300 helmets were in use and no armour.[7] The next inspection report merely states that the clothing is entirely new, and one might conclude that this refers to the new model of *habit* as described in 1803.[8] However, interestingly, and to contradict this, the inspection of *20 Thermidor An 13* (8 August 1805) observes that some of the *habits* worn in the regiment were still of the old model (i.e., long-tailed cavalry *habits*, with *revers*). Perhaps, to make an instant and lasting impression, the colonel had had everyone clothed identically in the new model for the 1804 inspection, but had retained the old *habits*, which were then simply continued in use as required. We note by the time of the 1805 review that 588 helmets were in service and 625 *cuirasses* for 656 men under arms.[9]

3ᵉ *Cuirassiers*

It had become *cuirassiers* on *20 Vendémiaire An 11* (12 October 1802). Inspected on *10 Fructidor An 11* (28 August 1803), the general reported that the clothing of the regiment was 'good but still not all of the new model'. Every man had their *cavalerie habit* and *surtout*, the inspector noted, who ordered the regiment was to receive 625 new *habits*, *surtouts*, and *gilets*, 601 stable coats and stable trousers, 625 pairs of *culottes de peau*, *chapeaux*, helmets, *bonnets de police*, *ceinturons* of the new model with slings, new model *portmanteaux* and pairs of boots. In essence, the regiment was to receive its '*cuirassier* start-up kit' by the time of the next inspection in batches of 625. In addition, 9 caissons of new-model sabres were at Compiègne awaiting delivery. Not a single *giberne* and *porte-giberne* was in use, nor had the regiment received a single *cuirass*.[10]

Inspected again on *1 Vendémiaire An 13* (23 September 1804), the regiment still had no *cuirasses*, but the clothing had 'much greater uniformity'. Of the 625 new *habits* authorised, 417 old *habits* were in use, and only 195 new items had been made, presumably 'more of the same' but perhaps with the tails cropped short.[11]

The regiment had 418 new helmets in use, and some 496 new-model *ceinturons* had been issued since 1803, a huge increase on the 32 allowed for. Despite official sanction, the regiment still had not received a single *giberne* and *porte-giberne*, and the *portmanteaux* were all of the old model.[12]

By the time of the next inspection on *11 Thermidor An 13* (30 July 1805) the regiment had received its armour and every man now had the new pattern sabre – almost two years since the 1803 decree. The mobilised men in the war squadrons mustered 485 rank and file, of which 433 were mounted and ready to be mobilised. Since 1804 84 new *habits* had been made, bringing the total up to 488. All of these must have been the old model. Furthermore, 224 new *surtouts* had been made, bringing the total up to 527 in existence, of which 477 were in good condition and 50 needed to be replaced. In total 232 new *surtouts* had been made up to 1804 and a further 224 since 1804, some 456 examples of new-model *surtouts*, which are arguably the *habit de cuirassier* of 1803. Of the *habits*, 195 were made new before the September decree so must be the *cavalerie* model, with a further 84 of these made since 1804. As the regiment marched to war, it had just 408

The Cavalry Reserve 173

Sapeur of *Grenadiers à Pied*. This elaborate uniform was only worn in Paris, and the *sapeurs* wore an undress uniform on campaign, with minimal lace to the collar and cuffs, and crossed axed badges to the sleeves and tails.

manteaux, of which 378 were in good condition, 30 had to be replaced and 113 were new. Clearly in the fighting to come, some men got wet and cold lacking a *manteau*. The men had 250 *gilets*, of which 175 were new and 40 were fit only for rags, 556 stable coats were in use, of which 313 were new and 150 were fit for nothing else. Some 296 new pairs of *culottes de peau* had been issued since 1804, making the total up to 530 pairs. Not a single *giberne* and *porte-giberne* existed, and some 408 pairs of gauntlets were in use. For headdress the regiment had 388 *chapeaux*, 499 helmets and 601 *bonnets de police*.[13]

Concerning the dress of the trumpeters, an archive document dated *30 Thermidor An 11* (18 August 1802) tells us 36fr had been spent on livery for the trumpeters applied to blue *habits*. A document of *1 Vendémiaire An14* (23 September 1805) tells us scarlet cloth had been bought for the trumpeters: presumably it was only now in summer 1805 that the trumpeters adopted reversed colours.[14]

5e *Cuirassiers*

Inspected on 25 *Thermidor An 11* (13 August 1803), the report shows that since its conversion to *cuirassiers*, hardly any new clothing had been made, and the old *cavalerie* items were in shreds: every single *habit* and *surtout* had to be replaced as life expired. As could be expected, the inspecting officer reported that none of the clothing conformed to the new model for *cuirassiers*. The same was true of the equipment.[15]

Inspected on *1 Vendémiaire An 13* (23 September 1804), the officer conducting the inspection noted that the *surtouts* and equipment were of the model authorised for *cuirassiers*. The officer noted that the regiment had received new *habits* on *7 Thermidor An 11* (26 July 1803), which conformed to the model. Surely these are the old-style garments with the tails cropped off as the new *habit-de-cuirassier* had yet to be formally introduced by decree.[16]

The 1805 inspection report of *8 Thermidor An 13* (27 July 1805) states that *habits* were not made according to the example supplied by the Ministry of War. This is most interesting for two reasons: it proves that the 1803 regulation concerning the cut of the new *habit* wasn't always strictly observed, and it also confirms that this regiment had been sent an actual example of the new 1803 *habit*, to use as a model to copy. Our conclusion is that for the practical reasons of wearing a *cuirass* on horseback, the regiment used the *surtout* and *habit* with the tails cropped off. About the men's riding ability we are told that 'the squadron leader Balthazar Roustan, a former French guard, has been in the corps for a little time, but he is a horseman and he manoeuvres well' and he was in charge of equitation. Presumably the men rode well.[17]

9e *Cuirassiers*

Inspected on *28 Prairial An 11* (17 June 1803), in use were 534 *habits* and 504 *surtouts*, the bulk of which were over 18 months old and were no doubt *cavalerie* items.[18] At the time of the inspection of 21 October 1804 the inspector reports that the clothing did not

Drum major of the *Grenadiers à Pied* in full dress, *c.*1805. This hugely costly ensemble was left behind in Paris on the orders of Colonel Hulin, the drum major wearing a far more sombre *surtout* on campaign.

conform to regulations. In use were 541 *habits courtes*, alongside 541 *habits-longues* and 457 *surtouts*, which were to be phased out. Reviewed on *17 Thermidor An 13* (5 August 1805), the inspector noted that 548 *habits courtes* were in use, alongside 538 *habits-longues* and 27 *surtouts*. The *habits courtes* are no doubt *habits de cuirass*. The trumpeters, it seems, had *surtouts*, so too adjutants. Presumably the old *cavalerie habits* were worn for dismounted duties, and by 1805 were four years old, being made during 1801.[19] A letter from the 9[e] *Cuirassiers Conseil d'Administration*, dated *16 Frimaire An 12* (8 December 1803), to the Minister of War asks whether the regiment should be able to wear plumes, and if so in what colour; ditto the same question for epaulettes, and whether or not their symbol on *habits* and *housses* should be the grenade. Finally, if the answer was yes to all these questions, they demanded funds to help pay for such items. The Minister for War replied in a letter dated *28 Frimaire* (20 December 1803), and stated that as *cuirassiers* were elite, every man was allowed scarlet-fringed epaulettes, grenade devices to the turnbacks and red plumes by all regiments, and it is probable that by 1805, all regiments had adopted these items.[20] The regiment received on *8 Prairial An 12* (28 May 1804) 625 *cuirasses* and helmets. Of these, 85 sets were defective and returned to the arsenal for repairs, and these were replaced on 6 March 1805.[21]

10[e] *Cuirassiers*

Inspected on *9 Thermidor An 13* (28 July 1805), the men were wearing 451 *habits-vestes* and 651 *surtouts* for the 619 men under arms. Clearly some men had two *surtouts*, and not every man had a *habit-veste*. Interestingly, only 584 helmets were in use and 546 *cuirasses*. Men must have been wearing *surtouts* under the *cuirass*, and some men clearly had helmets but no armour. Of interest, 610 *chapeaux* were in service. The regiment must have presented a far from uniform look.[22]

11e *Cuirassiers*

Reviewed on *22 Vendémiaire An 12* (15 October 1803), the regiment was still dressed as the 11e *Cavalerie*. We note the elite company swaggered wearing bearskins, and some 59 were in service. The regiment had 446 *habits* in service, of which 340 were in good condition, 43 needed repairs, 63 needed replacing and 74 had been made since 1802. Also, in service were 494 *surtouts*, 397 *manteaux*, 463 *gilets*, 479 stable coats, while every one of the *culottes de peau* in use had to be written off and replaced. Headdress comprised 464 *chapeaux*, and 470 *bonnets de police*. Not a single *schabraque* existed, 262 pairs of *chaperons* being in use along with 262 *housses* and 409 *portmanteaux*. The *habits* were all good for another year's service, the *surtouts* were passable, but the stable coats were all in need of replacement, as were the *portmanteaux*. Cloth in the depot comprised 673m 90 blue broadcloth, 140m 21 white broadcloth, 6m 50 yellow broadcloth, 405m 62 *blanc picquer de bleu* broadcloth for making *manteaux*, 12m 86 *rose* broadcloth, 93m 15 blue tricot, 1m 25 yellow tricot, 474m 55 white milled serge, 786m 93 *treillis*, and 166m 21 linen. The regiment to be converted to *cuirassier* needed 537 *habits*, 537 *surtouts* and *gilets*, of which 134 *habits* were authorised,

The Cavalry Reserve 177

Drummer of *Grenadiers à Pied* in full dress, *c.*1805. The drummers wore a sombre *surtout* on campaign.

269 *surtouts* and 134 *vestes*! Clearly equipping as *cuirassiers* would take time.[23] The regiment received 625 *cuirasses* and helmets on *30 Ventôse An 13* (21 March 1804).[24] However, when reviewed on *1 Thermidor An 13* (20 July 1805), the 588 men under arms had 516 helmets and 588 *cuirasses*, which included the trumpeters and corporal trumpeter. The men lacking helmets were wearing *chapeaux*, of which 610 existed!![25]

12ᵉ *Cuirassiers*

The *24 Vendémiaire An 13* (16 October 1804) inspection report states that this regiment had simply modernised its old cavalry *habits* by shortening and recutting the tails. However, elsewhere the inspector noted 'the clothing entirely conformed to the models and instructions sent by his excellency the Minister of War'. We noted 486 *habits* had been made since the 1803 review, bringing the total in use up to 498, and 589 *surtouts* were in use by the 594 men under arms. One oddity shown up in this inspection was that the regiment used 18m of chestnut brown broadcloth and 21m 10 of grey broadcloth in the production of clothing. Regimental archives note the presence of 231 pairs of gaiters: were they made from grey broadcloth? Possibly. The chestnut brown may have been destined for legwear. In addition, the report states the trumpeters were wearing 14 bearskins and 531 helmets were in service.[26] The regiment received on *21 Brumaire An 13* (12 November 1804) 625 *cuirasses*.[27]

Moving forward to the time of the next review, the regiment still had *habits a revers* and *surtouts* on *20 Thermidor An 13* (8 August 1805) as 512 *habits* existed, 54 being made since the previous review, and 612 *surtouts*, 105 of which were new. The inspector commented that the regiment's dress conformed entirely to regulation, so proof positive that the short-tailed *habit a revers* and *surtout* were considered regulation at this date.[28]

Carabiniers

The two regiments of *carabiniers* were formed in the middle years of the sixteenth century. They were cavalry armed with rifles – in French *carabine* – and at the battle of Neerwinden in 1693 the corps was commanded by Prince de Conti. The men were drawn from each regiment of cavalry into a provisional formation. Formed into an independent regiment in 1693, 13 May 1758 witnessed the regiment renamed Royal *carabiniers* de monsieur le Comte de Provence. In 1762 the Corps of *Carabiniers* was some 30 squadrons strong, formed in five brigades, which was reduced to a single regiment of 8 companies in 1776 – each company comprised 145 troopers and five officers. In 1779 the regiment was reorganised into two brigades, each of five squadrons. In 1788 the corps was renamed the *Carabiniers de Monsieur*, comprising two regiments, each of four squadrons. From then on, both regiments would serve side by side as a single cohesive brigade.

With the outbreak of the Revolution, the privileged Royal Corps and regiments were abolished; yet with King Louis XVI still nominally monarch, the *Carabiniers* were retained. On 18 August 1790 the National Assembly voted to retain the two regiments and their traditions, and were renamed the '*Grenadiers des troupes à cheval*', literally the grenadiers of the mounted troops, and were fitted out with scarlet-fringed epaulettes and bearskin caps. The two regiments had seniority over the rest of the cavalry. Always a hotbed of Royalists, the officers of the corps owed more allegiance to the crown than the state or Emperor. In the wars of the revolution, the *Carabiniers* fought mostly in the Army of Germany. In 1804 Louis Bonaparte was named Colonel General of *Carabiniers*; the two regiments led the coronation procession from the Tuileries to Notre-Dame, much to the chagrin of the *Grenadiers à Cheval* of the Imperial Guard.

We commented upon the dress regulations for both regiments in earlier chapters, suffice to say they wore blue *habits* with red facings, red grenadier epaulettes and swaggered under tall bearskin caps.

1ᵉ *Carabiniers*

The regiment was inspected on *5 Messidor An 11* (24 June 1803), when its clothing was as follows:[29]

Item	In good condition	In need of repair	To be written off	Total	Number made since 20 April 1802
Standards	4				
Habits	456	64	94	608	
Surtouts	267	87	227	588	94
Manteaux	453	85	88	556	47
Gilets en drap blanc	567	49	222	608	102
Gilets d'ecurie	196	83	446	584	8
Culottes de peau	608		8	616	606
Pantalons d'ecurie	563		6	569	569
Chapeaux	354		230	584	569
Bonnets a poil	463	32	96	584	64
Bonnets de police	209	10	383	576	48

In the same period 48 *habits* were made, 139 *surtouts*, 48 *manteaux*, 574 *gilets*, 378 stable coats, 624 pairs of *culottes de peau de mouton*, 475 pairs of stable trousers, 625 *chapeaux*, 222 bearskins and 319 *bonnets de police*. As in previous inspection returns, we have no clue as to the dress of trumpeters. The total lack of blue milled serge and the small amount of scarlet broadcloth used is proof positive that reverse colours were not used by both regiments. We can only assume they wore the same uniform as rank and file, but perhaps with lace to the collar and cuff of the *habit*. The lack of any period iconography is also a hinderance in making any comments about the uniform beyond it was not reversed colours.

2ᵉ *Carabiniers*

The early paperwork for the 2ᵉ *Carabiniers* cannot be located at the time of writing.

Chapter 13

Everything Else

Behind the glamour of the *hussards* or *cuirassiers*, came the support troops: the artillery, engineers, and the waggon drivers.

Artillery

Technically, the Corps of Artillery was still part of the infantry branch of service. Under the title of Royal-Artillerie, it ranked 64th in the list of infantry units. It was only in September 1790 that the Artillery became fully independent. Even then some confusion lasted almost throughout the entire period. Once the *amalgame* was put into effect, it resulted in all the former infantry regiments effectively disappearing – thus the artillery took the first rank in the army! The 1e *Artillerie à Pied* was formed on 25 February 1720, as were the 2e, 3e, 4e and 5e regiments. The 6e was formed on 1 January 1757, the 7e on 8 December 1762, and the 8e on 24 October 1784. Each regiment was organised into two battalions of ten companies. Each battalion was subdivided into two divisions of five companies.

Each company would include:

2 captains (one 1st class, and one 2nd class)
1 *lieutenant en premier*
1 sergeant major
1 *fourrier*
4 sergeants
4 corporals
2 drummers
24 gunners of 1st Class
45 gunners of 2nd Class

The foot artillery were armed with 12-pdr, 8-pdr and 4-pdr field guns. Each battery had eight field guns, and two howitzers. As well as the slow-moving foot artillery, from experiencing the highly trained Austrian artillery, the National Assembly recommended the formation of horse artillery on 28 September 1791. Minister of War Narbonne was enthusiastic, and in January 1792 allowed the formation of two companies in Metz. On 17 April, nine more companies were ordered to be created, the remaining seven being formed in May. Each of these companies was armed with six 4-pdr guns and a 6in howitzer. The new light artillery arm became operational on 7 February 1794,

Bandsman of *Grenadiers à Pied* in full dress, c.1805.

the existing companies being organised into eight regiments, each having six companies and a *dépôt*. The new regiments were numbered 1 to 8, and were organised during the summer of 1794. The gunners were dressed in fashionable hussar dress, and they rapidly developed a style and panache of their own.

Each gunner riding on their own horse proved to be especially costly: many in the War Ministry felt horses were better used by the cavalry and not gunners. Thus, we see in imitation of the Austrians, by 1798, the French had formed companies of *Artillerie Légère*. Rather than riding, the men rode into action seated on the ammunition, known as a 'Wurst waggon'. The gunners wore dragoon helmets and *chasseur*-style uniforms. The mounted light artillery was known as *Artillerie Volonte*.

Tactically the two types of horse artillery served different purposes: the *Artillerie Légère* was used to occupy positions with speed, while the *Artillerie Volante* had to follow the cavalry at all times. Despite operational flexibility, the 'wurst' waggons were done away with in 1801.

Organisationally, the guns were grouped into divisions, each consisted of 2 × 12-pdr, 6 × 8-pdr, 2 × 4-pdr and 2 × howitzers. One division of guns was allocated to each Army Corps Division: thus, a corps of three divisions had three divisions of artillery attached to it with associated personnel from the *train d'artillerie*. In a like manner, the cavalry divisions would have allocated a division of horse artillery, but of 4 × 8-pdr and 2 × howitzers. The most common calibre for both foot and horse artillery at Austerlitz was the 8-pdr.

The guns themselves were in the process of change. Experience gained of the existing artillery system designed forty years earlier showed weaknesses in the equipment: the 4-pdr was deemed to be of too small a calibre to be effective when used in close support of infantry,[1] and the 8-pdr to be too heavy for close support of infantry.[2] The 4-pdr, it was said, lacked range and hitting power when compared to heavier calibres of the enemy[3] and that a heavier gun was needed for infantry support.[4] General Sorbier went further and suggested that all 4-pdrs should be melted down and used to cast new 8-pdrs[5] as this was the favoured piece by the horse artillery (both artillery officers[6] and cavalry generals alike[7]), who were vehemently opposed to the removal of the 8-pdr. Ideas to arm the foot artillery and horse artillery universally with 8-pdrs was impractical for economic reasons, as compared to the proposed 6-pdr, the 8-pdr required more caissons for ammunition (thus more horses to move the ammunition), required a larger powder charge, making the 8-pdr more expensive to operate as compared to operating a 6-pdr, and were less mobile than the 4-pdr.

There were also other issues with the 8-pdr. Fundamentally, there was the problem of *encastrement*, whereby the 8- and 12-pdr gun tubes had to be moved forward on the gun carriage when being made ready for firing. This caused considerable delay for gun and battery emplacement and could cause problems in an emergency (the howitzers and 4-pdr did not have this problem as they only had one trunnion position on the gun carriage). The 12-pdr and 8-pdr had two sets of trunnion positions on the carriage as, when the piece was limbered, the muzzle of the gun tube tended to drag on the road.

Everything Else 183

Cymbalist of the *Grenadiers à Pied* in dull dress, *c*.1805. I cannot imagine this costume was worn on campaign.

In addition, when in the forward or firing trunnion position the weight of the gun tube was not distributed evenly between the carriage and limber; moving the gun tube back to the second trunnion position spread the weight better between the carriage and limber. Moving the gun tube took time and immense effort on the part of the gun crew, and made deploying the gun slower. For short moves on the battlefield (and undoubtedly for longer ones as neither commanders nor crews wanted to hump heavy gun barrels all day), the gun barrel was left in the firing position. Rather than limbering the gun, the horse artillery tended to drag the gun around the field with a *prolonge*: a thick rope connecting the trail end of the gun carriage to the limber axle. To overcome this General Marmont proposed a 6-pdr to replace both the 4-pdr and 8-pdr. All of this boiled down into the new artillery system of An XI, which witnessed a total redesign of the artillery equipment then in use. None of these new guns made it to the Grande Armée, however, and due to a process of logistical collapse, most of the field artillery with 1st Corps at Austerlitz were captured Hanoverian pieces. Bernadotte's Corps had 38 guns: 1st Division had 4 × 3-pdr, 4 × 6-pdr and 2 × howitzers, 2nd Division 5 × 3-pdr, 5 × 6-pdr and 2 × howitzers, the Ligh Cavalry 2 × 6-pdr, 2 × 3-pdr, 2 × howitzer and the reserve, 4 × 12-pdr, 2 × 6-pdr, 2 × 3-pdr and 2 × howitzers. Davout had French guns with him, 8 × 4-pdr, 24 × 8-pdr 8 × 12-pdr and 8 × howitzer. Soult likewise had French guns, 6 × 4-pdr, 18 × 8-pdr, 6 × 12-pdr and 8 × howitzers. The cavalry reserve under Murat had 2 × 4-pdr, 16 × 8-pdr, 2 × 12-pdr and 8 × howitzers and the reserve 8 × 4-pdr, 22 × 8-pdr, 18 × 12-pdr and 8 × howitzers. The Imperial Guard horse artillery was equipped with 6 × 4-pdr, 12 × 8-pdr, and 6 × howitzers.[8]

The artillery of France during the Napoléonic epoch was of a highly heterogeneous nature with guns and carriages of different generations used side by side with captured equipment. The success of the French artillery at the time lay not in the guns they used; the main and fundamental difference was in the way in which the guns were used and the mentality of the officer corps. The tactical use to which an individual battery could be used were many and various. In defence, it would be a powerful deterrent to attacking enemy infantry, the gunners always trying to fire into opposing infantry and cavalry masses rather than artillery. In this way, attacking enemy formations would be broken up and disorganised by the time they reached the French line. The sound of the bombardment would also reassure the French infantry.

In the defence of villages, the battery would be concealed by strong cover, if available. Normally, the battery would be placed on the flanks in order to give enfilade fire. The same tactic would be used in open country. Cross fires and enfilades were foremost in every gunner's mind. When used to support an infantry attack, the battery would once again seek to obtain a position where it could fire into the opposing troops' flank. The closer the battery could get to the selected target the better – get up close and shoot quick was one French artillerist's maxim. However, this tactic required quick reactions to guard against sudden counter-attacks. To some extent the danger of this tactic could be overcome by leapfrogging batteries forward in alternate sections or by approaching behind a cavalry or infantry screen, increasing the surprise factor, which could often rout

Velite – apprentice or cadet officer – of *Grenadiers à Pied* in full dress, c.1805.

an inexperienced enemy troop formation on its own. A more certain method was the adoption of the massed battery, but such tactical innovations were a few years off.

We have been unable to locate any details of the dress of the foot and horse artillery.

Train d'Artillerie

The second great innovation of the Consular years, after the introduction of *cuirassiers*, was the militarisation of the artillery train.

The desire to maximise returns led the contractors to neglect the drivers, their animals and equipment. To preserve their investment in material and horses, the contractors, frequently unhitched their guns and abandoned them at the first shot, leaving the gunners to manhandle the guns about the battlefield as best they could. At the battle of Novi (15 August 1799) the contractors abandoned their guns and caissons in a defile during a retreat, which led to the rearguard being cut off from its line of retreat. Upon becoming First Consul, Napoléon militarised the artillery train with the decree of 3 January 1800. Under the terms of the decree each battalion had an Elite company, usually attached to the mounted, or horse, artillery, the remaining three companies being attached to foot artillery, *dépôt* and parks.

Each battalion was a self-contained, cohesive organisation attached permanently to an artillery regiment. The decree of 20 September 1804 increased the number of Battalions to 10. The 1ᵉ Bataillon was reviewed at Lille on *13 Brumaire An 13* (4 November 1804). The men were dressed in 476 *habits* worn with a sleeveless *gilet*, 570 *capotes*, 408 stable coats, 234 pairs of *culottes de peau* and 230 pairs of stable trousers. Headdress was a *chapeau*, 504 being in use, the men wore dragoon boots, carried a *sabre briquet* from a cow hide waistbelt and were issued a *giberne* and *banderole*. Clothing was made from *gris de fer* and *bleu nationales* broadcloth. For stable duties, 500 pairs of shoes were issued.[9] We assume this was representative of all the battalions. In theory, each squadron had an elite company attached to the horse artillery, to:

> be composed of the strongest, most skilled and most experienced of men. Three others will be aimed at service parks, squares and artillery on foot, and the last will remain in the depot and will provide replacements.
>
> III. Each elite company will consist of eighty men, including sous-officiers, and will be commanded by a sergeant major, two sergeants and three corporals.[10]

Yet by July 1801 the elite companies had been disbanded.[11] The archive paperwork for the clothing and equipment of the train is hugely fragmented and very little can be found relating to the pre-1814 period.

The Imperial and Royal Guard

Marshal Bessières was nominal commander of the Guard: the *Grenadiers à Pied*, *Chasseurs à Pied* and Royal Guard formed the infantry contingent. The Grenadiers and *Chasseurs à Cheval*, along with the Mamelukes and Elite Gendarmes, provided the cavalry contingent.

Officer of *Chasseurs à Pied* in full dress, *c.*1805. The scarlet collar may be an artist's error.

The light artillery and Marines formed their own enclave of specialists supported by the artillery train. All in all, a force of 5,500 officers and men with 24 guns. The guard was small and elite.

Based in Paris in comfortable lodgings, the Imperial Guard did not suffer the same deprivations as the men of the *Ligne*, *Légère* and cavalry. Unlike the *Ligne*, we have an embarrassment of riches for the clothing of the guard, but we have almost nothing concerning its training, living conditions and morale in the weeks and months before the campaign began with which to compare to the troops of the line.

For a detailed examination of how the Guard was dressed during the campaign, the author's companion volumes on the Guard Infantry and Guard Mounted troops (published by Frontline) are recommended reading. The archives of the Italian Royal Guard were destroyed during the Second World War.

It is worth making some mention of how the *Garde Imperiale* was dressed at Austerlitz. Like their colleagues in the *Ligne*, they did not wear full dress. On *22 Prairial An 13* (11 June 1805) Colonel Hulin, in preparation for the coming campaign, ordered that the grenadiers were to have two pairs of shoes, one good pair to be worn, the other pair to be placed into the *havresac*, along with the smock, *veste* and linen *pantalons*. Covers for plumes and bearskins were to be made. The newly issued white broadcloth *culottes* were to be saved 'for best' and the old tricot *culottes* worn in their place.[12] A week or so later, General Hulin ordered on *6 Messidor An 13* (25 June 1805) that on route marches grenadiers were to wear the *surtout*, *veste*, black stock, grey gaiters and *chapeau*. Oddly, leg wear is not listed but must have been worn, and likely were white tricot *culottes* issued at the start of the year and their linen *pantalons*.[13]

As war loomed, on 24 August Hulin ordered that in the forthcoming campaign the grenadiers were to wear the *surtout*, black stock, grey gaiters and *chapeau*. The bearskins were to be placed in their case and carried on the *havresac*. The men were to carry their full equipment and campaign equipment, which included their *capotes*, *gamelles*, *marmites*, *grand bidons*, and *petit bidons*, as well as hatchets and shovels. A few days later, on *11 Fructidor An 13* (29 August 1805), General Hulin ordered that the men's *habits*, as well as *vestes* and *culottes* in white cotton and white gaiters were to be packed into bales organised into company, and placed into stores.[14] Clearly the grenadiers did not wear full dress at Austerlitz as it was left behind in Paris! They wore bearskins devoid of cords and plumes, *capotes*, linen *pantalons de route* and grey gaiters. We assume their *Chasseurs à Pied* colleagues followed suit.

Chapter 14

The School of Boulogne: Success or Failure?

While at Boulogne, the very nature of French government was changed: following the Cadoudal plot – masterminded by the Comte d'Artois and radicalised *émigres* from England – the Republic evolved into an Empire. The Consulship had already changed from three to one, and now the First Consul was Emperor of the French. It is undeniable that many officers and men at Boulogne were no lovers of Bonaparte, or the new Imperial regime. Beset by external and internal threats, the concentration of troops a few days' march from Paris gave the new Emperor a powerful force close to hand if needed to secure his position. Secondly, Napoléon spared no effort to bind the army to his cause, and inter alia the nation, and to shape their political and moral outlook. More than training men to be soldiers, the camp of Boulogne forged a sense of identity and sense of unified purpose among the army. In part this was created through conscription: joining the army – even if despised – transformed a peasant into a soldier: by being issued a uniform, he was responsible for its care and maintenance, providing a sense of discipline, duty and pride in a well turned out set of kit. Joining the army was – as with the armed forces today – a transformative experience: one that was hated and resented by many, but also embraced in huge numbers. Soldiers had a stake in their company, their regiment, their officers and their leader, the emperor, in a way that civilians did not. The relationship between soldier and the Bonaparte regime was forged here at Boulogne, and came to define France. France was militarised: France became not a nation with an armed force, but a nation in arms: a vast training camp of men and horses, being fed and clothed by an economy, which was directed to feed the ever-growing demands of the militarised state. This sense of identity and belief in Napoléon created here at Boulogne shaped France for the next decade to unify the armed forces and nation into a single military machine. The development of this sense of identity is beyond the scope of this work, but falling within its remit we must ask how successful was the camp at Boulogne at forging conscripts into soldiers?

The Infantry

General Duhesme reflected in 1806 on his own experience of his time at Boulogne, and drew a number of conclusions. Coming in for particular criticism was the reliance on the over-mechanical approach of the Prussian school, which he lamented had been excessively resorted to. 'Recruits were tormented for six months,' he noted, commenting bitterly 'their chests often damaged in order to teach them the first position, how to march in step and how to bear arms; every morning the poor devils were kept motionless

Chasseur à Pied in full dress, *c*.1805. As with the Grenadiers, they wore *surtouts* and overall trousers on campaign.

or in awkward positions for two or three hours at a time, enough to put off even those keenest on the military life.'[1]

The reality of the training programme, and how successful it may have been, is borne out by the following examples:

I Corps

The 1804 inspection revealed that the 8ᵉ *régiment de la Ligne* could drill very well according to the 1791 regulation, but the officers had trouble in keeping the lines dressed and their position. Colonel Outie gave his orders with great precision. The men executed charges with fury, it was reported, and fired very well. Schauenbourg ordered battalion fanions made from cloth were to be produced by the regiment to help the alignments and dressings. Schauenbourg also reminded the colonel that the accelerated pace of 120 paces per minute was not to be used for movements in line and the ordinary pace of 90 paces per minute was to be used, the accelerated pace to be only used in the charge.[2]

The same was true in the 27ᵉ *Légère:* General Rivaud remarked about the *sous-officiers'* abilities, 'that they lack skill and precision in acting as guides' and moreover lacked precision in 'dressing their companies [...] and keeping the lines straight' on manoeuvres. Rivaud recommended the *sous-officiers* attend classes to improve their theoretical and practical knowledge, and their failings, he reasoned, explained why the training of the men was not as good as it could have been. The officers also came in for criticism, and the colonel was ordered to make closer supervision of their training and to establish a school of instruction.[3] The regiment on manoeuvres conducted them at 120 paces a minute rather than 90.[4]

Similar comments were made about the 45ᵉ: the regiment's manoeuvres were described as good, and discipline as 'good and just'. Schauenbourg had to remind the colonel that the accelerated pace of 120 paces per minute was no longer used for movements in line and the ordinary pace of 90 paces per minute was to be used, the accelerated pace to be only used in the charge.[5] Almost exactly the same comments were made about the brigaded 54ᵉ *de Ligne*. The regiment's manoeuvres were described as 'passable' and it was well commanded by the superior officers and without exception by the *sous-officiers*. The inspector was very satisfied with the manner and conduct of the officers and *sous-officiers*, the way they gave commands, and the way the orders were executed. The officers, it was noted, used their épée to dress the lines, as well as to pass instruction. The rank and file needed better instruction in keeping the lines dressed – the soldiers who did not know their left and right were to be sent back to the depot. The placing of battalion guides by the adjutant and battalion commanders needed more precision, it was reported. To aid the guides, battalion fanions were to be made. Schauenbourg also reminded the colonel about the pacing regulations.

The 12ᵉ *de Ligne* was reviewed in early autumn 1804, when the inspector noted more training time was needed to be spent on the school of the platoon. He noted that the *sous-officiers* were diligently attending classes established by the major to improve their

Officer of Marines in full dress, c.1805.

theoretical and practical instruction. Of the men themselves, the cadre were considered 'solid and reliable' and carried out their movements well. However, the conscripts had much room for improvement and needed to lose bad habits and have their zeal tempered.[6] Reviewed almost a year later, the inspector noted many *sous-officiers* were German, and needed to study both French and the regulations to be more proficient at their duties. Both *sous-officiers* and men needed to spend more time learning the school of the platoon, and the officers were to strictly enforce the ordinary marching pace of '24 pouces and 76 paces a minute'. Battalion-level manoeuvres needed to be perfected.[7]

Clearly Bernadotte was marching his men faster than the regulations allowed for: was this a recent change to the regulation, or had he sought to modify the regulations to suit his own ends based on his field experience? In moving his men at a faster pace, was he hoping to make his corps more reactive to battlefield requirements?

III Corps

We imagine Davout's Corps as being the best in the army, but it was far from perfect: reviewed in early October 1804 by General of Brigade LaMartilliere, the 13ᵉ *Légère*'s *sous-officiers*, it was noted, needed to better apply their theoretical training – basically they lacked experience of command. In practice, their drill was good, but lacked uniformity, likewise of the men, which was largely down to the inexperience of the *sous-officiers*.[8] The 13ᵉ *Légère* was inspected again in summer 1805 at Gand by LaMartilleire, who reported enthusiastically on the improvements made in the training and instruction of the *sous-officiers* and men since he last reviewed them, thanks to regimental schools being established.[9]

When the 111ᵉ *de Ligne* was reviewed in early autumn 1804, the inspector noted that the men and officers had, for the major part, been in the service of the Sardinian Army, or came from Sardinia and spoke little French. The officers and men had bad habits, the officers' training in theory was 'passable' but that of the *sous-officiers* 'mediocre' and classes were to be set up to school the officers and *sous-officiers* in their jobs. Only 'the old soldiers' were good at their drills and theory, the inspector lamented, and they were the only ones who could run the school of the platoon. The inspector opined that the regimental schools should resolve a lot of the issues, especially language barriers.[10]

When the 21ᵉ *de Ligne* was reviewed at Cologne in summer 1805 discipline and drill was 'very satisfactory'. The majority of the regiment drilled very well, yet the inspector remarked that some officers, *sous-officiers* and men needed more instruction on theory and practice, especially corporals, many of whom who had no grounding in theory or practice of the regulations.[11]

The 85ᵉ *de Ligne* was reviewed on Bastille Day 1805, and the report remarks that the regiment's training was good and the officers knew and understood the *école de peleton*, as did the *sous-officiers*. However, the regiment's movements were carried out without any precision, which resulted from a lack of training and indecision of the *sous-officiers*. The *sous-officiers* were overall generally well versed in theory but many were far from

194 Napoleon's Army at Austerlitz

Marine in full dress, c.1805.

fully proficient in putting theory into practice. The inspector noted the regiment needed to work more at its drill and manoeuvres. Again, the inspector noted with much regret the *sous-officiers* delegated to teaching the new entrants also lacked the attributes and education needed for this task.[12]

Also coming in for criticism from Davout's command was the 51ᵉ *de Ligne* when it was reviewed on *12 Thermidor An 13* (31 July 1805). The inspector noted that the regiment's dressing was executed exactly as per the regulation of 1791, and added he was satisfied that the regiment could manoeuvre effectively and that the officers and *sous-officiers* were competent. However, when conducting battalion-level manoeuvres, the regiment struggled to keep the alignment and placing of companies and battalions in line of battle. Furthermore, he reported the drummers struggled to keep even time and the cadence would either slow or speed up. The drummers needed to better learn their trade, he recommended, and to learn the marching paces. He subsequently ordered that the battalion officers were to ensure that the correct intervals were maintained rather than allowing battalions to drift towards each other. To this end, the inspector ordered that the regiment's major was to drill the officers and men in the *école de peleton* and pay great attention to any irregularity, and to ensure the officers, *sous-officiers* and corporals knew their theory and practice thoroughly. It was clear, the inspector remarked, that 'the companies had not been drilled sufficiently well'.[13]

IV Corps

The only unit in Soult's command that came in for criticism was the 24ᵉ *Légère* when it was reviewed in late summer 1804. The inspector noted that the regiment faced discipline issues and warned the officers that they needed to be more vigilant in giving orders according to the regulation. They were instructed to establish a school to assist teaching the *sous-officiers* practice and theory.[14]

V Corps

When he came to review the 40ᵉ *régiment de Lignes*' drill in autumn 1804, General of Brigade Thiébault singled out sergeant majors Gadre, Poterie, Courtrois, and Grivel and corporals LaCroix and Duprette as being particularly weak in their theory of the 1791 regulation, as were the greater part of the *sous-officiers* of the two war battalions and the depot. The major needed to drill the officers and *sous-officiers* in the school of the *peleton* under the guidance of the adjutants. The grenadiers knew their drill, as one would expect from veteran soldiers, but the regiment needed to work hard on the *école du soldat*, i.e., rudimentary basic training, and also battalion drill. It was noted that previously regimental schools had helped train the regiment in executing the *école du bataillon*.[15]

Comment

Based on these inspections, Soult's IV Corps outclassed Davout's III Corps – although myth suggests Davout was the best officer in the army, it seems his corps was outclassed by Soult's. Again, if we ignore Bernadotte changing the regulations, I Corps drilled better than Davout's men. Quite clearly, training in the infantry was far from ideal, even among the regiments of the famed III Corps of Davout: it is clear the corps was struggling, and a long way from the perfection held in popular imagination.

Lack of motivation from officers and men to spend hours at drill, the huge influx of conscripts, and the discharge of veterans all impacted on the level of efficiency at drill across the army. We note from Napoléon's correspondence that both Ney and Marmont 'needed a kick up the rear' to get on with the task of instructing their troops. In spring 1804, Napoléon ranted to Ney after reviewing his corps: 'I hardly need tell you to manoeuvre your troops more diligently. The last time I saw them it looked as though they needed it.'[16] This is confirmed by a letter from General Loison, commanding the 2nd Division of Ney's Corps, who noted in late summer 1804 that the brigades 'manoeuvre quite well, but are weak on their alignments, marching in battle formation and marching to the flank'. More damning of Ney's laxity in drilling his corps, Loison continued to Berthier, the Minister of War:

> I have given orders to monitor this essential part of the officers' and men's education. The manoeuvres were well executed, particularly in 76^e, it entirely depended on the battalion commanders. The colonels are not yet capable of commanding evolutions in line, [...] Many captains are very weak in theory and practice of manoeuvres. They need a lot of practice to strengthen their knowledge [...] the colonel will be given orders so that the recruits are exercised twice a day in all the cantonments; Companies must manoeuvre at least three times a week and battalions twice. We will put the men in two ranks and make platoons of a narrower front whenever we will not be able to bring the whole battalion together, but it is important to make the battalion drill very often.[17]

Ney had 'taken his eye off the ball' when it came to training his command. Confirming the lack of drill, we find in reports and official correspondence, Fezenzac of the 59e tells us that his regiment hardly ever assembled for training, and carried out no skirmishing or marksmanship training.[18] Napoléon wrote to Marmont in March 1805: 'Recommend to your divisional commanders that they make their troops go through the firing drill twice a week, that they have target practice twice a week, and finally, that they perform drill evolutions three times a week. Have them form columns of attack by battalion, charge in column of attack, and deploy under the covering fire of the first division, with everyone firing upon reaching a line of battle.' He also told him to 'direct that each voltigeur company be instructed in promptly forming the square and immediately opening fire by files, so that skirmishers sent out in front of the battalion can quickly unite and fight off cavalry. Issue the necessary powder for these exercises and announce that these

Grenadier of the Italian Royal Guard. On campaign they wore overall trousers and a single-breasted *surtout*, as well as a greatcoat.

manoeuvres are most especially what I will have performed in my presence.'[19] In March 1805 Ney, perhaps to compensate for these failings, ordered:

> The Marshal Commander-in-Chief orders that the detail exercises by company are taken up in all the army regiments next Monday, the 27 of the month, and will take place, in the future, at least three hours every day. Corps commander will ensure the instructions of the *école du soldat* will be taught and all the lessons that successively follow; they will then attend to the *école du peleton*; and after that of the battalion, when the troop appears sufficiently educated. As long as detail exercises are deemed necessary for the instruction of the troop, they will take place four times a week. One day will be devoted for line steps, either by brigade or by division, as well as it will be ordered.[20]

One would have assumed such instructions would have been passed on a year or more earlier. Ney's ambitious plan relied on having effective instructors. We often think that the years of 1813 and 1814 were marked by a lack of veterans and instructors: not so. As early as 1805 the lack of competent *sous-officiers* to train conscripts, aligned with the pressing need to shorten training times to rapidly increase the size of the army, meant men marching to Vienna had to 'learn on the job' what was needed of them.

Keeping this in mind, for example the major of the 21e *de Ligne* admitted that 'the pressing needs of the war battalions too often oblige them to send absolutely raw recruits' to the war battalions.[21] We note similar issues in the 17e *Légère*, part of V Corps. General Laval reported that *sous-officiers* 'least able to undertake active serve, either by their infirmities or by their few talents' were sent to be training instructors, noting:

> as a result, the dépôt battalion is constantly devoid of officers and *sous-officiers*, and therefore the men in these battalions received neither means of instruction nor means of discipline. At this moment, the 3rd battalion of the 17e *Légère* is 667 men present under arms, and to command it there are only 14 officers, 16 sergeants and 47 corporals.[22]

As we noted earlier, a lack of trained cadre, often seen as a major issue in 1813, was already impacting on the army. For example, of the captains of the 12e *de Ligne*, it was noted in September 1804 that three were totally ignorant of the military regulations, and 'most of them were illiterate' and the battalion commanders were 'totally incapable of conducting manoeuvres'. One captain was 40 years old, 'had no morals' and was 'incapable of instruction', another was aged 51 and unable to fulfil his functions and a third aged 53 'an old soldier, who knows the service'. The major part of the old soldiers in the regiment were 'untutored', i.e., they had learned their trade in combat, which was not necessarily according to regulation.[23]

Removing officers who were judged unfit for command opened the way for officers educated by the invigorated military instructions in France, notably the school at

Fontainebleau and the *Ecole Militaire* in Paris. The officers who were removed were put on half-pay as supernumeraries and told to go home. Theoretically, they were to be recalled to active service to fill vacancies as they appeared. Many did indeed go home, but equally many wished to continue their careers. As in Italy in 1796, Napoléon set up an *ad hoc* all-officer formation for supernumeraries. By serving in this formation, these men could demonstrate their commitment to the regime, maintain contact with their comrades, and in sharing their hardships and dangers, hopefully win back an active command. This formation provided a pool of officers available as immediate replacements for battlefield attrition, even if they were not the best-trained individuals in the army.[24]

The Cavalry

As with the infantry, the quality of instruction relied on the quality of instructor: in the 2e *Hussard*, it was reported 'the equitation is quite good, however there is no one in this regiment to notice for their talents in equitation'. Garrisoned in Celle, near Hanover, the men were lodged with the townsfolk, the regiment was 'in good spirits and motivated in their affection for the government' and he noted 'the horsemanship is quite good'.[25] Concerning the 3e *Hussard*, it was noted that 'equitation is very well taught by Mr. Chevalier, an officer led by the most commendable zeal, and perfectly educated with everything that is detailed by the functions entrusted to him. It is done whenever time allows; however, the regiment does not have a covered riding school.' In the same regiment, a second lieutenant is noted as a 'very good horseman and good instructor'.

Among the officers in the 4e *Hussard*, 'there is an officer who knows the details of equitation perfectly, which he teaches in the regiment'.[26] General de Beaumont reviewed the 5e *Hussard* in summer 1803. The regiment's manoeuvres were good, the men overall rode well and cared well for their horses. Discipline in the regiment was good – in fact everything about the regiment met his satisfaction.[27] Similarly, in the 18e *Dragons*, it was noted that Lieutenant Zénon Lefebvre 'rides well on horseback', and in consequence the regiment rode well thanks to his instruction.

Conversely, the conscripts of the 16e *Chasseurs* who arrived at the barracks had received no instruction. Inspector General Bourcier ranted to the Minister of War over a lack of horses for the riding school and an instructor to teach them.[28] In a similar manner, the 21e *Dragons*' General Canclaux ordered the regiment to buy ten quiet and docile horses to teach the new recruits. The officers and *sous-officiers* were ordered by the inspector to pay better attention to the regulations and the riding master in teaching the men in their foot and mounted drills.[29] Reviewed in June 1803, the regiment's foot drill and arms drill was very well executed, according to General Oudinot. However, despite this promising improvement, Oudinot noted that the men needed more training as the movements lacked precision in their execution and the words of command given were not uniform. The officers could ride well, Oudinot noted, but the men needed more training to become proficient riders, adding that the regiment desperately needed new remounts.[30]

In autumn 1804 General Barageuy d'Hillier reported about the newly converted dragoon regiments – the 22e to 30e – that:

Colonel of the *Grenadiers à Cheval* in full dress, *c.*1805. On campaign officers wore a *surtout*, and the saddlery had blue lace rather than gold.

None of these regiments has yet perfected the spirit of the new arm in which he was placed. Some act like heavy cavalry in all their movements, the others are disorderly and disunited like light troops. I believe it would be useful (if possible) these regiments were united with three or four old regiments of dragoons at the end of the summer … so as to manoeuvre together during Vendémiaire and Brumaire. We think that this would do the greatest good to the esprit de corps, would arouse emulation, excite zeal, and destroy, better than ten inspections, the prejudices and the vicious *habits* that still persist that make training slow.[31]

By the time of the July 1805 inspection, this group of regiments were praised for their position on horseback, but the bulk of the men's equitation had yet to be mastered. The men also needed to pay more attention to their horses. The remaining men from the 13ᵉ *Cavalerie* were perfect in their training and manoeuvre, but overall, the regiment's evolutions as cavalry or infantry were deplorable.[32] The other regiments were still far from good soldiers or horsemen in summer 1805.[33] Lack of training would impact on the combat effectiveness of the 3rd and 4th Dragoon Divisions. Cavalry cost far more to equip than the infantry, and took far longer to become effective combat troops. It was to the hard core of the old *cavalerie* regiments – the new *cuirassiers* – that the bulk of the fighting in the forthcoming campaign fell. One gets the feeling that Napoléon never fully understood the needs of the cavalry: he often blindly assumed that a man on a horse was a competent trooper. Infantry conscripts could be taught to shoot and handle their muskets on the march and during 'down time'. The cavalry needed at least six months to bring a conscript up to a similar standard. Many commanders were forced to train their men on the march, a phenomenon that lasted until the end of the Empire. It is undeniable that although Napoléon had been able to regenerate his mounted arm quickly into the three arms he envisioned for it, it lacked training, experience and cohesion.

The reality of the situation the army faced as it mobilised in late summer 1805 was far from ideal. General Bourcier, commanding 4th Dragoon Division, informed Napoléon on *18 Fructidor An 14* (5 September 1805) that his division of dragoons was plagued with injured horses caused by the ignorance of the men, noting:

the number of injured horses is almost unprecedented. The colonels or commanders of corps to whom I expressed my surprise represented to me that it was due particularly to the fact that they had too many conscripts, the majority of whom were put on horseback without having received the first instructions on how to saddle and bridle and on the handling of weapons on horseback. In fact, there are far too many recruits and too few veterans in the division's regiments. It would be much to be desired, for the good of the service, that a part of the former could be exchanged for old dragoons, then there would be less numerical imbalance between the number of the old dragoons and new in each regiment.[34]

Adjutant-Commandant of the Imperial Guard in full dress. On campaign they wore a simple *surtout* with embroidery to the collar, and a *chapeau* rather than bearskins. The saddlery again had blue lace and not gold.

The School of Boulogne: Success or Failure? 203

Standard bearer of *Grenadiers à Cheval*, c.1805.

Bourcier, was in essence, complaining that the cuirassiers had kept the best men when the *cavalerie* had been converted; moreover, the regiments of dragoons that already existed had the monopoly on veterans, that could be usefully sent to the newly convered regiments. Bascially, the army lacked sufficient veteran soldiers to act as cadres. Again, we imagine this to be a problem primarily in 1813–14: not so. General de Beaumont, at the head of the 3rd Dragoon Division, adds:

> I must inform you, Monsieur le Maréchal, that I have many wounded horses. The main cause of this is that in the corps there are many men who have almost never sat on horseback […] about 150 men per regiment exercise well on foot, but know nothing on horseback, while the division of General Baraguey-d'Hilliers has at least 900 men per regiment trained on horseback.[35]

He asked that the men who could not ride be sent to the foot dragoons and replaced with men who could ride. Clearly the rapid expansion of dragoon regiments from 500 men in 1802 to almost 1,000 men had had disastrous consequences regarding training. The same story was true for the heavy cavalry. General Nansouty carried out a shakedown review of the cavalry reserve and found that it lacked mounts: of the 496 horses with the 1^e *Carabiniers*, 13 were considered too young for service and 43 too old. In the 2^e *Carabiniers*, out of 469 horses, 25 were too young, 30 too old and 34 sick. The regiment needed 100 horses on 28 August 1805, days before it was marched to war. In the 2^e *Cuirassiers*, of 530 horses only 470 were suitable for service, while in the 3^e *Cuirassiers* of 512 horses just 481 were available. The 9^e *Cuirassiers* needed 143 horses as it only had 367 available for service, of which 342 were with the war squadrons. In the 12^e *Cuirassiers*, out of 502 horses, 452 were available for service, with 365 in the war squadrons. If each regiment was to field 500 men per regiment, Nansouty noted, then the cavalry reserve needed horses. Nansouty noted he needed six months to complete the cavalry reserve.[36]

We are left wondering about the training level of the Grande Armée, and we must wonder if the appellation of 'best' should go to the men who survived Austerlitz, and spent much of 1806 undergoing drill. It is undeniable that Austerlitz 'winnowed the wheat from the chaff' and for those that survived, the time of peace in Germany thereafter was the crucible that made the Grande Armée and not the Camp of Boulogne.

Chapter 15

Desertion

As we noted earlier, the army at Boulogne, both at the coast and dispersed cantonments, had major issues with 'troop retention'. The French army of the time had two classifications of 'deserter' following the law of *6 Floréal An 11* (26 April 1803) relating to a levy of conscripts.

The *refractaire* was a conscript who went AWOL on his way to his depot after being conscripted. He, and his family, was treated differently to a true 'deserter'. The *refractaire*s family would be 'civilly responsible' for his conduct, and a fine of 1,500fr would be levied (rather pointlessly, as most families just didn't have that kind of money). Another method used against the families, or neighbours, was the imposition of *garnisaires*, a requirement to provide lodging for up to four soldiers. The National Guard were deployed to seek out these men and take them back to the army. Such was the scale of the problem, on *19 Vendémiaire An 12* (12 October 1803) eleven depots of refractory conscripts were established in Lille, Givet, Luxembourg, Strasbourg, Besançon, Briançon, Perpignan, Bayonne, Saint-Martin-de-Ré, Caen and Alexandria. The men were isolated from other troops, being confined to their barracks under guard. Here the men undertook military training and work for the state.[1]

A deserter, a soldier who had undergone basic training, been issued arms and uniform and had gone AWOL from camp or depot, would face a sliding scale of punishment if caught. According to the law of *17 Ventose An8* (8 March 1800), a fine of up to 1,500fr could be levied. The deserter under the law of *14 Floréal An 12* (4 May 1804) could be sentenced to the *Boulet*, for which he was shackled to an 8lb cannonball on a 2.5m chain and required to carry out public works either mending roads, digging canals or in a workshop of the state for eight to ten hours a day. They would not be in uniform, would wear clogs and their heads would be shaved. Notably, the men were not allowed to shave. The death sentence was implemented for the following: deserting to the enemy, deserting while on guard duty, leading a plot to desert, and deserting with arms.

Despite these penalties, men deserted by the thousand. A bounty of 12fr was to be paid to anyone who captured a deserter.

So bad was desertion that on *27 Germinal An 13* (17 April 1805) Lannes issued orders to strengthen camp guards to stop men getting away, and made arrangements to pay the bounty on capturing men as promptly as possible. He hoped paying the Gendarmes and other soldiers their bounty money 'there and then' would encourage a higher level of surveillance. The necessity of this action speaks volumes about the conditions in the camp.[2] Indeed, when the 28e *de Ligne* was reviewed in the middle weeks of September 1804, the major reported that over the previous year 86 men had died and a staggering

Trooper of *Grenadiers à Cheval* in full dress, *c.*1805. On campaign, the men wore *surtouts*, and the plumes and cords from the bearskins were stowed away. The lace cross on the *portmanteaux* may be an error.

636 had deserted.³ The 28ᵉ was not an isolated occurrence. Reviewed at Cologne in summer 1805, of 963 conscripts for *An 12* (1803–04) that the 21ᵉ *de Ligne* were allocated, the major noted 193 had deserted before reaching the corps, classed as refractory men, and 488 deserted while with the regiment and if caught faced the death penalty. Of the men already serving, desertion was still a problem. The major noted 103 men had quit their ranks, 88 men had died and a further 118 were sick in hospital. The reason for desertion and the high rate of sickness was by and large, the major noted, because many of the barracks were insufficiently ventilated; some rooms had no windows, while others had windows that could not be opened and were positioned high up on the wall, out of reach of the men. The men suffered from cold and bad rations.⁴

These episodes were not isolated incidents, as the following order from Napoléon to Berthier on *14 Frimaire An 12* (6 December 1803) attests:

> I beg you citizen minister to keep at the disposal of General Moncey a sum of 50,000 Fr to pay the gendarmes the 12 Fr for each deserter they will arrest. A hundred deserters at the Saint-Omer camp have already been arrested; make sure the gendarmes are paid immediately the gratuities due to them.⁵

A soldier deserted for a multiplicity of factors, beyond the most obvious being to escape the army and return home. The seminal study by Professor Alan Forrest on desertion and resistance to conscription is essential reading.⁶ Desertion carried the sentence of death if the soldier took with them their musket if caught, or 12 years' imprisonment in a chain gang. Despite these penalties, thousands set their minds to escaping the situation in which they found themselves. Undervalued in terms of renumeration compared to civilian employment, the poor living standards, lack of food as well as loss of status all contributed to the reasoning behind men deserting. As Forrest points out, the constant thread in soldiers' letters home was homesickness, the feeling of alienation, and the thirst for news from home. Failure to receive news from home, or bad news from home, put many conscripts in a state of agitation – we see this in their writing – which further influenced the desire to desert.⁷

The system in which conscripts were trained and fed was open to much abuse and no doubt contributed to many conscripts heading home. The instructors in the 8ᵉ *de Ligne* responsible for knocking the conscripts into shape literally did just that. These men were veterans with better martial ability than any skill at instruction, and were often ill-educated. Joining a regiment that had an already well-developed *esprit de corps* meant that for any new entrant the induction process was a painful one. To begin with, it is noted that at the Camp of Boulogne, the instructors in the 8ᵉ *de Ligne* were recorded as beating the conscripts who failed to obey orders, or struggled to learn their left and right.⁸ Facing a barrage of abuse from the *sous-officiers*, the new entrant found little respite in the barrack room. Regimental traditions could be hard on new arrivals. The most widespread induction ritual was that newcomers to the barrack room had to 'grease the pot', which meant standing the older soldiers a meal and drinks, which was open to rife abuse. Many

Trumpeter of *Grenadiers à Cheval* in full dress, c.1805. On campaign the trumpeters wore a *surtout*, and the saddlery was sky blue rather than crimson.

men deserted to escape the debts they had incurred 'to grease the pot' as they could never hope to discharge them.⁹ Conscripts already intimidated by their recent arrival could hardly refuse this rite of passage into the regimental bosom. One such conscript recounts it was:

> customary among old chasseurs, without which, they said, one could not become a good soldier. I consented to everything, and by acting and talking like them I became smart and got on the right side of my comrades, who showed me what I needed to know. Now I serve without complaint and live untroubled.¹⁰

These tests of masculinity also had another purpose: to make the point to young recruits that they would only be accepted into military society when they had been initiated into its codes. Despite some of the older soldiers being barely a few months' senior to the new arrivals, they nevertheless condescendingly addressed new comers as 'conscripts' and they were the target of their mockery. The bullied became the bullies in order to fit into military society. Young Sabon, who joined the 69ᵉ *Ligne* at Boulogne, was bullied and abused until he had proved his worth by being literate.¹¹ Major Dellard of the 46ᵉ *Ligne* emphasised education to prevent soldiers becoming bored and sought to limit violence towards conscripts.¹² Clearly, for the order to be written, abuse was an issue.

If the conscripts suffered at the hands of older soldiers in the barrack room, the *sous-officier* instructors on the parade ground were no gentler. *Sous-officiers* then and now would bark out the various sections of the manual, which the conscripts, who in some cases spoke French badly or not at all in case of the Gascons and those from Lorraine in the 40ᵉ *de Ligne*, simply did not understand what was being asked of them. In response, the instructors assaulted the conscripts, making cruel remarks and sarcastic comments, considering them 'dumb animals'. Thiébault ordered the *sous-officiers* to moderate their draconian ways, and required them to show more respect to both the men and officers.¹³ Similarly, when the 24ᵉ *Légère* was reviewed in late summer 1804, the inspector noted many men only spoke Basque, and did not understand the words of command from the officers and *sous-officiers*. The regiment's major reported that over the previous year 111 men had died, 282 had deserted, and 37 had been discharged from hospital as unfit for further service.¹⁴ Starving, sick, housed in muddy holes in the ground, unable to understand French and wondering when 'you were going home', is it little wonder the desertion rate was high?

Even when in barracks, life was little better.

Inspected on *19 Vendémiaire An 13* (11 October 1804), the 1ᵉ *Dragons* mustered 590 other ranks. Over the past year, 33 men had died, 96 had deserted, and 4 had been discharged from hospital as unfit for further service. Barracked at Rambouillet, the lodgings were in good condition, but warned the inspector, 'there exists not one blanket long enough to cover the men, they are all too short and in bad condition, it is necessary to replace these. However, the beds and furniture are in good condition. The food is acceptable and the register well maintained. The stables are good and well maintained.'

Kettledrummer of *Grenadiers à Cheval*, c.1805. This uniform was only ever seen in Paris, but remained in use till the regiment was disbanded in 1815. The kettledrums, banners, harness and uniform was made in 1805 and, as far as can be ascertained, never replaced.

The bread was described as good, made by bakers in Rambouillet with flour supplied from the stores at Versailles.[15] In the 16ᵉ *Dragons*, the inspector noted that the men were based in the citadel, but many of the barracks were in very poor condition, many rooms could not be occupied and the men had to lodge in corridors or in any room they could find. Every scrap of wood the regiment could obtain for heating and cooking had been burned. Being cold and damp perhaps explains the number of men deserting.[16] Rations, when available, were often far from ideal. In the 33ᵉ *de Ligne* the bread issued was considered bad as it was made from mouldy flour, but that was all that was available.[17] Supply and demand issues made prices rise: the generous and humane Marshal Bernadotte used his own funds to supplement the finances of his corps to ensure the men were fed.[18]

What follows are three case studies of how abuse was recognised and sought to be remedied to try and stem endemic desertion rates.

10ᵉ *Légère*

Lieutenant Charles d'Agoult, of the 10ᵉ *Légère*, recalls he was:

> tired of commanding drill for long, monotonous hours, and above all of seeing the poor conscripts tormented, robbed and humiliated. You cannot imagine how bleak was the fate of those unfortunate children at that time. If I recounted everything they had to bear in the way of thefts and sufferings, people would believe it an exaggeration.[19]

The archive of the regiment confirms this bleak impression. The 10ᵉ was reviewed on *19 Vendémiaire An 13* (11 October 1804) which tells us that since the 1803 inspection, 35 men had died of disease and 158 had deserted and 90 had been discharged from the regimental hospital as unfit for further service. Based at Corveux (?) the barracks were considered old, insufficient to house the men and immediate work was needed to make them fit for purpose. The furniture was noted as being in bad condition, and moreover 300 additional beds were needed, insufficient blankets existed and the mattresses all had to be replaced. Soldiers were deserting because they were cold, hungry and because of 'the severity of the discipline', which was inflicted 'for the slightest error or act of insubordination'. The colonel in essence 'beat' his men to obey orders and to be good soldiers.[20] Yet such methods went rewarded: General Saint-Hilaire reported that 'Colonel Pouzet's unit is the finest of the division' in a document of *26 Floréal An 13* (14 May 1805).[21]

3ᵉ *de Ligne*

Becoming a soldier either broke a conscript entirely and he deserted or 'he played the game' of bullying and abuse. The 3rd battalion had gained 773 men over the previous year, of which 183 were sick in hospital, 39 had died and 242 had deserted by *3 Brumaire An 13* (25 October 1804). The inspector noted that the *sous-officiers* who instructed the

Officer of *Chasseurs à Cheval* in field service dress, c.1805. This is how the regiment appeared at Austerlitz.

new conscripts did so with '*sang froid*' and the manner in which they gave out punishment was too harsh, yet, acknowledged the inspector, the zeal in which the men were trained got results as they were very proficient at drill. Also affecting desertion was the fact that the barracks at Meaux were designed to hold 400 men but held double that number, and were 'literally falling down'. Making matters worse, bedding and beds were in terrible condition, the bread issue was of bad quality, so too the meat.[22] Reviewed on *18 Thermidor An 13* (August 1805), the regiment had lost 46 men as deserters. Little wonder as the men suffered under the severe discipline of the regiment.[23] The colonel's reign of terror lasted into 1806, when Rapp reported to the Emperor that conscripts fled the regiment due to the harsh punishments.[24] Harsh justice, however, seems to have melded the 3e *de Ligne* into a crack regiment, its drill 'perfectly executed'.[25] Many readers who were in the armed forces can relate similar experiences.

40e *de Ligne*

The regiment was inspected on *19 Vendémiaire An 13* (11 October 1804), when the major reported that since the previous review 136 men had died of illness and 234 had deserted. Quartered in the Saint Charles district of Orleans, the lodgings needed major and immediate repairs. The beds, mattresses and blankets likewise all needed to be replaced. Bread and other rations were of low quality.[26]

Reviewed on *6 Thermidor An 13* (July 1805) by General Thiébault, he noted that since the last review, 62 men had died and 240 had deserted, with a further 125 discharged to their home from the regimental hospital as unfit for further service. Housed in the former convent of the Jacobins, the barracks were clean and in good condition, while those of the depot battalion were the best imaginable. The regimental library had 300 volumes, the books concentrating on history, 'the classics', the art of war 'and the other sciences necessary for an officer'. The colonel and major encouraged the officers to teach the men to read and write. The regimental school, established the previous year, was well stocked with pens, ink and paper under the care of Captain Lefevre and was teaching the men to read and write French rather than their native tongue. The officers had amassed 300 books into the regimental library. It stocked both literature and books on the military, and books of instruction. Reading gave the men something to do.[27]

Language barriers, being wrested from hearth and home by conscription, and seeking to escape the living conditions they encountered, all drove men to desert in the tens of thousands.

Mutilation
Alan Forrest, in his seminal study of soldiers' letters, comments:

> It is, indeed, surprising how many of the men in the revolutionary and especially in the Napoléonic armies seem to have considered the option of deserting at one time or another. For most of them the issue was far more a practical than a moral one,

and it was only fear of the terrible penalties that could be imposed on deserters – long years in gaol, forced labour, and the remote if ever-present threat of the death penalty – that made them grit their teeth and stay in their units. Yet there were times when almost any means of escape could seem attractive; and it could take very little, in the morose and depressed state in which so many of them found themselves, to make desertion seem a worthwhile option – a spell in hospital, the loss of a friend in battle, a mother's failure to reply to a letter, homesickness exacerbated by uncertainty.[28]

Rather than face the penalty of desertion, some men took ever more drastic steps: they self-mutilated to escape. Historians concentrate on this as an aspect of the conscripts of 1813 and 1814, yet it was a phenomenon at the Camp of Boulogne and across the army. The 72^e *de Ligne* based at the camp of Boulogne had major issues keeping conscripts in the ranks. In the year ending September 1804, 315 men had deserted and 41 had died: rather incredibly it was accepted and moreover, considered 'normal' at the time, that at least one soldier would die every week. a tragic waste of humn life. Conscript Antoine Thom cut off the fingers of his right hand with a hatchet to avoid military service. Thom was not alone in this extreme act of homespun surgery: Jacques Caron took a hatchet and cut off the first two fingers of his right hand so as not to be able to fire a musket. Louis Marinier did likewise, so too Pierre Panmier.[29] These were not isolated incidents.

Something was clearly terribly wrong in the world if this act was resorted to with the consequential impact on being able to earn a living in 'civvy street' and the risk of infection. As Forrest points out, self-mutilation, either before conscription or once with the army, was a 'ticket home'. Since 1798, self-mutilation to avoid conscription had begun to worry the war ministry in Paris.[30] At the camp of Boulogne it became endemic, much as it had been in the 1760s and 1770s to escape the militia ballot.[31] So serious was the issue that an imperial decree of *8 Fructidor An 13* (26 August 1805) stated that any conscript found guilty of having mutilated himself either when initially balloted or when arriving with their regiment would be gaoled, then taken to a port and from there 'transported to the French colonies, to be employed there in any military or maritime service'. Furthermore, article 4 of the decree of 6 January 1807 stated anyone found to have self-mutilated to avoid military service was to be imprisoned for five years. On release, the men were to serve five years working building roads or canals in the colonies.[32] For such decrees to have been necessary, with the formation of companies of mutilated men, speaks volumes about the nature and scale of the issue, which has long been relatively ignored in the study of the Grande Armée.

Comment
Starving, living in holes in the ground, or freezing barracks, seeing their comrades dying of fever in fetid hospitals, can we be surprised that men were gripped by what was termed at the time *melancholie* or *nostalgie* or simply went home?[33] This state of acute melancholia was believed to be contagious, and epidemics occurred at the camps in Bruges in 1804 and

Trooper of *Chasseurs à Cheval* in full dress, *c.*1805.

Trooper of *Chasseurs à Cheval* in field service dress, *c.*1805. Turned out with a colpack rather than *chapeau*, this is how the unit was dressed at Austerlitz.

Montreuil in 1805. A number of medical theses sought to find answers; the preventive remedy prescribed by the physicians was not to mistreat conscripts in the early days of their service, as had been the case in the 40ᵉ *de Ligne* [and also the 3ᵉ and 8ᵉ *de Ligne*]. The *sous-officier* instructors were instructed – as in this case with the 40ᵉ *de Ligne* – to behave in a gentle and father-like manner. The treatise stressed that the only known cure was to talk with the conscript in his native tongue and to evoke subjects that touched him. But the most successful remedy for the most severely affected was to send them back home.[34] Thiébault and Suchet clearly had read or been informed about these treatises and, as we have seen, put them into action in a bold attempt to lessen desertion rates.[35] When we look at Ney's VI Corps we see that desertion was running at 25 per cent in the 69ᵉ *de Ligne* (224 deserted from 910 conscripts),[36] 6ᵉ *Légère* (331 deserted from 1,289 conscripts)[37] as well as the 25ᵉ *Légère* (156 deserted from 637 conscripts)[38] and at 35 per cent in the 96ᵉ *de Ligne* (150 deserted from 421 conscripts).[39] Among the 39ᵉ *de Ligne*, desertion was over 50 per cent of all recruits in the year September 1803 to September 1804, when some 92 men out of 159 conscripts went AWOL.[40] In mid-*Pluviose* (early February) 1804, the '*Conseil de guerre special*' of VI Corps condemned two men from the 69ᵉ *Ligne* and two men from the 6ᵉ *Légère* to fines of 1,500fr per man, and all four were sentenced to the chain gang for seven years for the crime of desertion.[41]

One of Ney's brigade commanders, Villatte, ordered on *28 Nivôse An 12* (25 February 1804):

> In accordance with the Consul's decree dated 19 Vendémiaire year XII, the Special Council is summoned for tomorrow ten in the morning to judge the named Jean-Marie CH …, soldier at the 69th infantry regiment. The War Council will […] be made up of citizens: Brun, colonel of the 69e infantry regiment, Tirion, captain-adjutant major in the same, Pascal, captain in the same regiment, Philippe, captain in the same regiment, Lelarge, lieutenant in the same regiment, Labory, captain in the same regiment, Mich [illegible], lieutenant to the 10e regiment of *Chasseurs à Cheval*, Collet, captain in the 69e infantry regiment, fulfilling the functions of rapporteur and government commissioner.[42]

Brutal instructors, inaction breeding boredom and difficulty adapting to regimental life caused some conscripts to fall into a state of depression or desertion. In consequence of being often forcibly torn from native soil and everything the young conscript had known, joining the army for many was not an adventure and was greeted with abject fear. They hated the sudden change it had wrought in their lives, and instead longed for the habits and customs of earlier times: this form of depression wreaked havoc among contingents of conscripts. The young men pined for what they had lost – family, friends, sometimes a bride – and simply lacked the mental capacity to contemplate a brutal death on the battlefield far from their loved ones and a future life away from hearth and home. A soldier who knows why he is fighting – the cause for his enlistment – is far more efficient and understands why he has been called up, but for many of these young men,

Kettledrummer of *Chasseurs à Cheval*. This ensemble was made just once according to the regiment's archive and used at the Coronation and second marriage.

they could not grasp the reason that lay behind being taken from their loved ones, and being told they were now soldiers. Such was the scale of desertion that Marshal Moncey informed Napoléon in the new year of 1805 that he had arrested 25,036 deserters over the previous year.[43] The figure was undoubtedly much higher: we are ignorant of the number of men who made it home. Did they find happiness living a life on the run? As Forrest comments succinctly, the deserter could never be sure of obtaining their goal of returning to the bosom of their family. Of those caught:

> substantial numbers of deserters were sent to Corsica or herded into the citadel at Blaye. Conditions were miserable: men complained of damp cells, poor food and decaying clothing; often they had been robbed of such money as they had had and were at the mercy of their gaolers; and there was a terrible uncertainty about their future, condemned as they were to terms of seven or nine years in prison or to labouring on public works projects. Even if some consoled themselves with the thought that they were spared the terror of the front line, they had little sense of what the future held and knew that at any moment they might be sent back to battle.[44]

Was the penalty worth it? It must have been given the huge numbers involved. During the Great War of 1914–18 the French Army lost 66,678 men as deserters, an average of 16,699 a year: this is a gross oversimplification of the data, but shows the loss of manpower was as similarly endemic as the later conflict. Indeed, the losses for 1804 represent 37 per cent of the total loss of the Great War.

Men deserted as we noted due to homesickness as well as no doubt finding themselves living in 'hell on earth', which we discuss in our next chapter. That soldiers continued to desert despite the considerable risks and penalties of being captured, gives us ever more reason to look closely at the rationales they offered for their behaviour and the reasoning behind their risk taking. The system that placed men in the army had one major flaw: the French state simply failed to acknowledge that familial and civilian obligations did not end when a citizen became a soldier. If the French Armed Nation was to be fed, its uniforms made etc it needed men at home tending fields and being economically active. Stripping these men from the economy and placing them into the Armed Nation dislocated the moral economy, and in future years led to large-scale shortages of labour to work the land.

It is undeniable that compulsory military service was detested by many, who resorted to extreme acts to escape. Men did not go willingly to fight for glory and the 'father land' that mythos would have us believe. The huge upscaling of conscription to fill out the Grande Armée exacerbated resentment against state officials, the army and Napoléon. France was not unanimous in its adoration and adulation of the army or Emperor, and as the wars progressed, desertion and self-mutilation reached epidemic proportion. Men forced to fight do not make good soldiers, yet the numbers willing to fight voluntarily had been so low, that the Republic was forced to resort to compulsion to generate its armed forces.

Chapter 16
Death and Disease

Desertion was in part fuelled by the lure of hearth and home, yet other factors drove this phenomenon: escaping the living conditions of the camps themselves was a driving factor in the rationale behind the men's actions to desert.

By summer 1805, men had been living in their huts for over 18 months. It cannot have been a pleasant experience: men were rebuked for defecating in their huts, and told to keep them swept clean. Beyond reasonable doubt, human waste was seeping into the ground water, contaminating wells and other sources of water. It comes as no surprise therefore to learn that dysentery was a major problem, as a dragoon officer noted:

> I hope if I don't catch the type of dysentery that reigns here, I will declare myself satisfied. It is wreaking havoc among our dragoons despite all the precautions we've taken.
>
> We also prodigiously suffer from scabies. The land where we are is very sandy, the water is bad, and the wind, sun, rain freeze and burn us in turn.[1]

Scabies and other disease was, it seems, endemic: other archive documents show us that between December 1803 and March 1805 the number of men hospitalised with scabies was 3,217 individuals, or 9 per cent of all men hospitalised. The actual infection rate was much higher, and these figures are only the extreme cases. The major illness at the camps was 'fever' – likely typhus – with 22,698 men hospitalised, followed by 4,313 wounded – representing 12 per cent of the total, primarily through self-mutilation, broken limbs and other causes – and lastly 3,299 with syphilis and other sexually transmitted disease, again around 9 per cent of men hospitalised. These men probably showed no immediate signs before marching to war. This made a total of 33,527 men from the 127,230 in the various camps of IV and VI Corps, or 26 per cent of all men were hospitalised that joined one of the camps.

This figure overlooks notable variations in sickness rates: Ney notes that in VI Corps, 10 per cent suffered from scabies or other similar complaints, slightly higher than the overall average.[2] In comparison, Davout with III Corps at the Camp of Bruges reported 8,823 sick out of a force of 23,231 men, or sickness running at 37 per cent.[3] We do not have any figures from I or V Corps. From these facts and figures it is undeniable that the Camp of Boulogne was an unhealthy place to be: from regimental records, thousands of men died, as the following case studies demonstrate:

Officer of *Chasseurs à Cheval* in parade dress, c.1805.

17ᵉ de Ligne

Inspected on *18 Vendemiaire An 13* (8 October 1804) by General of Brigade Peionville in Brussels. He reported the regiment mustered 2,486 other ranks, of which 486 had joined in the previous year, 305 had died, 428 had deserted out of a total of 820 men the regiment had lost. Illness – malnutrition and contaminated water? – was a major killer for the 17ᵉ *de Ligne*. The regiment's manoeuvres were not carried out according to the regulations, he noted, this was largely because the battalions had large numbers of men missing due to sickness, some 358 men. He added that the men's quarters were bad, and due to lack of pay were in a state of acute privation as they could not afford to buy food to supplement the almost non-existent ration. It had been impossible, he noted, to establish the regulation issue of bread and meat, adding that the regiment's administration was in 'chaos'.[4]

Given a shake-down inspection on *9 Thermidor An14* (28 July 1805) by General Belliard, the 3rd battalion had 54 officers and 531 other ranks, and the 1st and 2nd 63 officers and 1,800 men, which included an 8-strong band. He reported that 335 men had joined the regiment since the previous inspection, 73 had died – hugely less than a year earlier – 33 had deserted and 18 were missing. Regimental administration was no longer chaotic, and the men were receiving their pay and regulation bread, meat, candles, wood and coal for heating. The improved health of the regiment is shown by the fact that all bar 64 men had been released from hospital as able to re-join the ranks.[5]

18ᵉ de Ligne

Drawn up in review on *26 Vendemiaire An 13* (18 October 1804), the major reported that of the 2,019 men, 165 were sick in hospital, and that in the preceding year 128 men had died from illness, 621 had deserted and 176 had been discharged as missing: indeed 1,126 men had left the unit, almost 50 per cent. Why was this? The soldiers' accommodation was unhealthy and needed immediate total replacement, the inspector ordered. The men were well fed, but sickly.[6]

Quartered in Paris at the time of the next review on *3 Thermidor An 14* (22 July 1805), the major reported 134 men were sick in hospital, 57 had died since the last review and 84 had deserted. The men's quarters needed new blankets and mattresses, he noted, but the men were receiving their allocation of bread and beans, although meat is not mentioned.[7]

25ᵉ de Ligne

Reviewed on *16 Brumaire An 13* (28 October 1804), the regiment had received 942 conscripts, 91 had deserted in transit, and 417 had deserted while with the regiment. A further 508 men had deserted from Mauberge, making a total of 1,033 who had deserted that year. A further 40 were dead from fever, with another 58 men discharged from hospital as unable to remain in the army. The barracks, designed to hold 1,200

Trumpeter of *Chasseurs à Cheval* in full dress, c.1805. On campaign they wore a sky blue habit rather than this costly *Hussard* ensemble.

men, were holding 1,743, so each room had five beds rather than four, but they were all heated and ventilated, the inspector commented. However, the beds were in need of replacement, and the blankets were almost totally useless due to their age. Each ordinary comprised 18 to 20 men, and each were obliged to spend 35 centimes on vegetables, or nearly half the budget, leaving nothing for meat once bread had been bought.[8] Reviewed on *13 Thermidor An 14* (1 August 1805), still garrisoned at Mauberge, the war battalions mustered 1,848 men. Since the last inspection, 37 men had died and 9 men had deserted, almost a 1,000 fewer. The beds and bedding were still in desperate need of replacement, and the barracks needed repairs. The meat and vegetable rations were considered very poor and infrequently issued, but the bread was of acceptable quality.[9]

28ᵉ *de Ligne*

Inspected on *1 Vendemiaire An 13* (23 September 1804), the major reported that since July 1803, 86 men had died, 636 men had deserted, 49 had been discharged from the regiment, 30 had been discharged as 'bad sorts', and 59 were missing: in total 1,052 men had quit the regiment in one way of another. What had caused this high number of desertions? Discipline was good and exacting, wrote the inspector, and drill only needed 'a few small details correcting' to be very good. Clearly, desertion was not due to draconian drill instructors. We find the answer later in the review: the inspector tells us the accommodation used by the regiment was unhealthy, and had to be totally replaced. Too small to accommodate the men, they were hot in the summer, and exposed to frosts, cold and rain in the winter. The men were either frozen, baked alive or soaked, he noted, and their equipment suffered as the shelves to store their clothing and effects had been burnt to keep the men warm. Clothing and leather work was mouldy and damaged after being stored badly, and the men's blankets were mouldy and not fit for purpose. The men were issued 5 sous per day per ordinary to buy white bread: this bought 14 loaves for 6 men, but of very bad quality. The men also received sausage and beans or peas every day.[10]

43ᵉ *de Ligne*

Drawn up in review at Bethune on *30 Vendemiaire An 13* (22 October 1804), General Schauenberg reported that since *2 Thermidor An 11* (21 July 1803), 64 men had died and 290 had deserted, a further 52 were AWOL on leave and 137 were discharged from the regiment. Of the 2,260 men under arms, 8 men formed the regimental band and 121 were sick in the regimental hospital. Perhaps this was because the barracks were cold, unheated and in consequence were damp. It was for this reason the men had to be lodged with the townsfolk. Where the barracks were habitable, each had 7 to 8 beds per ordinary of 16 men, which was allowed 22 centimes for food, which was of good quality, reported the inspector.[11] Inspected again on *21 Thermidor An 14* (21 August 1805), the regiment listed 2,336 men, and since the last inspection, 37 had died and 44 deserted. The barracks had been repaired and chimneys installed, however a major part of the beds, mattresses

Officer of Guard Horse Artillery in full dress, *c*.1805.

Gunner of Guard Horse Artillery in full dress, c.1805. Of interest, the sabretache carries the arms of the Emperor and not the expected eagle over cannon.

and blankets needed immediate replacement. Meat and vegetable rations were obtained with difficulty, but bread was plentiful and of good quality.[12]

45ᵉ *de Ligne*

Inspected on 4 *Vendemiaire An 13* (23 September 1804), the major noted the regiment mustered 1,786 men, and in the previous year 28 had died and 349 had gone AWOL, while a further 126 were suspected of desertion: some 532 men had left the regiment. The unit was camped at Saint-Omer, in wooden huts. However, despite the quality of the rations being considered good, 'much negligence' occurred with its distribution, which needed to be redressed. This may explain the high desertion rate.[13]

During late summer 1805, the regiment mustered 1,786 men, of which 130 were sick in hospital. Since the last review the major reported that 21 men had died, 320 men had deserted, 108 had been discharged as unfit for service and 6 had been sent home from hospital. The men were all lodged in the homes of the townsfolk of Verdun.[14]

48ᵉ *de Ligne*

Inspected on 5 *Brumaire An 13* (27 October 1804), the two war battalions mustered 61 officers and 1,296 other ranks, of which the band were 8 men. The 3rd battalion mustered 360 men, of which 44 were *enfant de troupe*. The war battalions were hugely understrength as 493 men were sick in hospital. Indeed, 42 men had died of diseases in the year before, 150 had deserted and 66 had never re-joined the ranks after admittance to hospital.[15]

About the barracks, the inspector told the ministry that the citadel at Anvers could reasonably accommodate 1,500 men and three regiments – 48ᵉ, 61ᵉ, 108ᵉ – were squeezed into the space. It was felt preferable to lodge officers and men with the townsfolk rather than the unhealthy barracks.[16] Inspected again on *10 Thermidor An 13* (30 July 1805) by General Mouton, the two war battalions were reduced to 927 men under arms with a further 141 sick in hospital. The regiment was plagued with ill health as since the last inspection 106 men had died and 71 had been discharged as unfit for further service after being hospitalised. We also note 52 men had deserted. The men ate in their rooms, the furniture in which was in bad condition, and the rooms were barely adequate.

To replace the men lost to ill health, just 129 conscripts had arrived. Perhaps reflecting the high rate of attrition from ill health, many of the *sous-officiers* had been promoted before they had learned their trade, and were unable to carry out their functions effectively.[17]

51ᵉ *de Ligne*

The regiment was inspected in early autumn in Ypres, when it mustered 60 officers and 1,529 men in the two war battalions, which included an 8-strong band. The inspector also tells us that 585 conscripts had joined the regiment, 50 men had died, 110 deserted,

Gunner of Guard Horse Artillery in field service dress, *c.*1805, as they appeared at Austerlitz, but perhaps with colpacks.

263 were sick in hospital and 42 had been discharged from hospital as they had never recovered full health. The inspector noted that due to supply and demand issues each ordinary was not being issued sufficient rations, and the officers were authorised to begin the production of bread. The officers were also to make sure the barrack rooms were kept clean, reported the inspector. The rooms could only accommodate eight men, lacked fireplaces and chimneys and were thus cold and damp. The beds were falling to pieces, while the blankets and mattresses were all very old, threadbare and in need of immediate replacement. Indeed, insufficient blankets existed for every man to have one. It was hoped to lodge the men with the townsfolk. This helps explain the high sickness rate.[18]

57ᵉ de Ligne

At the time of the 1804 review the major noted that since the previous inspection 70 men had died and 251 had deserted. The men's drill was 'mediocre and in many regards very bad' reported the inspector, who added that the accommodation at Lille was 'very damp and needed repairs'. The beds were in good condition, as were the blankets, but 'they needed cleaning'. Each ordinary mustered 16 men, allocated 5 sous, but rations of bread, meat and vegetables cost 8: bread was the costliest item.[19]

61ᵉ de Ligne

Inspected in early autumn 1804, the regiment mustered 46 officers and 1,197 other ranks in the two war battalions. The band mustered seven men. Since 1803 710 men had joined as conscripts, 50 men had died from illness and a further 311 were sick in hospital, 191 men had deserted, and 38 men had never recovered from their illness to return to ranks. Clearly, the cantonments at Anvers were far from a healthy place to be and a particular report about the conditions was sent to the Ministry. The beds, blankets and mattresses were in just about usable condition.[20] About the barracks, the inspector told the ministry that the citadel at Anvers could reasonably accommodate 1,500 men, but was housing three times this figure. He added that 28 officers were housed in the commandants' quarters, while the remainder were under canvas – *pavilion* – but it was felt preferable to lodge officers and men with the townsfolk rather than the unhealthy barracks. The inspector also noted that the men had not been paid between the years of An 8 and An 12, many being owed substantial sums.[21]

75ᵉ de Ligne

Reviewed on *4 Brumaire An 13* (26 October 1804) at Quesnoy, the inspector noted that over the last year, 937 men had joined the regiment, and 675 had left, with 1,749 men in the war battalions. Of those who had left, 247 had deserted, and 76 had died. Housed under canvas, the tents were in a good location but when it rained, water would pour into them, causing them to flood and ruin the soldiers' belongings. The officers were in small tents containing 2 or 4 large beds. The 'rooms' for the men held 12 to 14 beds but 'were very damp'. Blankets and bedding had been furnished by the townsfolk, the Inspector noted, but was old, needed repairing and was often wet with damp. The straw mattresses were mouldy due to damp. Each ordinary was paying 20 centimes for the washing of shirts and other items, and 30 to 35 sous per man for spirits, meat vegetables and bread.[22]

108e *de Ligne*

Reviewed on *18 Vendémiaire An 13* (18 October 1804), the regiment mustered 79 officers and 1,687 men in the three battalions. A further 450 men were in the regimental hospital, along with 6 officers. In the past year, 113 men had died of disease, 170 had deserted and 26 had been discharged from hospital as unfit for further duty.[23] About the barracks, the inspector told the ministry that the citadel at Anvers could reasonably accommodate 1,500 men, but was holding the three regiments. Hugely overcrowded, men became sick very easily, and it was felt preferrable to lodge officers and men with the townsfolk rather than the unhealthy barracks. The officers were under canvas. The inspector also noted the men had not been paid between An 8 and An 12, many men being owed substantial amounts.[24]

111e *de Ligne*

Reviewed on *19 Vendémiaire An 13* (11 October 1804), the inspector noted that the regiment had 62 officers and 1,173 men in the two war battalions, which were understrength as 651 men were sick in hospital, and noted in the past year 94 men had died from illness, 96 men had deserted and 23 had been discharged from hospital as unfit for further service. The inspector reported the barracks were 'incredibly bad, the rooms are falling down, very small, damp and very old but the furniture is good'. Food was acceptable but not good. Bad accommodation, that suffered from damp, clearly had a major impact on the regiment's manpower, but the inspector had no powers to change the situation. The 111[e] was clearly far from being even an 'average' regiment. Its men were ill, its drill bad, its officers and *sous-officiers* far from ideal.[25] Inspected again on *3 Thermidor* An 13 (22 July 1805), the regiment mustered 62 officers and 1,894 men in the two war battalions, which included the 6-strong regimental band. Just 7 men were sick in hospital: a huge reduction since the previous year. Indeed, since the previous inspection, 245 conscripts had joined the regiment, 99 men had died of disease, 29 had deserted, 141 had been discharged and 9 had left the regiment, unable to return to ranks after ill health. This is explained by the men's accommodation. Housed at Montmedy, the barracks were 'incredibly bad, the rooms are dreadful, small and old but the furniture is good'. Food was acceptable but not good. Bad accommodation and low-grade food no doubt explains the sickness and desertion rates. The inspector noted that the conduct and drill of the conscripts in the war battalions 'could have been better', but regimental discipline was good, as was the men's turnout.[26]

Trumpeter of Guard Horse Artillery wearing full dress, *c*.1805. This costume was packed away in Paris when the regiment left in summer 1805 for Austerlitz.

Officer of Guard Artillery Train. Of interest, the uniform is shown as Imperial Blue.

What is clear, is that at a time of 'peace and plenty' the systems designed to feed men and house them simply failed to do so. From the data presented, it seems undeniable that it was accepted as 'normal' that on average, every single regiment had one soldier a week 'dropped dead' at the Camp of Boulogne. Only when the death rate rose to over two soldiers a week did a colonel start to take interest in the causes. However, some corps were far better at keeping men alive than others: looking at just the *ligne* and *Légère*, Bernadotte's I Corps in Year 12 to 13 lost 2,054 men from effective strength: 152 men dead and 1,105 deserted, 192 missing and 605 sick. In the same period the 1st Division of III Corps lost 2,730 men from effective strength: some 478 dead – double that of I Corps – 912 deserted and 1,131 sick. In the 2nd Division, 3,318 were lost from effective strength, with 343 dead and 716 deserted, and 1,954 sick. In Davout's famed III Corps, one man a day 'dropped dead'. Clearly something was very wrong indeed with this command. In the period before leaving the camp the death rate had dropped, the 1st Division had 312 deaths, and the 2nd 297: when compared to the 134 dead in I Corps, we still see Davout's command was beset by ill health and acute supply issues for food. Bernadotte reported 338 men sick in hospital, while Davout in the same period, year 12 to 13, registered a minimum of 3,661 hospitalised. Gathering thousands of young men in a single area introduced many to new illnesses that proved fatal: in III Corps only the fittest conscripts survived: Davout lost from his effective strength 9,020 men in the year 12 to 13 – more men that Murat's cavalry reserve – and 3,008 in the next year. Soult lost 7,245 men from effective strength in the first period and 2,808 in the second. Higher than I Corps, but less than III Corps. By August 1805, the sickness rate had dropped to just under 1,500 – roughly 60 per cent less – in III Corps. In IV Corps the men hospitalised fell from 1,370 to 1,175 in comparison: significantly lower than III Corps. Yet history implies Davout, 'the Iron Marshal', led the best Corps in the French Army. Not so. You were unlucky indeed to be conscripted to serve under Davout as you had more chance of 'dropping dead' from illness or other factors than being killed in action.

Clearly across the various army corps the weakest had died and with better food, better resilience to illness, and better resilience to the military life, death rates had dropped by 50 per cent in the weeks before the camp was struck. How could it be that a peacetime army had a higher attrition rate than at the Battle of Waterloo? Roughly 3,000 men in the corps that fought at Austerlitz died in years 12 to 13 while in the various camps, and in the following months almost 2,000 more: almost 11,000 men went AWOL, and roughly 7,000 were hospitalised in year 12 to 13. Even at times of peace, this huge wastage of young lives was considered acceptable.

As this study stands, it is all too easy to be shocked by the figures. Without comparative data sets, we cannot judge the attrition levels, other than between corps. For this to be meaningful, what is needed now is a comparative study of the armed forces of other nations to place the French data into a broader context. In addition, a comparative study of the French army in other theatres of operations and dates is needed to provide a broader image of death rates, desertion etc across time and location.

Chapter 17

Conclusions

What then can we say about the Camp of Boulogne and the forging of the Grande Armée? Well, for many it was 'hell on earth'. Sickness and disease were rampant, while cold and starvation was a common theme for most. A lot of the problems the army faced at Boulogne had been faced before and would do so again: Consul Bonaparte was well aware of the conditions faced when assembling thousands of men into a single locale and the exhaustion of local supplies of wood, food and ground that had not been already used for latrines from the siege of Toulon. Keeping the men alive rested on good logistics, which would not come under army control until 1807. As Alan Forrest notes, for the soldiers, homesickness:

> made them sickly and disgruntled, a prey to every virus and fever that swept their unit, it also threw them open to temptation, above all to the temptation of desertion. Sunk in the depths of despond, their thinking dulled by fear and by the constant sound of gunfire, or their mood blackened by weeks spent in hospital, men talked of the regret they felt at having ever left home at all. In these expressions of regret there is more than a tinge of self-flagellation, a tendency to blame themselves for their misfortune.[1]

It is easy to see why when stationed in north France, cold, hungry and miserable, many simply went home, or while on the long march into Germany to join their units, simply 'slipped away' into the countryside. Troop retention was as much an issue for the French Armed Nation as keeping the troops alive before getting into action. The rapid condensing of training of conscripts meant that the army did not reach the level of perfection that is often ascribed to it by later writers. Luck, more than training and tactics, won the campaign for Napoléon. It was luck that saved the army from starvation when it arrived in the theatre of operations at the end of November.

Logistics

As we have seen in an earlier chapter, even at times of peace and plenty, the system for feeding the men simply could not cope. At times of war, the system simply collapsed. We evidence this with documents generated during the Austerlitz campaign.

During the march to destiny, desertion, starvation and sickness claimed men from the effective strength of regiments. Berthier admitted on *6 Vendemiaire An 14* (28 September 1805) that hard tack had to be issued as it was impossible to obtain fresh bread.[2] The following day, *7 Vendémiaire An 14* (29 September 1805), Vandamme informed Soult that his division had lost 146 men admitted to hospital since leaving Boulogne, while 42 had

Conclusions 235

Driver of Guard Artillery Train. This costume was virtually identical to the uniform worn across the artillery train as a whole.

Officer of Elite Gendarmes of the Imperial Guard, *c.*1805.

Trooper of the Elite Gendarmes, *c*.1805. The lace cross on the *portmanteaux* may be an error.

Trumpeter of Elite Gendarmes wearing full dress, *c*.1805. On campaign a scarlet *surtout* as worn.

deserted.³ On *10 Vendémiaire An 14* (2 October 1805), Davout issued orders to III Corps to requisition bread and other foodstuffs as the men had consumed all the rations they had begun the march with.⁴ Likewise, Soult with IV Corps on the *13 Vendémiaire* An 13 (5 October 1805) issued orders to requisition 10,000 loaves and 10,000 rations of meat, and obtain 15,000 loaves from the town of Offingen.⁵ Despite meticulous preparation, the supply of food on the march broke down in reality.⁶

Less than 30 days later, on *9 Brumaire An 14* (31 October 1805), Bernadotte reported that 642 men had dropped out from the line of march and had been admitted to hospital. General Suchet reported that of his 6,698 men, 1,079 had dropped out due to illness. Oudinot reported 972 men had been admitted to hospital from the *Grenadiers Réunis* and 332 were 'missing'.⁷ Hungry, cold and sick, is it little wonder men dropped out? The army was withering away before battle had commenced. Marching to war was costlier in lives than the battle to come.

It was only through the capture of Austrian stores at Brunn that Lannes was able to order on *3 Frimaire An 14* (24 November 1805) on his own initiative a full distribution of oats and hay for the cavalry.⁸ If the retreating Austrians had set the stores on fire, Lannes would have been unable to issue the first full ration since to his cavalry leaving Boulogne. More luck than planning, the Austrians failed to destroy huge stockpiles of food and clothing. It enabled the *Grenadiers Réunis* and every man in Lannes' corps to be issued a full ration of bread, biscuit and meat for the first time since leaving Boulogne.⁹ Two days later, on *6 Frimaire* (27 November), every man in V Corps was again issued rations.¹⁰

Clothing

As with keeping men alive, resource management and logistics were key to keeping the men well dressed. Yet, as we have seen, in terms of clothing and equipment, at least 50 per cent of the men who set off to Vienna in August or September were wearing uniforms that were ragged, or needed total replacement. They had to 'make do and mend' until peace came. On *4 Frimaire An 14* (25 November 1805), General Duroc ordered stocks of Austrian clothing captured at Brunn to be distributed to the army. The Division of *Grenadiers Réunis*, for example, were issued:

3,000 pairs of black gaiters
60 greatcoats made from broadcloth
780 greatcoats made from linen
300 greatcoats made from linen with lining
12,000 shirts
1,800 *sacs a distribution*
1,912 civilian greatcoats
884 pairs of civilian *culottes*
99 white *vestes*
Broadcloth to make 343 greatcoats.¹¹

Kettledrummer of Elite Gendarmes, *c.*1805. We cannot be certain the unit had such a personage in 1805.

Mameluke of the Imperial Guard, c.1805.

Mameluke of the Imperial Guard, *c.*1805.

Conclusions 243

Officer of line foot artillery.

As with feeding the men on campaign, the army 'lived off the land' when it came to replenishing clothing stocks: hardly an endorsement of the army's logistical systems. Wearing civilian greatcoats of differing cuts and colours, accompanied by civilian *culottes*, the 'Elite' battalions must have looked far from 'Elite': clearly 'make do and mend' was more important than regulation. How warm a linen greatcoat could have been we leave to the reader to imagine. On *6 Frimaire An 14* (28 November 1805) V Corps was allocated 45,700m of cloth to make greatcoats to be produced locally.[12] The time taken to make these greatcoats – several days if not more – suggests that any encounter with the Austrians and Russians was not at that stage considered. Indeed, the same day Marshal Murat issued identical orders to the cavalry to make new cloaks: he ordered every regiment to conduct a shake-down review to identify damaged or missing clothing, equipment and harness, and to obtain the required number of remounts needed.[13] How much was replaced we know not before the army broke its cantonments and marched to destiny.

Without the halt at Brunn, and the assimilation of captured Austrian clothing, as well as vital stockpiles of food, the Grande Armée would have been in a very 'sorry state indeed'.

A Last Word

There are stereotypes of Napoléonic history. One is of the splendid army, outfitted in their finest, going to battle. On the other hand, history shows jaunty hussars raping and pillaging for food: on *18 Brumaire An14* (9 November 1805) Murat ordered any men in the cavalry caught pillaging to be shot. He noted that officers had reported to him many troopers had threatened to kill civilians with their sabres if they did not hand over food and alcohol to them. Reports of rape had also been received. The Prince issued orders that any man suspected of rape would be shot, officers and *sous-officiers* were to take steps to prevent their men going off at the end of the day to pillage and to ensure their good conduct. Rations and supply were difficult on campaign, Murat admitted, but added that theft and rape was not becoming of French soldiers.[14] The need for such an order is damning evidence that 'living off the land' and the limited intendance system, simply did not work and soldiers resorted to the acts of violence to get food. As we have seen in these pages concerning the logistics, training, and diet of the Grande Armée, if this was the best army Napoléon ever fielded, then the worst must have been a shocking disgrace to humanity.

It seems therefore, based on the archive sources generated at the time, that the famous maxim Napoléon is reputed to have said, 'Amateurs study strategy. Professionals study Logistics' and the more wildly quoted 'An army travels on its stomach' as a guarantor of success, was more bluster than reality. As historian Ben Townsend comments:

> When you concentrate men you get disease, that's why you disperse when possible. When you march fast, you get wastage. If you are advancing, you can recover some

Officer of line horse artillery wearing full dress.

Gunner of line horse artillery wearing full dress.

drop outs, when you are retreating [...] In my route marching days, I saw men fracture bones in their ill-conditioned feet that effectively disqualified them from ever walking hard again. It takes years, not months, to train feet to distance.[15]

As we have seen, route marches did not figure largely on the training programme at Boulogne, nor were men dispersed. The training programme and the camps themselves contributed directly to the huge wastage of young lives. Relying on captured clothing and food stocks is hardly a sign of success: what if the stores were not there to be captured and the Austrians had had the good sense to burn it all? Chance and luck saved the French army from defeat. The halt at Brunn at the end of November allowed the men a chance to rest, to get new shoes, and a few decent meals before the campaign began again. That the French army won at Austerlitz speaks not of the genius of the French Emperor, but of broader failings among the allies in both command and control and not burning stores at Brunn. Capturing food and clothing at Brunn gave the French the shot in the arm it needed to rebuild morale. Had it not been for the failure by the Austrians to burn the stores, we must conclude the outcome of Austerlitz may well have been an allied victory.

Notes

Chapter 1
1. Service Historique de Armee du Terre (hereafter SHDDT) GR 1M 1420 Folio 63 Aperçu d'une expédition sur l'Irlande.
2. Archives Diplomatique (hereafter AD) Correspondance Politique Angleterre (hereafter CPA) 601 Folio 60. Rapport sur l'Irlande 17 Fevrier 1803.
3. Archives Nationales de France (hereafter AN) Af/IV /1672 plaquette 2, Folio 268–273. Rapport sur le voyage de M. Middleton en Angleterre, 1803.
4. Ibid. pièce 78 Folio 180–185 Mémoire de Duverne, chargé de mission en Angleterre 6 vendémiaire an XII.
5. Napoléon a Berthier 26 Germinal An XI, Bonaparte, *Correspondance générale, publiée par la Fondation Napoléon* (Paris, 2004–2013), No. 7579, IV, 103.
6. AN Af/IV/1195.
7. SHDDT GR 1M 1420 Note, projet de descente en Irlande, 14 Prairial an II.
8. AN Af/IV/1195.
9. SHDDT GR 1M 1420 Folio 78 Points de départ d'une expédition contre l'Irlande.
10. Ibid., Folio 44 Mémoire sur l'Irlande.
11. AN Af/IV/1672 Napoléon a Berthier 22 Nivôse An XII.
12. SHDDT GR 1M 1420 Emmet au ministre de la Guerre 4 Pluviose an 12.
13. Correspondence Napoléon, lettre n° 9246.
14. Correspondence Napoléon, lettre n° 9186.

Chapter 2
1. Owen Connelly (2012) *French Revolution and Napoleon* Routledge, London, p.43.
2. Hans Karl Weib pers comm 9 August 2014.
3. SHDDT Xs 525 Projet de décret portant création d'une compagnie de voltigeurs dans chaque bataillon des régiments d'infanterie de ligne.
4. SHDDT Xs 525. Circulaire 27 10bre 1807.
5. Ian Smith pers comm 23 September 2022.

Chapter 3
1. Alan I. Forrest (1989), *Conscripts and Deserters: The Army and French Society during the Revolution and Empire*, Oxford University Press, Oxford, p.31.
2. Ibid., pp.30–32.
3. SHDDT GR 21 YC 24 3ᵉ *régiment d'infanterie de ligne*, 24 vendémiaire an XII-13 messidor an XIII [17 octobre 1803–2 juillet 1805] (matricules 1 à 3000).
4. SHDDT Xb 347 3ᵉ de Ligne. An XII a 1810. Dossier An XII. Rapport 3 Brumaire An XIII.
5. SHDDT Xb 347 3ᵉ *de Ligne*. An XII a 1810. Dossier An XII.
6. SHDDT GR 21 YC 24 34ᵉ *régiment d'infanterie de ligne*, 17 thermidor an XIII [5 août 1805]–29 frimaire an XIV [20 décembre 1805] (matricules 1 à 3 000).
7. SHDDT Xb 349 4ᵉ *régiment d'infanterie de la Ligne*. Dossier An 13. Rapport 17 thermidor An XIII.
8. SHDDT GR 21 YC 24 88 8ᵉ *demi-brigade d'infanterie de ligne*, 26 thermidor an XI [14 août 1803]–7 octobre 1806 (matricules 1 à 3 000).
9. SHDDT GR 21 YC 383 45ᵉ *demi-brigade d'infanterie de ligne*, 12 pluviôse an X–1er prairial an XI [1er mai 1802–21 mai 1803] (matricules 1 à 1 800).

10. Ibid. GR 21 YC 384 45ᵉ *régiment d'infanterie de ligne*, 1er prairial an XI–1ervendémiaire an XIV [21 mai 1803–23 septembre 1805] (matricules 1 801 à 3 600).
11. SHDDT Xb 435 45ᵉ *de Ligne*. An XII a 1811. Dossier An XIII. Rapport 8 Fructidor An XIII.
12. SHDDT Xb 452 54ᵉ *de Ligne*. An XII a 1811. Dossier An XIII. Rapport 14 Vend An XIII.
13. SHDDT GR 21 YC 704 94ᵉ *régiment d'infanterie de ligne*, 22 nivôse an XII [13 janvier 1804]–4 novembre 1806 (matricules 1 à 3 000).
14. SHDDT Xb 512 94ᵉ *de Ligne*. Dossier An 13. Rapport 16 Thermidor An 13.
15. Every tenth day.
16. SHDDT GR 1M 2008-6. Instructions pour tous les Grades de l'Infanterie Républicaine.
17. Anon (1805) Manuel *Journalier* Chez Magimel, Paris.
18. Duc de Fezensac (1870), Souvenirs militaires de 1804 a 1814, Librairie militaire J. Dumaine, Paris, pp.17–18.
19. J-B. Boisson, Revue de l'Agenais, 1965–1967, pp.288–289, quoted in Aain Pigeard (1993), *L'armée napoléonienne*, édition Curandera, Paris, pp.343–344.
20. Anon, *Règlement concernant l'exercice et les manœuvres de l'infanterie du 1ᵉʳ août 1791*, Chez Magimel, Paris, p.138.
21. Etienne Alexandre Bardin (1808) *Manuel d'infanterie, ou Résumé de tous les règlements, décrets, usages, renseignements concernant l'infanterie, dans lequel se trouve renfermé tout ce que doivent savoir les sergents et caporaux*. Chez Magimel, Paris, p.335.
22. SHDDT Xs 526 Arrête 25 Avril 1806.
23. Ibid.
24. Anon (1795) *Reglement Arête pour le Roi pour l'habillement et l'equipment des ses troupes*. Imprimiere Royale, Paris, p.5.
25. Paul Lindsay Dawson (2019) Napoleon's *Imperial Guard Uniforms and Equipment: The Infantry*. Frontline, Barnsley, p.38.
26. Anon (1791) *Instruction provisoire sur l'Habillement des troupes 1 Avril 1791*. Imprimiere Royale Paris, p.13.
27. Ibid., pp.14–16.
28. Dawson (2019), p.45.
29. SHDDT Xs 525.
30. AN Af/IV/1600B plaquette 2. Mémoire sur les approvisionnements et l'organisation administrative de l'armée de Saint-Omer adressé au ministre de la Guerre Berthier par Pierre Daru, intendant général, le 9 prairial an XI.
31. SHDDT Xs 525 Décret 9 Thermidor An 8.

Chapter 4

1. SHDDT AG 1M fol. 1965 Arrette 1 Prairial An X.
2. SHDDT AG 1M fol. 1965 Arrette 1 Germinal An XI.
3. SHDDT AG 1M fol. 1965 Arrette 18 Brumaire An XII.
4. Ibid.
5. Perrot et Amoudru (1821) Histoire *de la ex-Garde* Deluany, Paris, p.35.
6. SHDDT 2C 432 Camp des côtes de l'Océan : minutes de la correspondance du ministre de la guerre major-général (12 octobre 1803–27 août 1805). Bourcier au Berthier 11 Nivoise An 13.
7. SHDDT 2C 432 Camp des côtes de l'Océan : minutes de la correspondance du ministre de la guerre major-général (12 octobre 1803–27 août 1805). Bourcier au Berthier 11 Nivoise An 13.
8. SHDDT C2 General Sebastiani to Berthier 15 Avril 1813.
9. SHDDT C2 Sebastiani to Berthier 25 Avril 1813.
10. «Jacques Chevillet (2004) *Souvenir d'un cavalier de la Grande Armée, 1800–1810*, Bibliothèque de l'histoire, Paris, p.9.
11. Anon (1793) *L'art militaire, ou trait complète de l'exercise d'infanterie, cavalerie, du canon de la bombe* et *des piques* Maxwell. Paris, p.100.

Chapter 5

1. SHDDT 2C 223 Correspondance et Ordres Marechal Soult, p.2. In metric 3.65m by 3.65m. Sunken into the ground by 91cm, with the lamp pit of 60cm radius. The excavated barracks for VI Corps measure 4m by 4m, so slightly larger.
2. Frédéric Lemaire, Archéoscopie d'un projet d'invasion: la fouille des baraquements d'infanterie du camp de Montreuil (1803–1805) in *Napoleonica. La Revue*, 2018/2 (N° 32), pp.5–48.
3. Op. cit. Kitchen's measure 3.65m by 1.82m. The kitchens of Vi corps from excavated remains measure 3m square.
4. AN 137 AP 2 Agenda of 3 Brumaire An 12.
5. Revue du Nord, tome 50, n°198, Juillet–septembre 1968. pp.435–447.
6. AN 137 AP 2 Agenda of 3 Brumaire An 12.
7. AN 275 AP/2 Correspondance General Marchand.
8. AN Af/IV/1600A État des effets de campements nécessaires pour l'armée des Côtes.
9. SHDDT 2C 223 Correspondance et Ordres Marechal Soult, p.20.
10. Ibid., p.21.
11. SHDDT C2 223 Correspondance et Ordres Marechal Soult, p.17.
12. Ibid., p.22.
13. Ibid., p.30.
14. Ibid., p.32.
15. Ibid., p.101.
16. Elie Brun-Lavainne (1855) *Mes Souvenirs* Lille: Lefebvre-Ducrocq, pp.44–45.
17. Ibid.
18. Montesquiou-Fezensac, p.45.
19. SHDDT 2C 223 Correspondance et Ordres Marechal Soult, p.103.
20. Ibid., pp.108–109.
21. Ibid., p.172.
22. AN 384 AP 211 8 Ventose An 13.
23. AN 384 AP 211 12 Ventôse An 13.
24. SHDDT 2C 223 Correspondance et Ordres Marechal Soult, p.321.
25. AN 137 AP 2 Lettre 4 jour complémentaire An XII.
26. AN 137 AP 2 Lettre 8 Vend An 13.
27. AN 137 AP 2 Lettre 23 Vend An 13.
28. AN, 137 AP 2. Lettre 17 Vend An 13.
29. Jean Stanislas (1907) *Vivien Souvenirs de ma vie militaire (1792–1822)*, Hachette, Paris, pp.116–120.
30. SHDDT GR C2 412 Registre d'Ordres 64ᵉ régiment de la Ligne.
31. François Vigo-Roussillon (1981) *Journal de campagne, 1793–1837* Editions France-Empire, p.135.

Chapter 6

1. Fermand Beaucour, 'Notes et souvenirs de Jean-Jacques Bellavoine, soldat du camp de Boulogne', in *Revue du nord*, vol. 198, July–September, 1968, p.440.
2. SHDDT C2 223 Correspondance General Soult, p.94.
3. AN 137 AP3 11 L'instruction militaire au camp de Montreuil d'après une lettre du général Ney du 13 floréal an XII.
4. AN 275 AP/2 Correspondance General Marchand, lettre 26 Pril. An 13.
5. AN 275 AP/2 Correspondance General Marchand, lettre 15 Vend An 13.
6. SHDDT GR 2C 224 Correspondance et Ordres Marechal Soult, Soult au Ministre de Guerre, 18 Thermidor An 13.
7. SHDDT 2C 223 Correspondance et Ordres Marechal Soult, p.176.
8. Ibid., p.206.
9. 9 SHDDT GR Xab 106 Registre de Délibérations 2ᵉ régiment Conscrit Chasseurs de la Garde Imperiale.
10. SHDDT 2C 412 registre d'ordres 64ᵉ de Ligne.
11. Pierre Charrie (2004) *Lettres de guerre, 1792–1815*, Nantes: éditions du Canonnier, p.132.
12. SHDDT GR C2 412 Registre d'Ordres 64e de Ligne.

Chapter 7

1. AN 137 AP3 11 ordre du jour 4 brumaire an XII.
2. Lemaire, pp.29–34.
3. AN AF IV 1602.
4. Chantal Prévot, 'Les femmes au camp de Boulogne, 1803–1809. Éléments de réponse d'après l'état civil des communes de Montreuil-sur-Mer, Étaples, Saint-Josse, Camiers, Dannes, Widehem', In Napoleonica. La Revue, vol. 32, no. 2, 2018, pp.49–63.
5. SHDDT 2C 223 Correspondance et Ordres Marechal Soult. pp.278–279.
6. SHDDT 2C 412 Registre d'Ordres 64e régiment de la Ligne.
7. Ibid., p.144.
8. Ibid., p.145.
9. Ibid., p.148.
10. Vivien, p.118.
11. SHDDT 2C 412 Registre d'Ordres 64e régiment de la Ligne.
12. Bellavoine, p.441.
13. Ibid., p.442.
14. Ibid., p.443.
15. SHDDT G2C 412 Registre d'Ordres 64e régiment de la Ligne.
16. Ibid.
17. Ibid.
18. Ibid.
19. AN 137 AP3 11 ordre du jour de la 2e division du 6 pluviôse.
20. Ibid.
21. Ibid.
22. L. Arnaud & P. Bonnet (1912) *La Femme sur la Champ de Bataille* Paris: Henri-Charles Lavauzelle, p.42.
23. L. Hennet, 'Vivandières et Blanchisseuses', in *Carnet de la Sabretache*, vol. 21 (1912), p.35.
24. Ibid,. pp.37–38.
25. Ibid., pp.39–40.
26. Ibid., p.47.
27. SHDDT 2C 412 Registre d'Ordres 64e régiment de la Ligne.
28. Prévot, pp.50–53.
29. SHDDT 2C 412 Registre d'Ordres 64e régiment de la Ligne.
30. Firewood of the Napoleonic Wars: the first application of archaeological charcoal analysis to a military camp in the north of France (1803–1805) in Antiquity, Volume 90 , Issue 353 , October 2016 , pp. 1334–1347.
31. AN, 137 AP 3 12, Roguet au général de division Malher 26 nivôse an XIII.
32. 1 hectolitre = 100 litres, 1 hectogram = 100 grams. 8 hectograms is 800g or 8kg.
33. SHDDT 2C 412 Registre d'Ordres 64e régiment de la Ligne.
34. Ruth Goodman (2021) *The Domestic Revolution : How the Introduction of Coal into Victorian Homes Changed Everything*, Liveright Publishing Corporation.
35. Lemaire, p.32.
36. SHDDT Xb 534 111e *de Ligne*. Dossier An 13. Rapport 3 Thermidor An 13.
37. AN Af/IV/1600B plaquette 2 État des effets de campements nécessaires pour l'armée des Côtes.
38. Ibid. Rapport au Premier consul sur les dispositions faites et sur celles restant à faire pour les camps projetés, daté de Paris le 7 thermidor an XI (26 juillet 1803) et signé Dejean, ministre de l'administration de la Guerre.
39. Ibid. État de l'approvisionnement en bestiaux des camps des côtes de l'océan à l'époque du 15 brumaire an XII (7 novembre 1803), signé du conseiller d'État et commissaire général Petiet,
40. Ibid. État général des grains, farines, biscuits, riz, légumes secs et sacs existants dans les magasins de l'armée au 10 brumaire an XII (2 novembre 1803), signé du conseiller d'État et commissaire général Petiet,
41. AN AP 275 Correspondence of General Marchand file 2.
42. www.napolcon series.org/military info/organization/France/Food/CaloricIntact.pdf accessed 26 January 2023.

43. AN Af/IV/1159. Table of pay year XII.
44. AN AP 275 Correspondence of General Marchand file 2.
45. Brun-Lavainne, p.44.
46. SHDDT 2C 412 Registre d'Ordres 64ᵉ régiment de la Ligne.
47. Baron Dellard (1892), *Mémoires militaires du général Baron Dellard sur les guerres de la République et de l'Empire*, La librairie illustrée, Paris, pp.194–195.
48. AN 275 AP/2 Correspondence General Marchand.
49. Charrie, p.132.
50. AN, 137 AP 3 12, Roguet au général de division Malher 26 nivôse an XIII.

Chapter 8

1. SHDDT 2C 17 Renseignements Bataille d'Austerlitz.
2. SHDDT GR 1M 627 Renseignements bataille d'Austerlitz. Dossier 1ᵉ Corps. Relevé de livre d'ordres.
3. SHDDT Xb 358 8e de Ligne 1792 a 1811. Dossier An 13. Rapport 8 Vend An 13.
4. SHDDT Xb 358 8ᵉ *de Ligne* 1792 a 1811. Dossier An 13. Rapport 30 Thermidor An XIII.
5. SHDDT Xb 435 45ᵉ *de Ligne* An XII a 1811. Dossier An XIII. Rapport 4 Vend An XIII.
6. SHDDT Xb 435 45ᵉ *de Ligne* An XII a 1811. Dossier An XIII. Rapport 8 Fructidor An XIII.
7. SHDDT Xb 452 54e de Ligne An XII a 1811. Dossier An XIII. Rapport 14 Vend An XIII.
8. SHDDT Xb 452 54e de Ligne An XII a 1811. Dossier An XIII. Rapport 12 Fructidor An XIII.
9. SHDDT GR 1M 627 Renseignements bataille d'Austerlitz. Dossier 1ᵉ Corps. Relevé de livre d'ordres.
10. SHDDT Xb 614 17ᵉ *Légère*. Dossier An 13. Rapport 5 Vend An 13.
11. SHDDT Xb 614 27ᵉ *Légère*. Dossier An 13. Rapport 19 Thermidor An 13.
12. SHDDT Xb 512 94ᵉ *régiment de Ligne* An XII a 1810. Rapport 16 Thermidor An XIII.
13. SHDDT Xb 512 94ᵉ *régiment de Ligne* An XII a 1810. Rapport 16 Vend An 14.
14. SHDDT Xb 512 94ᵉ régiment de Ligne An XII a 1810. Rapport 26 Vend An 14.
15. SHDDT Xb 512 94ᵉ *régiment de Ligne* An XII a 1810. Dossier 1807. Rapport 3 Décembre 1807.
16. SHDDT Xb 512 94e régiment de Ligne An XII a 1810. Dossier 1807. Rapport 3 Décembre 1807 etat de pirx des fournitures.
17. SHDDT Xb 514 95e régiment de Ligne An XII a 1810. Dossier An 13. Rapport 25 Thermidor An 13.
18. SHDDT GR 1M 627 Renseignements bataille d'Austerlitz. Dossier 1ᵉ Corps. Relevé de livre d'ordres.
19. SHDDT Xc 240 2ᵉ *Hussard*. Rapport 21 Thermidor An XIII.
20. SHDDT Xc 245 5ᵉ *Hussard*.
21. SHDDT Xc 244 4ᵉ *Hussard* 1791–1815.
22. SHDDT Xc 194 5ᵉ *Chasseurs à Cheval 1811* a 1815. Dossier An 13. Rapport 15 Thermidor An 13.

Chapter 9

1. SHDDT Xb 589 13ᵉ *Légère* An XI a 1811. Dossier An XIII. Rapport 11 Vendémiaire An 13.
2. SHDDT Xb 589 13ᵉ *Légère* An XI a 1811. Dossier An XIII. Rapport 9 Thermidor An 13.
3. SHDDT Xb 380 17ᵉ *régiment de Ligne* A n12 a 1808. Dossier An 13. Rapport 18 Vend An 13.
4. SHDDT Xb 380 17ᵉ *régiment de Ligne* An 12 a 1808. Dossier An 13. Rapport 9 Thermidor An 13.
5. SHDDT Xb 409 30ᵉ *régiment de Ligne* An 12 a 1808. Dossier An 13. Rapport 20 Vend An 13.
6. SHDDT Xb 409 30ᵉ *régiment de Ligne* An 12 a 1808. Dossier An 13. Rapport 8 Thermidor An 13.
7. SHDDT Xb 409 30ᵉ *régiment de Ligne* An 12 a 1808. Dossier An 13. Rapport 8 Thermidor An 13.
8. Musée de l'Armee, Fonds Rousselot.
9. SHDDT Xb 445 51ᵉ *de Ligne*. An 12 a 1809. Dossier An XII Rapport 14 Vend. An 13.
10. SHDDT Xb 445 51ᵉ *de Ligne*. An 12 a 1809. Dossier An XII Rapport 12 Thermidor An 13.
11. SHDDT Xb 468 61ᵉ *régiment de Ligne* An 12 a 1811. Dossier An XII. Report 16 Vendémiaire An 13.
12. SHDDT Xb 468 61ᵉ *régiment de Ligne* An 12 a 1811. Dossier An XII. Report 4 Fructidor An 13.
13. SHDDT Xb 593 13ᵉ *Légère*. Dossier An 13. Rapport 20 Vend An 13.
14. SHDDT Xb 593 15ᵉ *Légère*. Dossier An 13. Rapport 14 Thermidor An 13.
15. SHDDT Xb 413 33ᵉ *régiment de Ligne*. Dossier An 13. Rapport 10 Thermidor An 13.
16. SHDDT Xb 441 48ᵉ *régiment de Ligne* An 12 a 1808. Dossier An 13. Rapport 5 Brumaire An 13.
17. SHDDT XB 441 48ᵉ *régiment de Ligne* An 12 a 1808. Dossier An 13. Rapport 10 Thermidor An 13.

18. SHDDT XB 441 48ᵉ *régiment de Ligne* An 12 a 1808. Dossier An 14 Formation du *Voltigeur*s, 10 Brumaire An 14.
19. SHDDT Xb 441 48ᵉ *régiment de Ligne* An 12 a 1808. Dossier An 14. Lettre 10 Nivoise An 14.
20. SHDDT Xb 441 48ᵉ *régiment de Ligne*. Dossier An 12 a 1808. Dossier 1807. Rapport 1 Décembre 1807.
21. SHDDT Xb 534 111ᵉ *régiment de Ligne*. Dossier An 13. Rapport 19 Vendémiaire An 13.
22. SHDDT Xb 534 111ᵉ *régiment de Ligne*. Dossier An 13. Rapport 3 Thermidor An 13.
23. SHDDT Xb 534 111ᵉ régiment de Ligne. Dossier An 14. Rapport 1 Brum An 14.
24. SHDDT Xb 534 111ᵉ régiment de Ligne. Dossier 1807. Rapport 23 9bre 1807.
25. SHDDT Xb 532 108ᵉ *régiment de Ligne*. Dossier An 13. Rapport 18 Vendémiaire An 13.
26. SHDDT Xb 532 108ᵉ *régiment de Ligne*. Dossier An 13. Rapport 15 Thermidor An 13.
27. SHDDT Xb 532 108ᵉ *régiment de Ligne*. Dossier 1807. Rapport 30 Novembre 1807.
28. SHDDT Xc 133 1ᵉ *Dragons* An XII a 1811. Dossier An 13. Rapport 19 Vend An 13.
29. SHDDT Xc 133 1ᵉ *Dragons* An XII a 1811. Dossier An 13. Rapport 19 Thermidor An 13.
30. SHDDT Xb 601 21ᵉ *Légère*. Dossier An 13. Rapport 19 Vend An 13.
31. SHDDT Xb 601 21ᵉ *Légère*. Dossier An 13. Rapport 4 Thermidor An 13.
32. SHDDT Xb 367 12ᵉ *régiment de Ligne* An XII a 1808. Dossier An 13. Rapport 8 Vend An 13.
33. SHDDT Xb 367 12ᵉ *régiment de Ligne* An XII a 1808. Dossier An 13. Rapport 24 Thermidor An 13.
34. SHDDT Xb 367 12ᵉ *régiment de Ligne* An XII a 1808. Dossier 1808. Rapport 21 March 1808.
35. SHDDT Xb 391 21ᵉ *de Ligne* An XII a 1811. Dossier An XIII. Rapport 1 Thermidor An 13.
36. SHDDT Xb 399 25e *de Ligne* An XII a 1808. Dossier An XIII. Rapport 16 Brumaire An XIII.
37. SHDDT Xb 399 25ᵉ *de Ligne* An XII a 1808. Dossier An XIII. Rapport 13 Thermidor An 13.
38. SHDDT Xb 501 85ᵉ *de Ligne* An XII a 1811. Dossier An XIII. Rapport 25 Messidor An XIII b.
39. SHDDT Xc 186 1ᵉ *Chasseurs*. Rapport 10 Vendémiaire An XIII.
40. SHDDT Xc 186 1ᵉ *Chasseurs*. Rapport 3 Thermidor An XIII.
41. SHDDT Xc 250 7ᵉ *Hussard*. 8 Thermidor An XIII.
42. SHDDT Xc 188 2ᵉ *Chasseurs*. Rapport 9 Thermidor An XIII.
43. SHDDT Xc 208 12ᵉ *Chasseurs*. Rapport 2 Vend An 13.
44. SHDDT Xc 208 12ᵉ *Chasseurs*. Rapport 9 Thermidor An 13.
45. SHDDT Xc 157 15ᵉ *Dragons*. Dossier An 13. Rapport 15 Vendémiaire Year XIII.
46. SHDDT Xc 157 15ᵉ *Dragons*. Dossier An 13. Rapport 20 Thermidor An 13.
47. SHDDT Xc 161 17ᵉ *Dragons*. Dossier An 12. Rapport 6 jour complémentaire An 12.
48. SHDDT Xc 161 17ᵉ *Dragons*. Dossier An 13. Rapport 20 Thermidor An 13.
49. SHDDT Xc 164 18ᵉ Dragons. Dossier An X13. Rapport 4 Vend An 13.
50. SHDDT Xc 164 18ᵉ *Dragons*. Dossier An 13. Rapport 17 Thermidor An 13.
51. SHDDT Xc 166 19ᵉ *Dragons*. Dossier An 13. Rapport 26 Vend An 13.
52. SHDDT Xc 166 19ᵉ *Dragons*. Dossier An 13. Rapport 25 Therm An 13.
53. SHDDT Xc 166 19ᵉ *Dragons*. Dossier 1808. Rapport 17 Xbre 1807.
54. SHDDT Xc 174 25ᵉ *Dragons*. Dossier An 13. Rapport 24 Vend An 13.
55. SHDDT Xc 174 25ᵉ *Dragons*. Dossier An 13. Rapport 21 Thermidor An 13.
56. SHDDT Xc 176 27ᵉ *Dragons*. Dossier An XIII. Rapport 1 sansculottides An XII.
57. SHDDT Xc 176 27ᵉ *Dragons*. Dossier An XIII. Rapport 5 thermidor An XIII.

Chapter 10
1. SHDDT GR 1M 627 Renseignements bataille d'Austerlitz. Dossier IV Corps. Journal du marche du Marechal Soult.
2. Ibid., Journal du Marche IV Corps.
3. SHDDT 2C 17 Renseignements Bataill d'Austerlitz. Rapport 1 Vend An 14.
4. SHTDDT Xb 584 10ᵉ *Légère* An XII a 1809. Dossier An XIII. Rapport 19 Vend. An 13.
5. SHTDDT Xb 584 10ᵉ *Légère* An XII a 1809. Dossier An XIII. Rapport 30 Thermidor An 13.
6. SHDDT Xb 373 14ᵉ *de Ligne* An XII a 1809 Dossier An 13. Rapport 25 Vend An 13.
7. SHDDT Xb 373 14ᵉ *de Ligne* An XII a 1809 Dossier An 13. Rapport 2 Thermidor An 13.
8. SHDDT Xb 420 36ᵉ *de Ligne* An 12 a 1809. Dossier An 13. Rapport 10 Vend. An 13.
9. SHDDT Xb 420 36ᵉ *de Ligne* An 12 a 1809. Dossier An 13. Rapport 10 Therm. An 13.

10. SHDDT Xb 431 43ᵉ *de Ligne*. Dossier An 13. Rapport 30 Vend An 13.
11. SHDDT Xb 431 43ᵉ *de Ligne*. Dossier An 13. Rapport 21 Thermidor An 13.
12. SHDDT Xb 454 55ᵉ *régiment de Ligne* An XII a 1809. Dossier An XIII. Rapport 2 vendémiaire An 13.
13. SHDDT Xb 454 55ᵉ *régiment de Ligne* An XII a 1809. Dossier An XIII. Rapport 2 Fructidor An 13.
14. SHDDT Xk 15 Tirailleurs du Po. Dossier An 13. Rapport 21 Vend An 13.
15. SHDDT Xk 15 Tirailleurs du Po. Dossier An 13. Rapport 24 Messidor An 13.
16. SHDDT Xb 607 24ᵉ *Légère*. Dossier An 13. Rapport 1 Vend An 13.
17. SHDDT Xb 607 24ᵉ *Légère*. Dossier An 13. Rapport 10 Thermidor An 13.
18. SHDDT Xb 349 4ᵉ *régiment d'infanterie de la Ligne*. Rapport 1 Vendémiaire An XIII.
19. SHDDT Xb 349 4ᵉ *régiment d'infanterie de la Ligne*. Rapport 28 Messidor An XIII.
20. SHDDT Xb 349 4ᵉ *régiment d'infanterie de la Ligne*. Rapport 1 Brumaire An XIV.
21. SHDDT Xb 349 4ᵉ *régiment d'infanterie de la Ligne*. Lettre 10 Nivôse An XIV.
22. SHDDT Xb 349 4ᵉ *régiment d'infanterie de la Ligne*. Lettre au Colonel 2 Janvier 1806.
23. SHDDT Xb 405 28ᵉ *de Ligne*. Dossier An 13. Rapport 1 Vend An 13.
24. SHDDT Xb 405 28ᵉ *de Ligne*. Dossier An 13. Rapport 15 Thermidor An 13.
25. SHDDT Xb 437 46e *de Ligne* An XII a 1811. Dossier An XII Rapport 5 Sansculottides An XIIa.
26. SHDDT Xb 437 46e *de Ligne* An XII a 1811. Dossier An XII Rapport 5 Sansculottides An XIIb.
27. SHDDT Xb 459 57ᵉ *de Ligne* An XII a 1811. Dossier An XIII. Rapport 4 Vend. An XIII.
28. SHDDT Xb 459 57ᵉ *de Ligne* An XII a 1811. Dossier An XIII. Rapport 6 Fructidor AN XIII.
29. SHDT Xb 612 26ᵉ *Légère*. Dossier An 13. Rapport 4 Vend An 13.
30. SHDT Xb 612 26ᵉ *Légère*. Dossier An 13. Rapport 5 Thermidor An 13.
31. SHDDT Xk 17 Tirailleurs Corses.
32. SHDDT Xb 347 3ᵉ *de Ligne* An XII a 1810. Dossier An XII. Rapport 3 Brumaire An XIII.
33. SHDDT Xb 347 3ᵉ *de Ligne* An XII a 1810. Dossier An XII. Rapport 18 Thermidor An XIII.
34. SHDDT Xb 383 18ᵉ *de Ligne*. Dossier An 13. Rapport 26 Vendémiaire An 13.
35. SHDDT Xb 383 18ᵉ *de Ligne*. Dossier An 13. Rapport 3 Thermidor An 13.
36. SHDDT Xb 489 75ᵉ *de Ligne* An XII a 1811. Dossier An XII. Rapport 4 Brumaire An XII.
37. SHDDT Xb 489 75ᵉ *de Ligne* An XII a 1811. Dossier An XII. Rapport 27 Thermidor An XII.
38. SHDDT Xc 253 8ᵉ *Hussard*. Dossier An 13. Rapport 9 Fructidor An 13.
39. SHDDT Xc 206 11ᵉ *Chasseurs à Cheval*. Rapport 16 Vendémiaire An XIII.
40. SHDDT Xc 206 11ᵉ *Chasseurs à Cheval*. Rapport 29 Thermidor An XIII.
41. SHDDT Xc 217 16ᵉ *Chasseurs à Cheval*. An XI a 1811. Dossier An XIII. Rapport 2 Vendémiaire An XIII.
42. SHDDT Xc 217 16ᵉ *Chasseurs à Cheval*. An XI a 1811. Dossier An XIII. Rapport 3 Fructidor An 13.
43. SHDDT Xc 233 26ᵉ *Chasseurs*. Dossier An 13. Rapport 27 Vend An 13.
44. SHDDT Xc 233 26ᵉ *Chasseurs*. Dossier An 13. Rapport 12 Thermidor An 13.
45. SHDDT Xc 140 5ᵉ *Dragons*. Dossier An 14. Rapport 19 Brumaire An 14.
46. SHDDT Xc 145 8ᵉ *Dragons*. Dossier An 13. Rapport 8 Vendémiaire An 13.
47. SHDDT Xc 145 8ᵉ *Dragons*. Dossier An 13. Rapport 20 Thermidor An 13.
48. SHDDT Xc 149 9ᵉ *régiment de Dragon* 1792 a 1811. Dossier An XIII. Rapport 15 Vend. An XIII.
49. SHDDT Xc 149 9ᵉ *régiment de Dragon* 1792 a 1811. Dossier An XIII. Rapport 10 Thermidor An 13.
50. SHDDT Xc 149 9ᵉ *régiment de Dragon* 1792 a 1811. Dossier An XIII. Rapport 10 Thermidor An 13.
51. SHDDT Xc 151 12ᵉ *Dragons*. Dossier An 13. Rapport 5 Fructidor An 13.
52. SHDDT Xc 160 16ᵉ *Dragons*. Dossier An 12. Rapport 5 jour complémentaire An 12.
53. SHDDT Xc 160 16ᵉ *Dragons*. Dossier An 13. Rapport 13 Thermidor An 13.
54. SHDDT Xc 169 21e de Dragon An XIV a 1814. Dossier An XI. Rapport 20 Pluviôse An11

Chapter 11

1. SHDDT GR 1M 627 Renseignements bataille d'Austerlitz. Dossier Vᵉ Corps. Registre Historique.
2. SHDDT Xk 32 grenadiers réunis.
3. SHDDT Xk 32 grenadiers réunis.
4. SHDDT Xb 587 12ᵉ *Légère*. Dossier An 13 Rapport 12 Ven An 13 Grenadiers Réunis.
5. SHDDT Xb 593 15ᵉ *Légère*. Dossier An 12. Dossier Grenadiers Réunis.

6. SHDDT Xk 32 grenadiers réunis.
7. SHDDT Xk 32 grenadiers réunis.
8. SHDDT Xb 344 2e régiment de ligne. Dossier An 12. Proces verbal formation du bataillon d'elite.
9. SHDDT Xb 360 9e *de Ligne*. Dossier An 13. Rapport 1 Vend An 13.
10. SHDDT Xb 370 13e *de Ligne*. Dossier An 13. Rapport 1 Vend An 13.
11. SHDDT Xb 461 58e *de Ligne*. An 12 a 1809. Dossier An XIII. Rapport 7 Vendémiaire An XIII.
12. SHDDT Xb 495 81e de Ligne. Dossier An 13. Rapport 1 Vend An 13.
13. SHDDT Xb 571 4e *Légère*. Dossier An 13. Rapport 23 Vend An 13.
14. SHDDT Xb 571 4e *Légère*. Dossier An 13. Rapport 24 Messidor An 13.
15. SHDDT Xb 461 58e *de Ligne*. Dossier An 13. Rapport 22 Vend An 13.
16. SHDDT Xb 461 58e *de Ligne*. Dossier An 13. Rapport 7 Thermidor An 13.
17. SHDDT Xb 518 100e *de Ligne*. Dossier An 13. Rapport 20 Vend An 13.
18. SHDDT Xb 518 100e *de Ligne*. Dossier An 13. Rapport 1 Therm An 13.
19. SHDDT Xb 524 103e *de Ligne*. Dossier An 13. Rapport 8 Vend An 13.
20. SHDDT Xb 524 103e *de Ligne*. Dossier An 13. Rapport 8 4 Therm An 13.
21. SHDDT 2C 17 Renseignements Bataill d'Austerlitz. Rapport 1 Vend An 14.
22. SHDDT Xb 597 17e *Légère*. Dossier An 13. Rapport 15 Vendémiaire An 13.
23. SHDDT Xb 597 17e *Légère*. Dossier An 13. Rapport 28 Thermidor An 13.
24. SHDDT Xb 416 34e *de Ligne*, Dossier An 13. Rapport 7 Brumaire An 13.
25. SHDDT Xb 416 34e *de Ligne*, Dossier An 13. Rapport 24 Thermidor An 13.
26. SHDDT Xb 416 34e *de Ligne*, Dossier 1808. Rapport 7 Novembre 1807.
27. SHDDT Xb 427 40e *de Ligne*, An 12 a 1811. Dossier An XII. Rapport 19 Vendémiaire An XIII.
28. SHDDT Xb 427 40e *de Ligne* An 12 a 1811. Dossier An XII. Rapport 6 Thermidor An XIII.
29. SHDDT Xb 474 64e *de Ligne* An XII a 1808. Dossier An 13. Rapport 1 Ven An 13.
30. Bibliotheque Musée de l'Armee. Fonds Rousselot. Infanterie de la Ligne. Extraits de Livre d'Ordres du 64e de Ligne, pp.3–10.
31. SHDDT Xb 474 64e *de Ligne* An XII a 1808. Dossier An 13. Rapport 11 Thermidor An 13.
32. SHDDT Xb 474 64e *de Ligne* An XII a 1808. Dossier 1807. Rapport 9 Novembre 1807.
33. SHDDT Xb 427 40^e *de Ligne* An 12 a 1811. Dossier An XII. Rapport 6 Thermidor An XIII.
34. SHDDT GR 1M 627 Renseignements bataille d'Austerlitz. Dossier Ve Corps. Registre Historique.
35. SHDDT Xc 255 9^e *Hussard*. Dossier An 11. Rapport 20 Prairial An XI.
36. SHDDT Xc 255 9^e *Hussard*. Dossier An 13. Rapport 18 Fructidor An XIII.
37. SHDDT Xc 256 10^e *Hussard* 1793 a 1811. Dossier An XIII. Rapport 22 Thermidor An XIII.
38. SHDDT Xc 210 13e *Chasseurs*. Dossier An 13. Rapport 26 Vend An 13.
39. SHDDT Xc 211 13e *Chasseurs*. Dossier An 13. Rapport 10 Thermidor An 13.
40. SHDDT Xc 224 21e Chasseurs. Rapport 30 Messidor An XI.
41. SHDDT Xc 224 21e *Chasseurs*. Rapport 1 Vendémiaire An XIII.
42. SHDDT Xc 224 21e *Chasseurs*. Rapport 8 Fructidor An XIII.
43. SHDDT Xc 136 3e *Dragons*. Dossier An 11. Rapport 24 Messidor An 11.
44. SHDDT Xc 136 3e *Dragons*. Dossier An 13. Rapport 13 Thermidor An 13.
45. SHDDT Xc 136 3e *Dragons*. Dossier 1808. Rapport 30 Octobre 1807.
46. SHDDT Xc 142 6e *Dragons*. Dossier An 13. Rapport 20 Vend An 13.
47. SHDDT Xc 142 6e *Dragons*. Dossier An 13. Rapport 15 Fruct An 13.
48. SHDDT Xc 147 10e *Dragons*. Dossier An 13. Rapport 27 Vend An 13.
49. SHDDT Xc 147 10e *Dragons*. Dossier An 13. Rapport 9 Thermidor An 13.
50. SHDDT Xc 149 11e *régiment de Dragons* 1791 a An XII. Dossier An XIII. Rapport 23 Vend An XIII.
51. SHDDT Xc 149 11e *régiment de Dragons* 1791 a An XII. Dossier An XIII. Rapport 30 Thermidor An XIII.
52. SHDDT Xc 153 13e *Dragons*. Dossier An 10. Rapport 26 Floréal An 11.
53. SHDDT Xc 153 13e *Dragons*. Dossier An 10. Rapport 10 Nivôse An 10.
54. SHDDT Xc 154 13e *Dragons*. Dossier An 13. Rapport 29 Vend An 13.
55. SHDDT Xc 153 13e *Dragons*. Dossier An 13. Rapport 6 Thermidor An 13.
56. SHDDT Xc 171 22e *Dragon* An XIII a 1814. Dossier An XIII. Rapport 16 vendémiaire An XIII.
57. SHDDT Xc 171 22e *Dragon* An XIII a 1814. Dossier An XIII. Rapport 2 Thermidor An XIII.

Chapter 12

1. SHDDT GR 1M 627 Renseignements bataille d'Austerlitz. Dossier Reserve de Cavalerie. Registre Historique. See Also SHDDT GR 2C 240 Correspondance General Belliard; SHDDT 2C 241 Registre des Ordres du General Belliard; SHDDT GR 1M 628 Division des Grosse Cavalerie.
2. SHDDT GR 1M 628 Division des Grosse Cavalerie.
3. SHDDT Xc 91 1^e *Cavalerie Cuirassier*s. Dossier An X. Rapport 17 Germinal An X.
4. SHDDT Xc 91 1^e *Cavalerie Cuirassier*s. Dossier An IX. Rapport 23 Messidor An XI.
5. SHDDT Xc 95 1^e *Cuirassiers*. Dossier An X.
6. SHDDT Xc 95 1^e *Cuirassiers*. Dossier An XIII. Rapport 7 Thermidor An 13.
7. SHDDT Xc 97 2^e *Cuirassiers*. Dossier An XII. Rapport 20 Thermidor An 13.
8. SHDDT Xc 97 2e *Cuirassiers*. Dossier An XII.
9. SHDDT Xc 97 2e *Cuirassiers*. Dossier An XIII.
10. SHDDT Xc 99 3e *Cuirassier*s. Dossier An XI. Rapport 10 Fructidor An XI.
11. SHDDT Xc 99 3e *Cuirassier*s. Dossier An XIII. Rapport 1 Vendémiaire An 13.
12. SHDDT Xc 99 3e *Cuirassiers*. Dossier An XI.
13. SHDDT Xc 99 3e *Cuirassiers*. Dossier An XIII.
14. SHDDT GR 1M 1927 Registre Preval.
15. SHDDT Xc 103 5e *régiment de Cuirassiers*. Dossier An XI.
16. SHDDT Xc 103 5e *régiment de Cuirassiers*. Dossier An XI.
17. SHDDT Xc 103 5e *régiment de Cuirassiers*. Dossier An XIII. Rapport 27 Juillet 1805.
18. SHDDT Xc 110 9e *Cuirassiers*. Dossier An XI. Rapport 28 Prairial An XI.
19. SHDDT Xc 110 9e *Cuirassiers*. Dossier An 13. Rapport 17 Thermidor An 13.
20. Ian Smith Pers Comm 6 January 2018.
21. SHDDT Xc 110 9e *Cuirassier*s. Dossier An XI.
22. SHDDT Xc 112 12e *Cuirassier*s. Dossier An 13. Rapport 9 Thermidor An 13.
23. SHDDT Xc 113 11e *Cavalerie*. Dossier An XII. Rapport 22 Vend An XII.
24. SHDDT Xc 114 11e *Cuirassiers*. Dossier An XI.
25. SHDDT Xc 114 11e *Cuirassiers*. Dossier An XI Rapport 1 Thermidor An 13.
26. SHDDT Xc 116 12e *régiment de cuirassier*s. Dossier An XIII. Rapport 24 Vendémiaire An XIII.
27. SHDDT Xc 116 12e *régiment de cuirassier*s. Dossier An XII.
28. SHDDT Xc 116 12e *régiment de cuirassier*s. Dossier An XIII. Rapport 20 Thermidor An XIII.
29. SHDDT Xc 90 1e *Carabinier*s. Dossier An XI. Rapport 5 Messidor An XI.

Chapter 13

1. Coutanceau et al (1905) *La Campagne de l'armee du Nord 1794*, R. Chapelot & Co., France, p.229, notes that due to the terrain encountered the 4-pdr was the only truly mobile gun in the 1794 campaign in Germany but it lacked any effect on the enemy troops.
2. Allix *Observations sur le Nouveaux System d'artillerie Francaise* in *Journal Science Militaire* Vol XXVIII Juillet 1832, p.7.
3. SHDDT 2W 84 General Saint Hilaire to General Marmont 16 September 1803.
4. Ibid. General Soult to General Marmont 21 September 1803.
5. SHDDT 2C 213 General Sorbier to Marmont 29 September 1803.
6. SHDDT 2w 84 General Saint Maurice to Marmont 21 November 1803.
7. SHDDT 2C 213 General Nansouty to Marmont 8 December 1803.
8. SHDDT 2C 470 Etat du Matériel de l'Artillerie de la Garde Armée, 22 Fructidor An 13.
9. SHDDT Xd 48 1e *train d'artillerie*. Dossier An 13. Rapport 13 Brum An 13.
10. SHDDT Xd 48 1e *train d'artillerie*. Proces verbal d'organisation 13 Nivôse An VIII.
11. SHDDT Xd 48 1e *train d'artillerie*. Arrête 16 Thermidor An IX.
12. SHDDT C2 221 Ordre du jour 22 Prairial An 13.
13. SHDDT C2 222 Ordre du Jour 6 Messidor An 13.
14. SHDDT C2 222 Ordre du Jour 6 Frcut An 13.

Chapter 14

1. Duhesme (1814) *Essai sur l'infanterie légère*, Paris, Chez Magimel, p.202.
2. SHDDT Xb 358 8ᵉ *de Ligne* 1792 a 1811. Dossier An 13. Rapport 5 Vend An 13.
3. SHDDT Xb 614 17ᵉ *Légère*. Dossier An 13. Rapport 5 Vend An 13.
4. SHDDT Xb 614 27ᵉ *Le Légère*. Dossier An 13. Rapport 19 Thermidor An 13.
5. SHDDT Xb 435 45ᵉ *régiment de Ligne* An XII a 1811. Dossier An XIII. Rapport 8 Fructidor An XIII.
6. SHDDT Xb 367 12ᵉ *régiment de Ligne* An XII a 1808. Dossier An 13. Rapport 8 Vend An 13.
7. SHDDT Xb 367 12ᵉ *régiment de Ligne* An XII a 1808. Dossier An 13. Rapport 24 Thermidor An 13.
8. SHDDT Xb 589 13ᵉ *Légère* An XI a 1811. Dossier An XIII. Rapport 11 Vendémiaire An 13.
9. Légère Dossier An XIII. Rapport 9 Thermidor An 13.
10. SHDDT Xb 534 111ᵉ *de Ligne*. Dossier An 13. Rapport 19 Vendémiaire An 13.
11. SHDDT Xb 391 21ᵉ *de Ligne* An XII a 1811. Dossier An XIII. Rapport 1 Thermidor An 13.
12. SHDDT Xb 501 85ᵉ *de Ligne* An XII a 1811. Dossier An XIII. Rapport 25 Messidor An XIII.
13. SHDDT Xb 445 51ᵉ *de Ligne*. An 12 a 1809. Dossier An XII Rapport 12 Thermidor An 13.
14. SHDDT Xb 607 24ᵉ *Légère*. Dossier An 13. Rapport 1 Vend An 13.
15. SHDDT Xb 427 40ᵉ *de Ligne* An 12 a 1811. Dossier An XII. Rapport 19 Vendémiaire An XIII.
16. SHDDT GR 2C 197 Correspondance de la grande armée 1 fructidor an XI au 27 nivôse an XIII (29 août 1803–17 janvier 1805).
17. SHDDT 2C 192 Lettres et instructions adressées par le ministre de la Guerre aux ministres, aux généraux, aux chefs d'état-major et aux principales autorités, relativement aux opérations du camp de Saint-Omer, du 11 fructidor an XI au 27 nivôse an XIII (29 août 1803–17 janvier 1805). Loison au Berthier 15 Nivoise An 13.
18. Fezenzac, p.33.
19. SHDDT GR 2C 198 Correspondance de la grande armée 27 nivôse an XIII a 1 Vend XIV.
20. AN Af/IV/1602. Ordre du Jour 21 Ventôse An 13.
21. SHDDT 2C 197. Laval au Berthier, 10 Nivoise An 13.
22. SHDDT 2C 197. Laval au Berthier, 1 Nivoise An 13.
23. SHDDT Xb 367 12ᵉ *régiment de Ligne* An XII a 1808. Dossier An 13. Rapport 8 Vend An 13.
24. SHDDT GR 2C 247 bis.
25. SHDDT Xc 240 2ᵉ *Hussard*. Rapport 21 Thermidor An XIII.
26. SHDDT Xc 244 4ᵉ *Hussard* 1791–1815.
27. SHDDT Xc 245 5ᵉ *Hussard*. Rapport 30 Thermidor An XI.
28. SHDDT Xc 217 16ᵉ *Chasseurs*. Dossier An 13. Rapport 8 Fructidor An 13.
29. SHDDT Xc 169 21ᵉ *de Dragon* An XIV a 1814. Dossier An XI. Rapport 1 Nivôse An XI.
30. SHDDT Xc 169 21ᵉ *de Dragon* An XIV a 1814. Dossier An XI. Rapport 9 Messidor An11.
31. SHDDT GR 2C 197 Correspondance de la grande armée 1 fructidor an XI au 27 nivôse an XIII (29 août 1803-17 janvier 1805). Barageuy d'Hillier au Berthier 18 Vendémiaire An 13.
32. SHDDT Xc 171 22ᵉ *Dragon* An XIII a 1814. Dossier An XIII. Rapport 2 Thermidor An XIII.
33. SHDDT GR 2C 201 Barageuy d'Hillier au Berthier 18 fructidor An 13.
34. SHDDT GR 2C 202 Correspondance de la grande armée du 16 fructidor an XIII au 7 nivôse an XIV (3 septembre–28 décembre 1805). Bourcier au Napoléon 18 Fructidor An 13.
35. SHDDT GR 2C 201. Beaumont au Napoléon 21 Fructidor An 13.
36. SHDDT GR 2C 432. Nansouty au Berthier 10 Fructidor An 13.

Chapter 15

1. Marc Lebrun, 'Révolution, Empire et mauvais soldats' in *Revue historique des armées*, volume 244, 2006, pp.112–123.
2. SHDDT GR 2C 412 Registre d'Ordres 64ᵉ *régiment de la Ligne*.
3. SHDDT Xb 405 28ᵉ *régiment de Ligne*. Dossier An 12. Rapport 3 Jour Complémentaire An 12.
4. SHDDT Xb 391 21ᵉ *régiment de Ligne* An XII a 1811. Dossier An XIII. Rapport 1 Thermidor An 13.
5. AN Af/IV/1601 Napoléon au Berthier 14 Frimaire An XII.
6. Forrest (1989), p.152.
7. Alan Forrest (2002) *Napoleon's Men London*, Hambledon Consortium, pp.161–167.

8. SHDDT Xb 358 8ᵉ *de Ligne* 1792 a 1811. Dossier An 13. Rapport 5 Vend An 13.
9. Forrest (2002), p.96.
10. Chevillet, pp.29–30.
11. J.-L. Sabon, 'Mémoires du Petit Louis ou l'apprenti horloger de Genève devenu musicien et chef de musique dans le 69e régiment d'infanterie de ligne de la Grande Armée de Napoléon Ier', in *Soldats suisses au service étranger*, Geneva, 1910.
12. Dellard, p.199. See Also ibid. pp.200–204 and p.51.
13. SHDDT Xb 427 40ᵉ *de Ligne* An 12 a 1811. Dossier An XII. Rapport 19 Vendémiaire An XIII.
14. SHDDT Xb 607 24ᵉ *Légère*. Dossier An 13. Rapport 1 Vend An 13.
15. SHDDT Xc 133 1ᵉ *Dragons* An XII a 1811. Dossier An 13. Rapport 19 Vend An 13.
16. SHDDT Xc 160 16ᵉ *Dragons*. Dossier An 12. Rapport 5 jour complémentaire An 12.
17. SHDDT Xb 413 33ᵉ *régiment de Ligne*. Dossier An 13. Rapport 10 Thermidor An 13.
18. SHDDT Xb 514 95ᵉ *régiment de Ligne* An XII a 1810. Dossier An 13. Rapport 25 Thermidor An 13.
19. Charles d'Agoult (2001), *Mémoires*, Paris, Mercure de France, p.107.
20. SHTDDT Xb 584 10ᵉ *Légère* An XII a 1809. Dossier An XIII. Rapport 19 Vend. An 13.
21. SHDDT GR 2C 201 Expedition d'Angleterre. Correspondance du Marechal 16 Fructidor An 13 au 7 Nivoise XIV. Saint Hilaire a Soult 24 floréal An 13.
22. SHDDT Xb 347 3ᵉ *de Ligne* An XII a 1810. Dossier An XII. Rapport 3 Brumaire An XIII.
23. SHDDT Xb 347 3ᵉ *de Ligne* An XII a 1810. Dossier An XII. Rapport 18 Thermidor An XIII.
24. AN Af/IV/1591, fol. 2, 4, 11, 22. Reports from Rapp to Napoléon, July 1806.
25. Op. cit.
26. SHDDT Xb 427 40ᵉ *de Ligne* An 12 a 1811. Dossier An XII. Rapport 19 Vendémiaire An XIII.
27. SHDDT Xb 427 40ᵉ *de Ligne* An 12 a 1811. Dossier An XII. Rapport 6 Thermidor An XIII.
28. Forrest (2002), p.179.
29. SHDDT Xb 487 72ᵉ *de Ligne*. Dossier An 13.
30. Forrest, pp.136–137.
31. Ibid., p.10.
32. Lebrun, pp 113–114.
33. Forrest, pp.95–96.
34. François Houdecek (2023) *Vivre la Grande Armée. Être soldat au temps de Napoléon* CNRS Editions, Paris.
35. D. F. N. Guerbois (1803), *Essai sur la nostalgie appelée vulgairement maladie du pays*, médical thésis, Paris.
36. SHDDT Xb 483 69ᵉ *de Ligne* Dossier An 13.
37. SHDDT Xb 574 6ᵉ *Légère*. Dossier An 13.
38. SHDDT Xb 610 25ᵉ *Légère*. Dossier An 13.
39. SHDDT Xb 516. 96ᵉ *de Ligne*. Dossier An 13.
40. SHDDT Xb 425 39ᵉ *de Ligne*. Dossier An 13.
41. AN 137 AP 3 11 ordres 15 Pluvoise An 12.
42. AN 137 AP 3 11 ordres du Jour 28 Nivoise An 12.
43. AN Af/IV/1155. Moncey au Napoléon 15 nivoise An 13.
44. Forrest (2002), p.182.

Chapter 16
1. Marie Antoine Reiset (1899) *Souvenirs, 1775–1810* Calmann Lévy, pp.164–166.
2. AN 137 AP 3 11 ordre du jour de l'armée du 18 prairial An XII.
3. AN Af/IV/1602.
4. SHDDT Xb 380 17ᵉ *régiment de Ligne* An 12 a 1808. Dossier An 13. Rapport 18 Vend An 13.
5. SHDDT Xb 380 17ᵉ *régiment de Ligne* An 12 a 1808. Dossier An 13. Rapport 9 Thermidor An 13.
6. SHDDT Xb 383 18ᵉ *de Ligne*. Dossier An 13. Rapport 26 Vendémiaire A n13.
7. SHDDT Xb 383 18ᵉ *de Ligne*. Dossier An 13. Rapport 3 Thermidor An 13.
8. SHDDT Xb 399 25ᵉ *de Ligne*. An XII a 1808. Dossier An XIII. Rapport 16 Brumaire An XIII.
9. SHDDT Xb 399 25ᵉ *de Ligne*. An XII a 1808. Dossier An XIII. Rapport 13 Thermidor An 13.
10. SHDDT Xb 405 28ᵉ *de Ligne*. Dossier An 13. Rapport 1 Vend An 13.
11. SHDDT Xb 431 43ᵉ *de Ligne*. Dossier An 13. Rapport 30 Vend An 13.

12. SHDDT Xb 431 43ᵉ *de Ligne*. Dossier An 13. Rapport 21 Thermidor An 13.
13. SHDDT Xb 435 45ᵉ *de Ligne* An XII a 1811. Dossier An XIII. Rapport 4 Vend An XIII.
14. SHDDT Xb 435 45ᵉ *de Ligne* An XII a 1811. Dossier An XIII. Rapport 8 Fructidor An XIII.
15. SHDDT Xb 441 48ᵉ *régiment de Ligne* An 12 a 1808. Dossier An 13. Rapport 5 Brumaire An 13.
16. SHDDT Xb 468 61ᵉ *régiment de Ligne* An 12 a 1808. Dossier An XII. Report An 12 61ᵉ et 108ᵉ de Ligne.
17. SHDDT Xb 441 48ᵉ *régiment de Ligne* An 12 a 1808. Dossier An 14. Lettre 10 Nivoise An 14.
18. SHDDT Xb 445 51ᵉ *de Ligne* An 12 a 1809. Dossier An XII. Rapport 14 Vend. An 13.
19. SHDDT Xb 459 57ᵉ *de Ligne* An XII a 1811. Dossier An XIII. Rapport 4 Vend. An XIII.
20. SHDDT Xb 468 61ᵉ *régiment de Ligne* An 12 a 1811. Dossier An XII. Report 16 Vendémiaire An 13.
21. SHDDT Xb 468 61ᵉ régiment de Ligne An 12 a 1811. Dossier An XII. Report An 12 61ᵉ et 108ᵉ de Ligne.
22. SHDDT Xb 489 75ᵉ *de Ligne* An XII a 1811. Dossier An XII. Rapport 4 Brumaire An XII.
23. SHDDT Xb 532 108ᵉ *régiment de Ligne*. Dossier An 13. Rapport 18 Vendémiaire An 13.
24. SHDDT Xb 468 61ᵉ *régiment de Ligne* An 12 a 1811. Dossier An XII. Report An 12 61ᵉ et 108ᵉ de Ligne.
25. SHDDT Xb 534 111ᵉ *de Ligne*. Dossier An 13. Rapport 19 Vendémiaire An 13.
26. SHDDT Xb 534 111ᵉ *de Ligne*. Dossier An 13. Rapport 3 Thermidor An 13.

Chapter 17
1. Forrest (2002), pp.175–176.
2. SHDDT GR 2C 3 Correspondance Grande Armee 21ᵉ – 30 Septembre 1805. Berthier a Songis 6 Vend An 14.
3. SHDDT GR 2C 3 Correspondance Grande Armee 21ᵉ – 30 Septembre 1805. Vandamme a Soult 7 Vend An 14.
4. SHDDT GR 2C 4 Correspondance Grande Armee. 1ᵉʳ–1 0 octobre 1805. Ordre de Mouvement 10 Vend An 14.
5. Ibid., Soult Au Saint Hilaire 13 Vend An 14.
6. SHDDT GR 2C 3 Correspondance Grande Armee 21ᵉ – 30 Septembre 1805. Ordre du March IV Corps . Vend An 14.
7. SHDDT GR 2C 6 Correspondance Grande Armee 31 – 31 Octobre 1805. Rapport 9 Brumaire An XIV.
8. SHDDT GR 1M 627 Renseignements bataille d'Austerlitz. Dossier Vᵉ Corps. Livre d'ordres. Ordre du Jour 3 Frimaire An 14.
9. Ibid., Ordre du Jour 4 Frimaire An 14.
10. Ibid., Ordre du Jour 6 Frimaire An 14.
11. SHDDT GR 1M 627 Renseignements bataille d'Austerlitz. Dossier Vᵉ Corps. Livre d'ordres.
12. Ibid., Ordre du Jour 6 Frimaire An 14.
13. SHDDT 2C 241 Registre d'Ordres. Ordre du Jour 6 Frimaire An 14.
14. SHDDT 2C 241 Livre d'Ordres. Ordre du Jour 18 Brumaire An 14.
15. Ben Townsend pers comm 27 September 2023.

Bibliography

Bibliotheque Musée de l'Armee
Fonds Rousselot. Infanterie de la Ligne. Extraits de Livre d'Ordres du 64e de Ligne

Service Historique de la Armee du Terre
AG 1M fol. 1965
GR 1M 627 Renseignements bataille d'Austerlitz.
GR 1M 1420 Folio 63 Aperçu d'une expédition sur l'Irlande
GR 1M 2008-6

GR 21 YC 24 3e régiment d'infanterie de ligne, 24 vendémiaire an XII-13 messidor an XIII [17 octobre 1803–2 juillet 1805] (matricules 1 à 3000).
GR 21 YC 33 4e régiment d'infanterie de ligne, 17 thermidor an XIII [5 août 1805]–29 frimaire an XIV [20 décembre 1805] (matricules 1 à 3 000).
GR 21 YC 24 88 8e demi-brigade d'infanterie de ligne, 26 thermidor an XI [14 août 1803]–7 octobre 1806 (matricules 1 à 3 000).
GR 21 YC 383 45e demi-brigade d'infanterie de ligne, 12 pluviôse an X-1er prairial an XI [1er mai 1802–21 mai 1803] (matricules 1 à 1 800).
GR 21 YC 384 45e régiment d'infanterie de ligne, 1er prairial an XI-1ervendémiaire an XIV [21 mai 1803–23 septembre 1805] (matricules 1 801 à 3 600).
GR 21 YC 704 94e régiment d'infanterie de ligne, 22 nivôse an XII [13 janvier 1804]–4 novembre 1806 (matricules 1 à 3 000).

Xb 342 1e *régiment d'infanterie de la Ligne*
Xb 344 2e *de Ligne*
Xb 345 2e *de Ligne*
Xb 346 2e *de Ligne* 1814–1815
Xb 347 3e *de Ligne* An XII a 1810
Xb 348 3e *régiment de Ligne* 1813 a 1815
Xb 349 4e *régiment d'infanterie de la Ligne*
Xb 352 5e *régiment d'Infanterie de la Ligne*
Xb 353 6e *de Ligne*
Xb 356 7e *de Ligne* An 12 a 1810
Xb 358 8e *de Ligne* 1792 a 1811
Xb 360 9e *de Ligne*
Xb 361 9e *de Ligne*
Xb 362 10e *de Ligne*
Xb 365 11e *de Ligne*
Xb 367 12e *de Ligne* 1792 a 1808
Xb 368 12e *de Ligne* 1808 a 1812
Xb 369 12e *de Ligne* 1812 a 1815
Xb 370 13e *de Ligne*
Xb 373 14e *de Ligne* An XII a 1811
Xb 375 15e *de Ligne* An XII a 1811
Xb 378 16e *de Ligne*
Xb 380 17e *de Ligne*
Xb 383 18e *de Ligne* An XII a 1811
Xb 386 19e *régiment de Ligne* An XII a 1812
Xb 387 19e *de Ligne* 1812 a 1815
Xb 388 20e *de Ligne*
Xb 391 21e *de Ligne* An XII a 1811
Xb 392 21e *de Ligne* 1811 a 1815
Xb 393 22e *de Ligne* An XII a 1811
Xb 395 23e *de Ligne*
Xb 397 24e *de Ligne* An XII a 1809
Xb 398 24e *de Ligne* 1809 a 1812
Xb 399 25^e *de Ligne* An XII a 1808
Xb 401 26^e *de Ligne*
Xb 403 27^e *de Ligne* An 12 a 1811
Xb 405 28e *de Ligne* An 12 a 1810
Xb 407 29^e *de Ligne*
Xb 409 30^e *de Ligne* An 12 a 1808
Xb 410 30^e *de Ligne* 1808 a 1815
Xb 411 32^e *de Ligne*
Xb 412 32e *de Ligne*

Xb 413 33ᵉ *de Ligne* An 12 a 1808
Xb 414 33ᵉ *de Ligne* 1808 a 1813
Xb 415 33ᵉ *de Ligne* 1813 a 1815
Xb 416 34ᵉ *de Ligne* An 12 a 1811
Xb 417 34ᵉ *de Ligne* 1812 a 1815
Xb 418 35ᵉ *de Ligne*
Xb 420 36ᵉ *de Ligne* An XII a 1811
Xb 421 36ᵉ *de Ligne* 1811 a 1815
Xb 422 37ᵉ *de Ligne*
Xb 424 37ᵉ *de Ligne* 1812 a 1815
Xb 425 39ᵉ *de Ligne*
Xb 427 40ᵉ *de Ligne* An 12 a 1811
Xb 429 42ᵉ *de Ligne* An XII a 1811
Xb 431 43ᵉ *de Ligne*
Xb 433 44ᵉ *de Ligne*
Xb 435 45ᵉ *de Ligne* An XII a 1811
Xb 436 45ᵉ *de Ligne* 1811 a 1815
Xb 437 46ᵉ *de Ligne* An XII a 1811
Xb 438 46ᵉ *de Ligne* 1812 a 1815
Xb 439 47ᵉ *de Ligne*
Xb 444 48ᵉ *de Ligne*
Xb 442 48ᵉ *de Ligne*
Xb 443 50ᵉ *de Ligne* An 12 a 1811
Xb 444 50ᵉ *de Ligne* 1811 a 1815
Xb 445 51ᵉ *de Ligne*
Xb 448 52ᵉ *de Ligne*
Xb 450 53ᵉ *de Ligne*
Xb 452 54ᵉ *de Ligne* An XII a 1811
Xb 454 55ᵉ *régiment de Ligne* An XII a 1809
Xb 455 55ᵉ *de Ligne* 1809 a 1815
Xb 456 56ᵉ *de Ligne* An XII a 1809
Xb 457 56ᵉ *de Ligne* 1808 a 1813
Xb 459 57ᵉ *de Ligne* An XII a 1811
Xb 461 58ᵉ *régiment de Ligne*
Xb 463 59ᵉ *de Ligne* An XII a 1809
Xb 464 59ᵉ *de Ligne* 1809 a 1812
Xb 465 59ᵉ *de Ligne* 1812 a 1815
Xb 466 60ᵉ *de Ligne* An XII a 1811
Xb 467 60ᵉ *de Ligne* 1812 a 1815
Xb 468 61ᵉ *de Ligne*
Xb 469 62ᵉ *de Ligne* An 12 a 1808
Xb 470 62ᵉ *de Ligne* 1808 a 1810
Xb 471 62ᵉ *de Ligne* 1810 a 1815
Xb 472 63ᵉ *de Ligne* An XII a 1811
Xb 473 63ᵉ *de Ligne* 1811 a 1815
Xb 474 64ᵉ *de Ligne* An XII a 1809
Xb 475 64ᵉ *de Ligne* 1810 a 1815
Xb 476 65ᵉ *de Ligne*

Xb 477 65ᵉ *de Ligne* 1812 a 1815
Xb 478 66ᵉ *de Ligne*
Xb 480 67ᵉ *de Ligne*
Xb 482 69ᵉ *de Ligne*
Xb 485 70ᵉ *de Ligne*
Xb 487 72ᵉ *de Ligne*
Xb 489 75ᵉ *de Ligne* An XII a 1811
Xb 491 76ᵉ *de Ligne*
Xb 493 79ᵉ *de Ligne*
Xb 495 81ᵉ *de Ligne* An 12 a 1812
Xb 496 81ᵉ *de Ligne* 1812 a 1815
Xb 497 82ᵉ *de Ligne*
Xb 499 84ᵉ *de Ligne*
Xb 500 84ᵉ *de Ligne*
Xb 501 85ᵉ *de Ligne* An XII a 1811
Xb 502 85ᵉ *de Ligne* 1812 a 1815
Xb 503 86ᵉ *de Ligne*
Xb 505 88ᵉ *de Ligne* An X a 1811
Xb 507 92ᵉ *de Ligne*
Xb 509 93ᵉ *de Ligne*
Xb 510 93ᵉ *de Ligne*
Xb 511 93ᵉ *de Ligne*
Xb 512 94ᵉ *régiment de Ligne* An XII a 1810
Xb 514 95ᵉ *de Ligne* An XI a 1811
Xb 516 96ᵉ *de Ligne*
Xb 518 100ᵉ *de Ligne*
Xb 519 100ᵉ *régiment d'Infanterie de la Ligne* 1812 a 1815
Xb 520 101ᵉ *de Ligne*
Xb 522 102ᵉ *de Ligne*
Xb 524 103ᵉ *de Ligne* An XI a 1811
Xb 527 105ᵉ *de Ligne*
Xb 529 106ᵉ *de Ligne*
Xb 532 108ᵉ *de Ligne*
Xb 534 111ᵉ *de Ligne*
Xb 536 112ᵉ *de Ligne*

Xb 571 4ᵉ *Légère*
Xb 584 10ᵉ *Légère* An XII a 1809
Xb 587 12ᵉ *Légère*
Xb 589 13ᵉ *Légère* An XI a 1811
Xb 593 15ᵉ *Légère*
Xb 597 17ᵉ *Légère*
Xb 614 27ᵉ *Légère*
Xb 601 21ᵉ *Légère*
Xb 607 24ᵉ *Légère*
Xb 612 26ᵉ *Légère*

Xab 106 Registre de Délibérations 2ᵉ régiment Conscrit Chasseurs de la Garde Imperiale.

Xc 23 *Cavalerie*
Xc 90 1ᵉ *Carabinier*s
Xc 91 1ᵉ *Carabinier*s
Xc 93 2ᵉ *Carabinier*s
Xc 94 1ᵉ *Cavalerie*
Xc 95 1ᵉ *Cuirassier*s
XC 97 2ᵉ *Cuirassier*s
Xc 98 3ᵉ et 4ᵉ *Cavalerie*
Xc 99 3ᵉ *Cuirassier*s
Xc 101 4ᵉ *Cuirassier*s
Xc 102 5ᵉ *Cuirassier*s
Xc 104 6ᵉ *Cuirassier*s
Xc 106 7ᵉ *Cuirassier*s
Xc 108 8ᵉ *Cuirassier*s
Xc 109 9ᵉ *Cavalerie*
Xc 110 9ᵉ *Cuirassiers*
Xc 110 10ᵉ *Cavalerie*
Xc 112 10ᵉ *Cuirassier*s
Xc 113 11ᵉ *Cavalerie*
Xc 114 11ᵉ *Cuirassier*s
Xc 115 12ᵉ *Cavalerie*
Xc 116 12ᵉ *Cuirassier*s

Xc 132 1ᵉ *Dragons* 1791 a An XI
Xc 133 1ᵉ *Dragons* An XII a 1811
Xc 134 2ᵉ *Dragons* 1792 a An XI
Xc 135 2ᵉ *Dragons* An XI a 1815
Xc 136 3ᵉ *Dragons*
Xc 137 4ᵉ *Dragons* 1791 a An XI
Xc 138 4ᵉ *Dragons*
Xc 139 5ᵉ *Dragons*
Xc 140 5ᵉ *Dragons*
Xc 141 6ᵉ *Dragons*
Xc 142 6ᵉ *Dragons*
Xc 143 7ᵉ *Dragons*
Xc 144 7ᵉ *Dragons*
Xc 145 8ᵉ *Dragons* 1791 a 1811
Xc 146 9ᵉ *Dragons* 1791 a 1811
Xc 147 10ᵉ *Dragons* 1791 a An XI
Xc 148 10ᵉ *Dragons*
Xc 149 11ᵉ *Dragons*
Xc 150 11ᵉ *Dragons* An XII a 1815
Xc 151 12ᵉ *Dragons* 1791 a An XI
Xc 152 12ᵉ *Dragons*
Xc 153 13ᵉ *Dragons* 1791 a An XI
Xc 154 13ᵉ *Dragons*
Xc 155 14ᵉ *Dragons* 1791 a An XI
Xc 156 14ᵉ *Dragons*
Xc 157 15ᵉ *Dragons* 1791 a An XI
Xc 158 15ᵉ *Dragons* An XII a 1815

Xc 159 16ᵉ *Dragons* 1791 a An XI
Xc 160 16ᵉ *Dragons*
Xc 161 17ᵉ *Dragons* 1791 a An XI
Xc 162 17ᵉ *Dragons*
Xc 163 18ᵉ *Dragons* 1791 a An XI
Xc 164 18ᵉ *Dragons*
Xc 165 19ᵉ *Dragons* 1791 a An XII
Xc 166 19ᵉ *Dragons* An XII a 1815
Xc 167 20ᵉ *Dragons* 1791 a An XI
Xc 168 20ᵉ *Dragons*
Xc 169 21ᵉ *Dragons* An IV a 1814
Xc 170 21ᵉ *Dragons*
Xc 171 22ᵉ *Dragons* An XII a 1814
Xc 172 23ᵉ *Dragons* An XI a 1814
Xc 173 24ᵉ *Dragons* An XI a 1814
Xc 174 25ᵉ *Dragons* An XII a 1814
Xc 175 26ᵉ *Dragons* An XII a 1814
Xc 176 27ᵉ *Dragons* An XII a 1814
Xc 177 28ᵉ *Dragons* An XII a 1814
Xc 178 29ᵉ *Dragons* An XII a 1814
Xc 179 30ᵉ *Dragons* An XII a 1814

Xc 186 1ᵉ *Chasseurs*
Xc 188 2ᵉ *Chasseurs*
Xc 194 5ᵉ *Chasseurs à Cheval*
Xc 206 11ᵉ *Chasseurs à Cheval*
Xc 208 12ᵉ *Chasseurs*
Xc 210 13ᵉ Chasseurs
Xc 217 16ᵉ *Chasseurs à Cheval* An XI a 1811
Xc 224 21ᵉ *Chasseurs*
Xc 233 26ᵉ *Chasseurs*

Xc 240 2ᵉ *Hussard*
Xc 245 5ᵉ *Hussard*
Xc 244 4ᵉ *Hussard* 1791–1815
Xc 250 7ᵉ *Hussard*
Xc 253 8ᵉ *Hussard*
Xc 255 9ᵉ *Hussard*
Xc 256 10ᵉ *Hussard* 1793 a 1811

Xd 48 1ᵉ *train d'artillerie*

Xk 15 Tirailleurs du Po
Xk 17 Tirailleurs Corses
Xk 32 grenadiers réunis

Xs 525
Xs 526
Xs 528

2C 3 Correspondance Grande Armée 21ᵉ – 30 Septembre 1805
2C 4 Correspondance Grande Armée 1ᵉʳ – 10 Octobre 1805
2C 6 Correspondance Grande Armée 31 – 31 Octobre 1805
2C 17 Renseignements Bataille d'Austerlitz
2C 192 Lettres et instructions adressées par le ministre de la Guerre aux ministres, aux généraux, aux chefs d'état-major et aux principales autorités, relativement aux opérations du camp de Saint-Omer, du 11 fructidor an XI au 27 nivôse an XIII
2C 197 Correspondance de la Grande Armée 1 fructidor an XI au 27 nivôse an XIII
GR 2C 201 Expedition d'Angleterre
GR 2C 202 Correspondance de la Grande Armée du 16 fructidor an XIII au 7 nivôse an XIV (3 septembre-28 décembre 1805). Bourcier au Napoléon 18 Fructidor An 13
2C 213 Correspondance et Ordres
C2 221 Correspondance et Ordres General Hulin
C2 222 Ordres du General Hulin
2C 223 Correspondance et Ordres Marechal Soult
2C 224 Correspondance et Ordres Marechal Soult, Soult au Ministre de Guerre, 18 Thermidor An 13
2C 247 Bis Habillement
2C 412 registre d'ordres 64ᵉ de Ligne
2C 432 Camp des côtes de l'Océan
2C 470 Etat du Matériel de l'Artillerie de la Garde Armée

2w 84 Artillerie
Archives Diplomatiques
Correspondance Politique Angleterre, 601

Archives Nationales de France

Af/IV/1155	Af/IV/1600A	137 AP 2
Af/IV/1159	Af/IV/1600B	275 AP
Af/IV/1195	Af/IV/1602	384 AP 211
Af/IV/1591	Af/IV/1672	

Printed Material
Anon, *Règlement concernant l'exercice et les manœuvres de l'infanterie du 1ᵉʳ août 1791*, Chez Magimel, Paris.
Anon (1791) *Instruction provisoire sur l'Habillement des troupes 1 Avril 1791*. Imprimerie Royale Paris.
Anon (1793) *L'art militaire, ou trait complète de l'exercise d'infanterie, cavalerie, du canon de la bombe et des piques* Maxwell. Paris.
Anon (1795) *Reglement Arête pour le Roi pour l'habillement et l'equipment des ses troupes*. Imprimerie Royale, Paris.
Anon (1805) Manuel *Journalier* Chez Magimel, Paris.
Charles d'Agoult (2001), *Mémoires*, Paris, Mercure de France.
L. Arnaud & P. Bonnet (1912) *La Femme sur la Champ de Bataille* Paris: Henri-Charles Lavauzelle.
Allix Observations sur le Nouveaux System d'artillerie Francaise in *Journal Science Militaire* Vol XXVIII Juillet 1832.
Etienne Alexandre Bardin (1808) *Manuel d'infanterie, ou Résumé de tous les règlements, décrets, usages, renseignements concernant l'infanterie, dans lequel se trouve renfermé tout ce que doivent savoir les sergents et caporaux*. Chez Magimel, Paris.
Fermand Beaucour, 'Notes et souvenirs de Jean-Jacques Bellavoine, soldat du camp de Boulogne', in *Revue du nord*, vol. 198, Juillet-Septembre, 1968.
Elie Brun-Lavainne (1855) *Mes Souvenirs* Lille : Lefebvre-Ducrocq.
Correspondance générale, publiée par la Fondation Napoléon (Paris, 2004–2013).
Pierre Charrie (2004) *Lettres de guerre, 1792–1815*, Nantes : éditions du Canonnier.

Jacques Chevillet (2004) *Souvenir d'un cavalier de la Grande Armée, 1800–1810,* Bibliothèque de l'histoire, Paris.

Owen Connelly (2012) *French Revolution and Napoléon* Routledge, London.

Coutanceau et al (1905) *La Campagne de l'armée du Nord 1794,* R. Chapelot & Co., France.

Paul Lindsay Dawson (2019) *Napoléon's Imperial Guard Uniforms and Equipment: The Infantry.* Frontline, Barnsley.

Baron Dellard (1892), *Mémoires militaires du général Baron Dellard sur les guerres de la République et de l'Empire,* La librairie illustrée, Paris.

Duc de Fezensac,(1870) *Souvenirs militaires de 1804 a 1814,* Librairie militaire J. Dumaine, Paris.

Duhesme (1814) *Essai sur l'infanterie légère,* Paris, Chez Magimel.

Alan I. Forrest (1989), *Conscripts and Deserters: The Army and French Society during the Revolution and Empire* Oxford University Press, Oxford

Alan Forrest (2002) *Napoléon's Men London,* Hambledon Consortium, pp.161–167.

Ruth Goodman (2021) *The Domestic Revolution: How the Introduction of Coal into Victorian Homes Changed Everything,* Liveright Publishing Corporation.

D. F. N. Guerbois (1803), *Essai sur la nostalgie appelée vulgairement maladie du pays,* médical thésis, Paris.

L. Hennet, 'Vivandières et Blanchisseuses', in *Carnet de la Sabretache,* vol. 21 (1912).

François Houdecek (2023) *Vivre la Grande Armée. Être soldat au temps de Napoléon* CNRS Editions, Paris.

Marc Lebrun, 'Révolution, Empire et mauvais soldats' in *Revue historique des armées,* volume 244, 2006, pp.112–123.

Frédéric Lemaire, Archéoscopie d'un projet d'invasion: la fouille des baraquements d'infanterie du camp de Montreuil (1803–1805) in *Napoléonica. La Revue,* 2018/2 (N° 32), pp.5–48.

Perrot et Amoudru (1821) Histoire *de la ex-Garde* Deluany, Paris.

Aain Pigeard (1993), *L'armée napoléonienne,* édition Curandera, Paris.

Chantal Prévot, *Les femmes au camp de Boulogne, 1803–1809. Éléments de réponse d'après l'état civil des communes de Montreuil-sur-Mer, Étaples, Saint-Josse, Camiers, Dannes, Widehem,* In *Napoléonica. La Revue,* vol. 32, no. 2, 2018, pp.49–63.

Marie Antoine Reiset (1899) *Souvenirs, 1775–1810* Calmann Lévy.

J.-L. Sabon, 'Mémoires du Petit Louis ou l'apprenti horloger de Genève devenu musicien et chef de musique dans le 69e régiment d'infanterie de ligne de la Grande Armée de Napoléon Ier', in *Soldats suisses au service étranger,* Geneva, 1910.

Jean Stanislas (1907) *Vivien Souvenirs de ma vie militaire (1792–1822),* Hachette, Paris.

François Vigo-Roussillon (1981) *Journal de campagne, 1793–1837* Editions France-Empire.